The Fall Out of Redemption

The Fall Out of Redemption

Writing and Thinking Beyond Salvation
in Baudelaire, Cioran, Fondane,
Agamben, and Nancy

Joseph Acquisto

Bloomsbury Academic
An imprint of Bloomsbury Publishing Inc

B L O O M S B U R Y
NEW YORK · LONDON · NEW DELHI · SYDNEY

Bloomsbury Academic

An imprint of Bloomsbury Publishing Plc

1385 Broadway
New York
NY 10018
USA

50 Bedford Square
London
WC1B 3DP
UK

www.bloomsbury.com

BLOOMSBURY and the Diana logo are trademarks of Bloomsbury Publishing Plc

First published 2015

Library of Congress Cataloging-in-Publication Data
Acquisto, Joseph, 1975-
The fall out of redemption : writing and thinking beyond salvation in
Baudelaire, Cioran, Fondane, Agamben, and Nancy / Joseph Acquisto.
pages cm
Includes bibliographical references and index.
ISBN 978-1-62892-652-1 (hb : alk. paper) 1. Salvation in literature.
2. Redemption in literature. 3. Literature–Philosophy. I. Title.
PN56.S34A65 2015
809'.93382–dc23
2014041028

ISBN: HB: 978-1-6289-2652-1
ePub: 978-1-6289-2653-8
ePDF: 978-1-6289-2654-5

Typeset by Integra Software Services Pvt. Ltd.
Printed and bound in the United States of America

Contents

Note on Translations

All translations are mine unless otherwise indicated. For *Les Fleurs du Mal*, I quote William Aggeler's translation, *The Flowers of Evil* (Fresno: Academy Library Guild, 1954) and for *Le Spleen de Paris*, Edward K. Kaplan's *The Parisian Prowler* (Athens: University of Georgia Press, 1997). Page references are given in the text.

Permissions

Introduction

Recent developments in literary theory and continental philosophy, while remaining decidedly atheistic in orientation, have brought a renewed concern with the theological. In the wake of studies such as Charles Taylor's *A Secular Age*, scholars have called into question the secularization hypothesis whereby the birth of modernity in the West represented a definitive break with the religious worldview in favor of a thoroughgoing secularization of thought and practice that attempts to draw the consequences of the "disenchantment" of the world, in Max Weber's famous phrase borrowed from Friedrich Schiller (Weber 117). This is not to deny, of course, that many philosophers, writers, and artists maintained religious belief or a religious outlook, but it is to say that the main currents of art and thought since the mid-nineteenth century tended to discard theological engagement in favor of new secular models of inspiration. Recent continental thought, however, has suggested that no such definitive break occurred and that, while art and thought may be atheistic in orientation, it cannot be said merely to have put aside or surpassed the theological. In fact, modern art and thought might even be said to depend on it. From the outset, Friedrich Nietzsche's famous claim that "God is dead, and we have killed him" (*Gay* 167) is shot through with the traditional theological resonance of the innocent God taking on the sins of guilty humanity and dying to redeem them, and Nietzsche's own writings are full of theologically resonant vocabulary, from notions of transfiguration and redemption in *The Birth of Tragedy* to the quasi-biblical prose of *Thus Spoke Zarathustra*. This is not to say that Nietzsche's atheism is not sincere, but Nietzsche's entanglement in the discourse he was trying to surpass complicates a simple division between theism and atheism and the possibility of a simple passage from one to the other.

A recent study of contemporary French philosophers, Christopher Watkin's *Difficult Atheism*, argues convincingly that thinkers such as Jacques Derrida, Alain Badiou, and Jean-Luc Nancy retain more than a trace of theological heritage in their atheistic thought. Watkin demonstrates the persistence of theological orientation in contemporary thought, of the force of theology as a *structure* of thought even as this thought divorces itself from questions of religious belief and practice: "There is a new move in French philosophy today to come to terms with the death of God more rigorously than ever, and it cannot be understood under the banner of 'atheism.' No longer can we think in terms of a monolithic atheism or of a single agenda of thinking 'without God,' for what we see developing is a plurality of perhaps incommensurable approaches to thinking after God" (Watkin 1). The term "atheism" itself of course establishes a relation with theism by its very semantic structure; the semantics also reveal the extent to which the concept of atheism itself depends upon the theological. In that sense, the fact that there *is* no other word for atheism that does not define it in terms of theism is revealing about the difficulty of shaking off the traces, and more than the traces, of the theological as a structure of thought.

Recent work by continental philosophers from Slavoj Žižek to Giorgio Agamben, Alain Badiou, and Jean-Luc Nancy has taken up considerations of Christian theology quite explicitly. In contrast to thinkers such as Michel Henry and Jean-Luc Marion, who work within the bounds of theism and seek to redefine it while preserving the notion of a deity, Žižek, Agamben, and Badiou have taken up, within an explicitly *atheistic* context, questions such as Pauline theology, the betrayal of Judas, the foundational myth of the garden of Eden, early monasticism, and incarnation, giving these notions philosophical and sometimes political valence in ways that go far beyond simple questions of belief. To judge by these writers, atheism has reached a stage where it can move beyond the by turns aggressive and defensive insistence that God does not exist and engage with the import of theologically inflected thought in the contemporary world. At the same time, there has recently been increased attention to the pluralities of esthetic and intellectual practices typically labeled as "modern." Antoine Compagnon's book *Les Antimodernes* identifies a countercurrent within modernity of those who take up ideas or practices typically associated with the "modern" in a critical, which is not always to say reactionary, way. From some of these writers and thinkers, a paradoxical situation arises whereby those who are strongest in their critiques of aspects of modernity such as progress, secularization, technological development, and so on are also those most readily identified with the foundation of *esthetic* modernity. (Compagnon's earlier work, such as the *Five Paradoxes of Modernity*, was also sensitive to this irony.) It would seem not quite accurate, or at least overly reductive, to call these writers antimodern, given that a long tradition of the most innovative practices in the arts of the "modern" period find inspiration in these writers' works.

What I propose in this study is very much in the spirit of those writers who take the theological as a major and abiding current in the "modern" period but who divorce it from questions of belief in anything that might be identifiable as a form of Christianity. The theological as it emerges here will be of a philosophical and esthetic kind, one that operates as a structure of thought, sometimes in accordance with, and other times in opposition to, more typically philosophical systems of thought. To the extent that this gesture represents a move back toward a "pre-modern" unification of theology and philosophy, it too both participates in and calls into question the kinds of divisions of sacred and secular putatively established in the "modern" period. Contemporary esthetic philosopher Paul Audi calls attention to the way in which knowledge and artistic creation are inscribed in a theological framework by the move that they accomplish from the virtual to the actual: "Au paradis, non seulement tout est possible mais *la possibilité est tout ce qu'il y a* […]. Dans la mesure où nous agissons, et parce que nous sommes toujours en situation de jugement et d'actualisation des possibles, il est un fait que nous sommes toujours—que nous sommes « toujours déjà »—*expulsés du paradis*" ["In paradise, not only is everything possible, but *possibility is all there is* […]. Insofar as we act, and because we are always in a situation of judgment and realization of possible things, it is a fact that we are always—that we are 'always already'—thrown out of paradise"] (242). He goes on to clarify that his use of terms such as paradise and hell is, as I have been suggesting, more than metaphorical but distinct from anything that could appropriately be labeled belief: "Paradis, enfer, purgatoire, ce sont ici des cadres conceptuels, des « districts » de l'esprit, qui permettent de situer des *enjeux de conscience*" ["Paradise, hell, purgatory: these are conceptual frames, 'districts' of the mind, that allow us to situate the *stakes of consciousness/conscience*"] (243). My contention is that Charles Baudelaire is a key figure in the reimagining of theological discourse in a way that divorces it from a recognizable Catholicism yet retains the force of theological language as it seeks to recast the relationship between the metaphysical and esthetic questions in play in literary creation. By initiating this realignment, Baudelaire casts himself as neither modern nor antimodern but rather *amodern*, just as he could be said to be an atheological writer: in both of those terms, the presence of the modern and the theological is retained at the same time that the terms attempt to cancel their traditional connotations. The terms suggest the kinds of complications that Baudelaire, and those who follow him, introduce for anyone seeking to employ "theological" or "modern" as straightforward concepts that divide cultural or esthetic history into neat periods of "before" and "after." Indeed, as we shall see, a questioning of any neatly linear progression of time is one of the consequences of the move that Baudelaire makes in his complex engagement with the theological.

Reading Baudelaire through this lens allows us to give renewed attention to aspects of his work that are too easily neglected if one concentrates exclusively on the areas in Baudelaire's poetry that make him unflinchingly modern—the registration of the shock of modern urban experience, the complicated split subjectivity at play in his poetry, and so on—at the expense of a more holistic reading. In teasing out these radically innovative aspects of the modern Baudelaire, Fredric Jameson dismisses the "second-rate post-Romantic Baudelaire, the Baudelaire of diabolism and of cheap *frisson*, […] of a creaking and musty religious machinery which was no more interesting in the mid-nineteenth century than it is today" (Jameson 223). A more compelling reading of Baudelaire would seek to do justice to the duality that is always at hand in his work, not as a clearly set opposition but rather as a simultaneous duality, which Baudelaire claims is itself humanity's condition as a result of the permanent and irreparable fall from grace and which plays a determinative role in Baudelaire's depiction and theorization of the modern. On this view, Baudelaire's Satanism is not a holdover from romanticism but rather, I shall argue, an ultimately futile attempt to revolt in the face of the impossibility of redemption. Baudelaire's devil is no more "real" than his God, but both function powerfully in a larger metaphysical and esthetic view that attempts to imagine what a portrait of humanity without the possibility of redemption might look like. This attempt at constructing an aredemptive worldview is among Baudelaire's most innovative moves as a writer, poet, and thinker, and the "religious machinery" to which he has frequent recourse is a crucial aspect of that move, given the ways in which he rebuilds that machinery and assigns to it a radically different function from the one at play in earlier writers or those invested in a secularized notion of progress. This rewriting of theological discourse is what Jérôme Thélot has called Baudelaire's "religion without religion: deprived of all authority and all teaching, deprived even of any finished text" (*L'immémorial* 31), an attempt at what Yves Bonnefoy has called "the difficulty of modern poetry," which is that it has to define itself simultaneously "via Christianity and against it" (cited in *L'immémorial* 127).

This project of thinking and writing both by and against Christianity resonates far beyond Baudelaire into our own time, and it often generates a kind of writing that situates itself beyond easily definable categories of literary or non-literary writing, between what we could call poetry and criticism. Much of the writing I consider in this study lies at the liminal space between the two, as esthetic nonfiction (chiefly aphorism or essay) or philosophically inflected poetry. Baudelaire prefigures this double status of writing when he claims in his essay on Richard Wagner that "tous les grands poètes deviennent naturellement, fatalement, critiques" ["all great poets become naturally, fatally, critics"] (OC2: 793). Contemporary critical theory continues this tradition of esthetically inflected philosophical writing, and often those given to such a style also take up the question of thinking by and against Christianity. Foremost among these in our own time is Jean-Luc Nancy in his work on the self-deconstruction of Christianity:

> It is not a question [...] of being somehow interested in Christianity for itself, or for some religious, moral, spiritual, or saving virtue in any of the senses that the professions of Christian faith have left us with. In order to end, we give what remains of Christianity its leave, and this is why we can maintain that it is deconstructing itself. But in deconstructing itself, it dis-encloses our thinking: whereas Enlightenment reason, and following it the reason of the world of integral progress, judged it necessary to close itself off to all dimensions of the "outside," what is called for now is to break the enclosure in order to understand that it is from reason and through reason that the pressure, the drive (this *Trieb* of reason that Kant wants to uphold) of the relation with the infinite outside comes about, and does so *in this very place*. Deconstructing Christianity means opening reason to its very own reason, and perhaps to its unreason. (*Adoration* 24–5)

Nancy's view would thus establish more of a continuum than a rupture between sacred and secularly inflected thinking: "The only thing that can be actual is an atheism that contemplates the reality of its Christian origins" (*Deconstruction* 140), but at the same time, Christianity contains its own deconstruction, the emptying out of its own transcendence. The notion of a continuum between Christianity and atheism has implications for every branch of thought from metaphysics to ethics, esthetics, and politics.

It is my contention that the origin of this combined intellectual and esthetic project lies in Baudelaire and that the key marker of the shift away from traditional Christianity is not an affirmation of secularism but rather the removal of redemption (by any means, whether divine, esthetic, or political) as a conceptual or actual possibility. In 1943, Georges Bataille recorded, in *Inner Experience*, a conversation he had with Maurice Blanchot in which the latter identifies three aspects of the foundation of contemporary atheistic spiritual life, "which can only:—have its principle and its end in the absence of salvation, in the renunciation of all hope,—affirm of inner experience that it is authority (but all authority expiates itself),—be contestation of itself and non-knowledge" (102). With Baudelaire we have the first definitive sketch of what such a spiritual world without the possibility of redemption would look like. It is an unsentimental approach to experience that, while it may have moments of nostalgic longing for the comforts of older visions, recognizes them as nostalgic returns rather than actual possibilities—an outlook which, once again, will find its full flowering in twentieth century art and thought. Bataille links salvation not only to nostalgia but also to an altered attitude to suffering: "The nostalgia for salvation responds perhaps to the increase of suffering (or rather to the incapacity to bear it). The idea of salvation comes, I believe, from one whom suffering *breaks apart*. He who masters it, on the contrary needs to be broken, to proceed on the path towards rupture" (Bataille 43). This move to a Nietzschean affirmation of suffering, prefigured in Baudelaire and made explicit here in Bataille, refuses nonetheless the comforts of redemption via art, which Nietzsche affirms in ways that place him among theorists of redemption rather than among those, such as Baudelaire, who attempt to think and write beyond it.

The stakes are high when writers and thinkers aim to move beyond the logic of salvation toward what I will call *asoteriology*, a paradigm that refuses to entertain the possibility of redemption, as opposed to soteriology, the term for the study of redemption. The work of all of the writers I consider in this study could be said to be a prolonged attempt to draw out the full consequences of the move to asoteriological thinking, which becomes as urgent as it is difficult, given how deeply embedded in Western thought and writing the notion of redemption is. I will concentrate above all on a double set of consequences, metaphysical and esthetic, as they play themselves out in the authors I consider. To rethink salvation is ultimately to rethink the question of endings, since the logic of redemption maps onto a linear sense of time and a sense of progression from a fall to a redemption. This has its parallel in the progression of an essay or poem from the beginning of the exposition, through a development that leads us to the sense of an ending that gives retrospective meaning to the progression of words that will have led us to where we ultimately end. In other words, we read while trusting that by the end of our reading, there *will have been* meaning, just as the end of linear time, on traditional accounts of redemption, gives meaning and completion to the development of chronological, historical time and thus leads it on to its end. A break with the logic of redemption profoundly disrupts this linear sense of time and its concurrent notions of development and progress, and indeed a refusal of progress is a constant concern of the authors who figure in these pages.

A move away from linearity also forces a new relationship to time, since both secular narratives of progress and Christian notions of redemption depend on a similarly linear conception of time that is necessarily disrupted when redemption is removed. A Nietzschean eternal return of the same is just one of many ways to reconceive our relation to time beyond historical progress or redemption, and many of the writers I consider do not adopt such a framework, opting instead, like Walter Benjamin, for a catastrophe-driven notion of a series of calamities to which one might wish to put an end but which it appears impossible to stop. Thus another major concern of these writers is despair, an obvious problem that emerges when redemption is removed, since the traditional virtue of hope was directly linked to the notion of redemption. Without the redemptive event, or a secular equivalent of some kind, little stands in the way of human beings succumbing to despair at the view of the world that emerges from an aredemptive standpoint. Refuge in the work of art is one possibility, and again Nietzsche is a major theorist of such an option, but such an approach makes us fall back into redemptive logic rather than allowing us to get past it. The narrative of esthetic redemption has to be refused just as systematically as its political or religious equivalents in order to draw all of the consequences of the move beyond redemption. Asoteriological writing thus values lucidity above all. This lucidity is seldom comforting. Catholic philosopher Gabriel Marcel rejects the worldview contained in Emil Cioran's writing precisely on the grounds that its conclusions risk rendering life unlivable. He struggled with embracing Cioran as a friend while feeling the need to reject the conclusions of his work and writes poignantly about the "painfully felt divorce between my unfailing consideration for the man, for my friend, and the rejection of a thought to which I could not subscribe without renouncing all my reasons for living" (Marcel 223).

While there can be no redemption in esthetics, literary writing clearly plays a key role for the writers I consider here; one of its essential functions is to serve as an experimental ground for the working through of some of the consequences of the move out of redemptive logic. I have already identified how a sense of ending is troubled when the notion of redemption is refused; the consequences of a new approach to endings are esthetic as much as metaphysical. The refusal of redemption is played out at the level of form when writers rethink the way a literary work ends or concludes. In Baudelaire, this trouble with endings reveals itself both at the level of the individual poem and at the level of *Les Fleurs du Mal* as a whole, which, as I will demonstrate, turns in on itself rather than progressing toward an ending that could be derived from a linear reading of the poems. In fact, the poems themselves, in their complex system of echoes among poems from sometimes vastly different parts of the collection, direct readers on to new interpretive paths that actively defy an attempt to read a linear "plot" in the collection, all the while affirming nonetheless that there is a sense of interrelation among the parts that compose the whole. Another key figure in my analysis, Emil Cioran, likewise complicates our sense of an ending by complicating the relation of parts to wholes, this time via collections of aphorisms rather than poems. Like poems in a collection, aphorisms supposedly stand on their own as a unit, often with a definitive conclusion that gives the individual aphorism its particular force, but they also function as parts of a whole that is not necessarily meant to be interpreted according to a logic of linearity. Collections of aphorisms thus have no definitive beginning or end and are thereby a particularly fruitful genre for exploring the consequences of the refusal of redemption. Their refusal of a definitive endpoint echoes their refusal of definitive logical conclusion, and thus Baudelaire's lyric poetry collection and Cioran's volumes of aphorisms also perform one of the intellectual consequences of the refusal of linearity, the fall into an endlessly prolongable discourse, where conclusions can only be tentative in the wake of a refusal of systematic approaches to thought.

If the fall is irredeemable, then it is also eternal, as poems and aphorisms end rather than conclude and as readers are drawn into a labyrinthine artistic form. Thus the form of these works echoes a key traditional theological notion of sin, that of fallen humanity as *incurvatus in se*, turned in on itself. The idea stems from Paul and plays a key role in Augustine, according to whom the sinful subject seeks all things for its own sake rather than relating to God as the ground and center of our existence.[1] Such an idea is fully consonant with the atheological vision that the authors I consider shape through their works; in fact, a doubled self-torturing subject figures prominently in Baudelaire's writings. In the face of an atheology of impossible redemption, such is the portrait of subjectivity that emerges; it is one of the consequences of the impossibility of redemption. Fittingly, such a torturous subjectivity is worked out in literary forms that can also be described as *incurvatus in se*, not in the sense of a hermetically closed object that attempts to cut off reference to the external world but rather in the sense of a form that turns in on itself rather than proceeding linearly to a conclusion.

This kind of subjectivity, new in Baudelaire at least insofar as it presents itself as an incorrigible model rather than a temporary and corrigible state, is not a self-actualization in and through language and thus cannot carry any esthetic redemptive value any more than it can preserve the hope of divine redemption. This is a crucial aspect of Baudelaire's rupture with the romantics, for whom a powerfully transformative relationship to language emerges through the poetic word. As Jérôme Thélot describes it:

> it is only by language […] that subjectivity attains itself and freely reflects itself: it is thus only by language that romantic man will redeem his era. […] Romanticism, spurred on by the end of history which is its golden age—and this being what *is not* since it is *to come* and thus *to be said*—has as its task to return into a redemptive language the analytic discourse of science, which empties the world of its life, and the systematic discourse of philosophical rationalism, which is only the last aberration of the concept: this redemptive language is named "poetry." (*L'immémorial* 318)

Baudelaire and his descendants sometimes assert the power of the transformative and transcendental poetic word as his romantic predecessors did,[2] but in the context of the *Fleurs du Mal* in their entirety, such a faith in the power of poetry, much like Baudelaire's faith in God, cannot be sustained in the face of those other moments that powerfully call those into question. Those moments come, significantly, at the end of the "Spleen et Idéal" ["Spleen and Ideal"] section and at the end of "La Mort" ["Death"] which closes the collection; in other words, at precisely those culminating moments when one might expect a conclusion that affirms the transformative power of the poetic word, we have those poems that most powerfully question it. They do so by their inability to conclude, by the way in which they turn in on themselves, condemned to perform that kind of doubled-back-on-itself subjectivity into which the Baudelairean subject has permanently fallen.

In the face of such lucidity, the moments where Baudelaire seems to aspire toward transcendence cannot help but ring hollow. What, then, becomes of the role of poetic creation? Asoteriology does not simply cancel the creative powers of the writer, after all. As we saw above, the act of creation can survive the death of God because it retains the force of the theological account of creation even beyond the removal of God from that account. As Paul Audi claims, paradise cannot be desirable for the artist because everything remains there in the realm of the changeless virtual possibility, as opposed to the actualization of reality (and of creation) that needs to separate itself from the virtuality of paradise in order to realize itself. On this view, artistic creation is not rendered less powerful by the removal of the redemptive possibility of poetry; rather, the aredemptive nature of the work of art is precisely what becomes its very condition of possibility. Poetic language is thus more limited than it had been in the romantic framework, because it carries no redemptive power, but it also becomes a powerful vehicle for lucidity and thus a way to give form to an *incurvatus-in-se* subjectivity, one that is fully aware of the illusory nature of poetic creation and embraces that very production of illusion as the condition of possibility of poetry. And not just of poetry: as I have been implying, the question of the impossibility of redemption inextricably links esthetic concerns to questions of lived experience as those are conceptualized in writers whose work implicates both metaphysics and ethics. Commenting on the work of Giorgio Agamben, Thanos Zartalouids gives voice to the way redemption is linked to esthetic questions as well as modes of living in the world:

> It is not recognition any longer that "saves us," but the realization that we cannot recognize ourselves in any savior-sign, let alone return to it. Unlearning is needed, for this proposition is not to be confused with empty nihilism or other horrors that remain deep scars on the face of our degraded culture and poverty of experience. (132)

Removing redemption, then, does not cancel esthetic production; it could in fact be said to enable it by complicating, in ways at which I have already hinted and which I develop further in Chapter 3, the possibility of an ending, and thus putting into play a condition of eternal proffering of language shaped by the writer, not in any attempt at redemption of whatever by whomever but rather as an act of participation in the creative order which reinforces our move away from the purported "paradise" of the virtual and pushes us more solidly toward the world of the actual, the only one left for us to inhabit.

Released from any collusion with the salvific or the transcendent, poetic language reinforces its link with the "nonliterary" language of criticism, as I have already suggested, allowing us to read across the genres of "literature" and "criticism" or "theory" in ways that permit us to see the thought value of the former and the creative gestures inherent in the latter. Along these lines, we can also profitably read interhistorically, bringing texts of different periods into dialogue with each other.[3] Such an approach is fully consonant with these authors' own rejection of linear time in favor of a more dynamic model that questions "progress" and thus allows us to reduce the conceptual distance that separates two chronologically distinct periods. It is interhistorical reading that allows us to claim Baudelaire as, in some important ways, our contemporary; it is also what allows fruitful readings of, say, Baudelaire and Cioran in similar terms despite the differences in the particularities of their historical situations. And it is what allows literary theory to engage powerfully, meaningfully, and dynamically with the literary texts on which it comments. My contention, then, is that the kind of working through of asoteriological atheology that is taking place in recent critical theory is in direct relation to sometimes much older writing that is involved in the same sorts of working through of this idea. In that sense, Nancy's notion of the self-deconstruction of Christianity is pertinent, since it implies that the move away from a theism that still preserves a theological framework for thought is already operative in Christianity itself. Such theoretical models refuse a logic of the either/or that would endorse a progression from a theological to an atheological metaphysics or esthetics. By rejecting such linear *conceptual* (as well as historical) moves, contemporary thought gets beyond a mode of thought motivated by its conclusion; this, too, is an important consequence of thinking beyond redemption and its messianic logic of temporal progression, for thought that rejects the possibility of definitive conclusion must be asystematic, and indeed, all of the writers I examine here explicitly or implicitly reject systematic philosophy.

This refusal to conclude definitively and the impetus to proliferate the conversations that can be had across genres and across time periods encourages the kind of dynamic relation that I trace between literature and thought, most immediately visible in genres such as Cioran's aphorisms but also very much at work in Baudelaire's poetry and in the other writers I examine as well. Ulrich Baer underscores the link between meaning making and the collapse of systematicity in Baudelaire's poetry: "Philosophical writers may indeed vainly attempt to claim a position that will not come undone. Baudelaire's poetry, however, generates its very sense and meaning—its claim to reach through and above time—from this collapse of its position" (101). The fact that much of the work of the writers I examine sits solidly between literary and philosophical writing is in part a result of their refusal to adopt any system that would risk reducing or arresting the dynamism at work in their texts, a productive result of the inability definitively to conclude that I argue is one of the consequences of moving beyond redemption. By now it should be clear that I am not reading Baudelaire, or any of the literary writers I consider, in an attempt to tease out philosophical concepts from his writing, nor to see him as an "example" of one or another idea that is expressed already in another writer's philosophical or theological writing. Rather, my argument depends on the blurring of precisely the boundaries that are implied in the distinction between "literary" and "philosophical" writing, and when I claim that the consequences of the refusal of redemption are both esthetic and philosophical, I would like to suggest an interdependence of the two and to demonstrate a working through of one set of consequences by way of the other. The way that the writers I engage encourage us to see the literary in the philosophical and vice versa is one of their hallmark features.

Inasmuch as the fall out of redemption inaugurates an altered approach to temporality and to the possibility of concluding, it enables a new and particular amodernity. Before proceeding, let us pause for a moment over this concept, which is, as I indicate above, distinct from antimodernity. Elisabeth Goodstein's subtly argued study of boredom and modernity seeks to claim boredom as a specifically modern phenomenon, different in kind from earlier experiences such as *taedium vitae* or acedia:

> If rationality is the sustaining myth of modernity, boredom, as an everyday experience of universalized skepticism, constitutes its existential reality. An heir to Enlightenment, the bored subject rejects the everyday world yet finds in it (negative) metaphysical significance: the experience of boredom fosters a nihilistic dynamic that makes such disaffection seem a timeless feature of the human condition. (3–4)

For Goodstein, "the language of boredom is secular, materialist, and resigned to the loss of meaning" (5), and while the bored subject makes universal claims about boredom's metaphysical significance, those claims are historically specific in ways that the modern bored subject's very boredom renders him or her incapable of seeing. While I do not dispute the historical origins of this particular experience of boredom, I wish to complicate the either/or implied by the opposition between metaphysical and historical experience, and in this I take my lead from the very authors I consider in this study, those of both the nineteenth century and our own time. I would begin by qualifying the notion that the language of boredom is secular. If Baudelaire is to be considered a major figure in the inauguration of modern boredom, as Goodstein's several references to him and to his major interpreter Walter Benjamin suggest, then "secular" cannot be understood as opposing itself to, or divorcing itself from, a religious framework. Baudelaire and those that follow him force us to redefine what we mean by terms such as "secular": while Baudelaire is at best ambivalent about God's existence and while he denies the hope of redemption, and in that sense cannot be said to be Christian in orientation, he and those who write in his wake retain a powerfully theological framework that structures their thought and writing even as it distances itself from questions of religious belief or practice.

Goodstein herself refers to "the incomplete way in which religious and other metanarratives have actually been overcome" in modernity (10); my own task will be to identify the consequences of such incomplete overcoming of the logic of redemption specifically. To begin to do that, we need to distinguish writers such as Baudelaire and Cioran from what we would call secular and modern writers in a more casual sense. These writers often oppose themselves powerfully to the modern world when it is characterized in terms of a secularized notion of the linear development of history that reflects progress. While this might incline us to label them "antimodern," such a label would be no more complete a descriptor than "modern," since the former term implies a reactionary conservativism that is not really in line with these thinkers' thought, Baudelaire's lip service to Joseph de Maistre in his autobiographical notes notwithstanding.[4] A better descriptor of writers such as Baudelaire and Cioran would be *amodern*, a term which suggests that only by passing through the experience of the historical modern—the political, economic, and industrial events of the eighteenth and early nineteenth centuries— do these authors come to articulate their paradoxical position as prototypically modern writers giving voice to the very kinds of experience they often react against without in any way seeking to return to a putatively "better" earlier period. The fact that their fundamentally ahistorical view of human history as an inevitable series of calamities and cruelties is of course historically inflected, inasmuch as it arises from a particular set of historical circumstances, does not alter their ability (or ours) to enter into the esthetic and metaphysical conclusions to be drawn from their alinear perspective. For Goodstein, "the historicity of boredom is visible only from a position outside the nihilistic dynamic of the experience—a position that permits reflection on the discursive regime in which this peculiar experience came to be" (18). What is at stake, then, is our own contemporary ability to remove ourselves from the position of that "nihilistic dynamic" identified by the writers I engage here, that is, the degree to which Baudelaire could be said to be our "contemporary." The interhistorical reading I propose puts into dialogue writers in the nineteenth century, the early twentieth century, and our own day, but not in the sense of contemporary writers commenting on an earlier tradition that we are now able to analyze from that "outside" position that Goodstein evokes. Rather, writers from each of these periods are implicated in the same kind of project of coming to terms with the persistent residue of a salvational framework. Žižek, Agamben, and Nancy are not ahistorical thinkers any more than Baudelaire or Cioran, but they do all attempt, I would argue, to articulate history in terms of metaphysics while also giving voice to the way metaphysical concerns manifest themselves in historically specific ways. It is this back-and-forth between history and philosophy, as well as the hesitation between philosophy and literature, that is one important site of continuity that enables an interhistorical approach to these writers, an approach whereby Baudelaire may have as much to tell us about Agamben as Agamben does about Baudelaire.

With the impossibility of redemption comes a notion of a fall that is perpetual. The writers in question here define the nature of that fall differently but always in some kind of relation to knowledge and thus to something fundamental about human interaction with the world in which we act. As Elissa Marder remarks about Baudelaire, "the 'ancient fall' is conceived as a fall both *into* time and *out* of it. One falls into time by becoming conscious of it, but the moment one becomes conscious of time, one falls out of it because consciousness of time prevents one from being able to live in it" (20). This allows us to take a first step toward seeing why the kind of consciousness of time that is necessary in order to historicize properly is impossible to maintain perpetually, since the very act of contemplating removes us from the time for which we hope to account, thus forcing another attempt at historicizing *that* moment, and onward toward a future of which we could only have knowledge from the perspective of the end of time, which is precisely the perspective refused when we refuse the possibility of redemption. The position that Marder articulates here is one developed by Cioran as well, for whom the fall's relationship to time is double: first, a fall into time, and then a fall from it, as we shall see in more detail in Chapter 4. If nothing redeems the fall into knowledge (and especially, for most of them, knowledge via language), then human beings are always already falling, and thus anything we could say about our relation to the world is necessarily limited by that condition, which restricts our ability to step out of that fallen condition in order to see, from some sort of Archimedean point, how we might historicize this view of humanity's relation to the world in which it operates. While it certainly is possible to examine such a position historically for a moment, such historicization is, for the writers I consider here in the wake of the impossibility of redemption, ultimately collapsible back into the philosophical concerns. In other words, a dynamic relationship establishes itself between historical and philosophical concerns that never allows the historical definitively to override the philosophical.

Putting an end to that dynamism by claiming that what appears to be ahistorical reflection on the part of these writers is actually, and only, deeply historical does not reduce the force of those philosophical reflections. To claim as much would be implicitly to affirm the very sort of linear model of historical progression these writers seek to deny: it would be to claim that we used to think the positions we announced pretended to universality, but now we know better than that. To deny linear progress is to call such a view into question and to deny the comfort of settling into a definitive position, that is, that historicization puts an end to all universal claims. The possibility of concluding is, as I have suggested already and will explore in far more detail, precisely what is called into question when the logic of redemption is denied. It follows from the fall's logic of duality that we need to maintain the tension between universalizing and historicizing approaches, where the attempt to historicize can never be permanent but rather always ready to open on to the possibility of another interhistorical conversation. The realm of literary writing, whether in the form of poetry, aphorism, or critical writing that manifests a strong "literary" mode, is a privileged site in which to explore the ways the philosophical claims and their particular historical manifestations interact. That esthetic terrain is the one that is most conducive to holding dualistic oppositions in creative tension and to enabling interhistorical reading; it is thus no accident that it is the preferred mode of writing for all of the authors I explore here.

My first chapter lays the groundwork for understanding what is at stake in Baudelaire's refusal of redemption and sets up an interhistorical nexus by reading Baudelaire's *Journaux intimes* and his lyric poetry in relation to Walter Benjamin's early writings as well as Paul de Man's work on modernity and Giorgio Agamben's recent essay on the relationship of creation to redemption. The *Journaux intimes* provide a crucial starting place because they set out the theme of the fall without redemptive grace and its implications for Baudelaire's view of history, politics, and progress. These notes, which I read as *de facto* aphorisms, present the theologically inflected view that he had been developing throughout his poetic career, as my look back to the *Fleurs du Mal*, which precede the autobiographical notes by over a decade, will indicate. What also emerges between these texts is a sense of human solidarity, if not equality, stemming from the irredeemable original sin that defines humanity and accounts both for particular acts and larger historical movements. Original sin emerges from these texts not only as a political but also as an epistemological problem, since it is linked to, and even stems from, the question of knowledge. Baudelaire, as both poet and critic, helps us think through not only the epistemological but also the esthetic implications of living and writing under the condition of original sin and the condemnation to knowledge that it brings. Agamben's reflections on the interdependence and simultaneity of the creative and critical act resonate with Baudelaire's and extend the poet's theologically inflected atheology of creation by claiming that redemption effectively cancels itself because, since the work of creation (esthetic or otherwise), is destined to pass away, redemption can be operative only on itself, a pure saving of nothing.

This self-destruction in turn echoes de Man's notion of modernity and history "condemned to being linked together in a self-destroying union that threatens the survival of both" (151). De Man discusses the difficulty of theorizing modernity precisely in the Baudelairean terms of the eternal and the transitory, a characterization that both requires and renders impossible a movement outside the modern in order to contemplate and characterize the modern. The postulation of an existence both within and outside time chimes with the notion of simultaneity that Baudelaire's cancelation of a linear notion of times engenders. My analysis brings together several threads of this discussion, including irony, the satanic, contemplation, and the *néant* in a reading of Baudelaire's poetry that both inaugurates and, in its way, provides critical comment on the implicit conversation between the mid-nineteenth and late-twentieth centuries.

The second chapter returns to the question of how Walter Benjamin's early writings, ones not explicitly concerned with Baudelaire, can be put in dialogue with the poet's proto-theological stance on questions of knowledge, the fall, and redemption. I read the poet and the critic together in order to suggest that some of Benjamin's comments on Baudelaire in, for instance, his notes on the *Arcades* project can benefit from being read in light of the theological orientation of Benjamin's earlier writings, of which more than a trace of a theological approach remains later, despite Benjamin's move toward a materialist stance. Theological concepts open up productive possibilities for interpreting Baudelaire but also show the limits of Benjamin's approach, given his implicit concern with messianism, which is precisely the kind of position that Baudelaire would reject. I turn, by contrast, to a poet and critic active at the same time as Benjamin, the Romanian-born French writer

Benjamin Fondane, whose magnum opus, his book-length study of Baudelaire, was eclipsed at the time of its publication by Jean-Paul Sartre's book on Baudelaire and has since lived in the long shadow cast by Benjamin's highly influential essays on the poet. Fondane foregrounds metaphysical questions more than historical ones, and, like Baudelaire, engages theology as a mode of thought rather than a generator of belief or practice. Fondane reads Baudelaire in a lineage that gives weight to early existentialist writers such as Pascal, Kierkegaard, and Dostoyevsky; with and through Baudelaire's writings, Fondane attempts to react against the hopelessness of the *néant* that plays such a key role in Baudelaire, even while he operates in the knowledge that the attempt may be doomed to failure. His existential reading of Baudelaire, markedly different from Sartre's existentialist take, sees value in suffering and questions how to avoid despair in the face of the lack of redemptive grace. I thus argue that Fondane accounts better than Benjamin does for the refusal of the possibility of redemption in Baudelaire; his reading has important implications for the ambiguous status of revolt in Baudelaire and the role of political violence, a question of particular urgency given Fondane's haste to finish the Baudelaire book before being murdered at Auschwitz-Birkenau. The last section of the chapter extends the consideration of suffering in the wake of impossible redemption by reading Fondane's poetry of the 1930s, where we can see, as we do in Baudelaire, the poetic working out of a worldview that mediates between, or even calls into question the distinction between, metaphysical reflection and lived experience.

The following chapter continues to negotiate the terrain of a poetic metaphysics and a metaphysical poetics by deepening the simultaneous engagement of esthetic and philosophical or theological concerns as they relate to the question of the end of the poem. The notion of endings is common ground in both theology and poetry, and in this chapter I read Baudelaire together with Giorgio Agamben in order to inquire about the esthetic consequences of an asoteriological view. Agamben's notion of messianic time not as the view from the end of time but rather as the time it takes for time to come to an end has powerful consequences for the way poems end, and Agamben emphasizes the paradox that poems both drive on toward their end and resist that end, since the end of the poem is the moment when language falls back into prose or into silence. Here, as in the other chapters, I read Baudelaire not merely as a confirmation of, or case study for, Agamben's ideas, but rather as a partner in the working through of these ideas, unique in the way he allows us to extend Agamben's ideas through his approaches to bringing his poems to an end. These esthetic questions are intricately entwined, for Baudelaire as for Agamben, with metaphysical questions, and not just because death is an important subject of the last poems of *Les Fleurs du Mal*. The role of metaphysical considerations is not just thematic but also *formal* for both the critic and the poet. Once redemption is removed from the poet's worldview, there is a profound effect on the way poems end, or rather how they struggle to come to their end. This chapter considers the ways poems end—or resist ending—in Baudelaire, from formal questions of structural repetition, to the sense of endless falling suggested by several of his most innovative poems, and on to the poems that conclude the 1857 and 1861 editions of *Les Fleurs du Mal*. In both editions, the final poems resist definitive ending by sending the reader back to poems earlier in the same section, thus creating a sort of spiraling back that resists closure and, with it, the calming assurance of death or the *néant*, which, as I explore in Chapter 1, is as desirable as it is impossible for Baudelaire.

The struggle to accept the impossible is at the heart of Emil Cioran's engagement with the notion of redemption, and it is to him that I turn in Chapter 4. A Romanian immigrant to Paris, Cioran published his collections of aphorisms and essays in French from the 1940s to the 1980s. One of the most distinctive stylists of his generation, he was hailed by Maurice Nadeau as "the prophet of the concentrational era and of collective suicide [...], the bringer of bad news" (Nadeau 211). His work is often philosophical in orientation but Cioran refused the label "philosopher" on account of the systematic nature of philosophical thought, which he categorically refused in favor of the fragment. His work frequently foregrounds notions of despair and pessimism and, like Baudelaire, Cioran works within a Christian theological frame while refusing religious belief and practice. As such, he returns obsessively to the idea of impossible redemption; I demonstrate that this idea grounds his writing, which we can see as an extension of Baudelaire's project, reconceived in light of the cultural, intellectual, and political history that transpired between the poet's time and Cioran's. I begin by tracing Cioran's investment in the idea of lucidity about the human condition, a position that brings him close to a version of nihilism but that distances him from a thinker with whom he is sometimes associated, Friedrich Nietzsche. With Nietzsche we have an approach to redemption that is fundamentally different from that of the other thinkers I explore, since Nietzsche does affirm the possibility of redemption in the form of the esthetic. I argue that such an approach, which leans heavily on the notion of the transfiguration of reality, merely reproduces the logic of redemption rather than allowing us to get past it. This is a position that Cioran himself criticizes in his rejection of Nietzsche on grounds of the philosopher's naiveté. Cioran's own approach to asoteriology is linked, like Baudelaire's, to a self-tortured subjectivity eternally divided against itself, and, like Baudelaire, Cioran works out the consequences of the impossibility of redemption via the form he chooses, in his case the aphorism which, like Baudelaire's approach to his collection of lyric poetry, puts in question the notion of coming to an end and disrupts the possibility of a simple linear reading. For Cioran, form is an importance consequence of the fall that he theorizes, and redemption becomes, paradoxically perhaps, an intellectual and spiritual temptation, one that we find reassuring but that not only results in falsehood but also blocks esthetic creation. From this it might seem to follow that the knowledge that there is no redemption is itself a kind of redemption for Cioran, especially given the value he places on lucidity. But Cioran demonstrates the impossibility of coming to rest in such an affirmation, an impossibility generated by the fall itself which, while it condemns us to seek knowledge, also relegates us to a position of skepticism from which we cannot even affirm the salvific effect of being freed from the notion of redemption but rather will always see it as an irreparable loss.

Chapter 5 expands these considerations of Cioran in order to establish the crucial role that fiction plays in relation to lucidity and to read Cioran's work more directly in the light of his crucial middle-period essays on the fall. In light of the despair that haunts Cioran's vision of the world, it is fiction that allows us to live in the world, not by providing some sort of escapist fantasy that would merely be akin to the comforts of traditional Christianity, but by providing temporary nourishment by which we may continue to act in the world. Cioran distinguishes between nourishing and poisonous fictions; my analysis will illuminate the particular role that poetry specifically has to play in this bridging of conceptual and lived experience. Poets, perhaps like Cioran himself, can, by their creation which emerges from an act of destruction, become a model for how to mitigate between the lucidity that leads to total inaction in the world and a sense of agency that risks leading to illusion. The problem of the fall as Cioran poses it is, as it had been for Baudelaire and Fondane as well, a problem of knowledge, and thus literature becomes both a way of knowing our fallen state and a way of working out how we might live in what we might call lucid delusion. This doubled state is of course a consequence of the fall itself, which Cioran, like Baudelaire, theorizes in terms of doubleness. Cioran takes a step beyond other thinkers, however, by positing the fall *itself* as double: it is a fall first into, and then out of, time. The second fall repeats, rather than correcting, the first, and thus is to be distinguished from a messianic end of time that would cancel the fall into linear time. The conceptual restlessness to which we are condemned by the fall as Cioran portrays it allows him to consider a number of potential earthly forms of redemption, but all of them are temporary at best, and thus Cioran's thought comes to a series of provisional conclusions about an accessible redemption but cancels them all by turn in the affirmation that none of them can be definitive or eternal, a move that brings us back to the notion of an eternal fall.

The final chapter broadens onto ethical concerns, reading Baudelaire and Cioran together in order to articulate the way in which their emphasis on the notion of irredeemable original sin, while giving rise to anguish and despair, ultimately uses that shared notion of despair as a kind of basis for ethical relations to others. Paradoxically, these two writers, often labeled misanthropes, arrive at a vision of solidarity based precisely on the notion of unredeemed original sin as the common denominator of humanity, one that does not allow for division between believer and atheist, Christian and non-Christian, or saved and unsaved. The quasi-secularized notion of asoteriology does give rise to a certain nihilism, but it is not the nihilism of unqualified destruction or quietism. Rather, in our eternal falling lies a potential moment of relation to the other that is first expressed, for these authors, in esthetic terms. For it is the work of esthetic creation that provides the model of violent action that tears us away from the pure potentiality of paradise. I appeal to contemporary philosophers Paul Audi and Jean-Luc Nancy and return once more to Agamben to articulate a critique of potentiality. Baudelaire and Cioran provide the link between esthetic creation, which is also in some sense a violent destruction of the given world, and lived experience with others. Through an analysis centered on Baudelaire's prose poems, I demonstrate the way the esthetic, rather than distancing these writers from lived experience, allows them to enter it more fully. This is not a triumph over nihilism or despair but rather an articulation of the way we can live appropriately within the very particular kinds of conclusions wrought by the theorizing of the impossibility of redemption that I will have traced throughout the book. It would be misleading to label either Baudelaire or Cioran a humanist, and I in no way seek to "redeem" or cancel their deep-seated despair and tendency toward nihilism in the sense of a longing for nothingness. Rather, I demonstrate the way the removal of the category of redemption transforms that nihilism into a productive kind, one that makes room for artistic creation and shared human experience without seeking redemption in either one and in fact guarding against the long-standing tendency to do so.

The book's entire cast of characters returns in the final chapter, where we reach the fullest implication of my interhistorical reading. That reading uses the question of redemption to avoid the pitfalls both of a Christian framework of thought *and* the frameworks that attempted to replace it through the long period of modernity dating from the mid-nineteenth century and still very much unfinished. We best avoid these pitfalls, I argue, by shifting the ground on which we ask questions about knowledge and belief, metaphysics and ethics, fiction and reality. Baudelaire holds the key to a new style of thinking, previously underrecognized, and to be sure ambiguous, a thought worked out not via a system but rather in literature, which becomes a model for this new kind of thought while resisting any attempt to become a new model of redemption itself.

Saving Nothing: Baudelaire, Benjamin, de Man, Agamben

Philosopher John Gray has claimed that "if anything defines 'the West' it is the pursuit of salvation in history. It is historical teleology—the belief that history has a built-in purpose or goal—rather than traditions of democracy or tolerance, that sets western civilization apart from all others" (*Black* 73). Both capitalism and communism "were messianic movements, using the language of reason and science, but actually driven by faith" (1). When the object of that faith is progress, and when the stakes involve war and bloodshed, lucidity when we are tempted to take our guiding myths as fact is particularly important, and for Gray, "belief in progress has become a mechanism of self-deception that serves only to block perception of the evils that come with the growth of knowledge" (*Heresies* 5). This critique of self-deception leads Gray back to a more accurate foundational myth, that of original sin, fully acknowledged in its mythical status but nonetheless operative and useful as a corrective to more potentially dangerous modern myths of progress. There is much is Gray's diagnosis of our contemporary world that is expressed in sometimes similar ways in Baudelaire; as I will show in this chapter, Baudelaire's own refusal of the idea of historical, scientific, or technological progress leads to an emphasis on original sin that is not simply a vehicle for a poetry steeped in devils and the macabre but rather a complex vision that seeks to articulate the intersection of metaphysics with lived experience, in a way that both belongs to his particular historical moment and transcends it, allowing us to establish a dialogue between Baudelaire and thinkers from other key moments when the shape and nature of modernity was called into question.

This first chapter lays the Baudelairean groundwork for exploring these issues, concentrating in particular on the critique of progress, its relation to original sin, the implications of the critique of knowledge, the status of the theological, and, most importantly, the consequences of removing redemption from this nexus of ideas. It is this last aspect of Baudelaire's thought which is his most original: Baudelaire is the first to attempt to push to its limit a refusal of redemption; this results in what is perhaps the most radically heretical variation on Christian thought, cutting as it does at the very heart of the Christian faith. While Baudelaire's pessimism and antimodernity will figure in our analyses throughout the book, his effort to draw all the consequences from a refusal of redemption, and other thinkers' travels on that path, will be the most important guiding thread. In answer to the all-too-easy alternative of simply substituting a different *kind* of redemption for the traditional theological one, whether that be revolutionary political dreams or the estheticism of either art for art's sake or its later nineteenth and early twentieth-century manifestations, Baudelaire challenges us to consider how we might think unredemptively, or rather a-redemptively.

Let us begin by considering Baudelaire's characterization of the modern in light of his critique of progress. While he is often evoked as the first "modern" poet and his characterization of the "painter of modern life" has become canonical, there is also a deeply antimodern strain in Baudelaire. We must resist the urge to see the two in simple opposition, however, and recognize that, as Antoine Compagnon has remarked, "the antimoderns are not just any adversaries of the modern, but indeed the thinkers and theoreticians of the modern" (Compagnon 24). Modernity is thus defined and even constituted by antimoderns, if we take care to avoid making this term simply synonymous with vituperative cultural and political reactionaries.[1] Part of being antimodern is positing a critical relationship to history, but what makes the case of Baudelaire unique is that while working out ideas on history, he is also working through new notions of time, a question inextricably interwoven with theological and moral considerations. Hence the particularly modern kind of antimodernism that the Baudelaire of the 1850s and 1860s espouses: not simply ahistorical or antihistorical nor a critique of progress or revolution but a deeper pessimism that is worked out through a new relationship to writing, and to theological discourse, that finds one of its best expressions in the fragmentary writings of the *Journaux intimes* [*Intimate Journals*].

To be antimodern is, at the very least, to posit a critical relationship to history. As far as revolutionary intervention into history is concerned, we can trace a shift in Baudelaire's views, from the young man eager to go to the barricades in 1848 to the older man who claimed in a now-famous remark in a letter that the 1851 coup d'état by Napoléon III "m'a physiquement dépolitiqué" ["physically depoliticized me"] (*Corr* 1: 188). Beyond the political engagement of Baudelaire the man, the writings themselves accomplish a shift from the consideration of history to the consideration of the notion of time more generally. And it is a certain divided relation to time that marks, for theorists such as Matei Calinescu, the concept of modernity in its broadest outlines. Calinescu asserts that modernity "is reflected in the irreconcilable opposition" between "objectified, socially measurable time of capitalist civilization" and "the personal, subjective, imaginative *durée*, the private time created by the unfolding of the 'self'" (Calinescu 5), and recognizes that "although the idea of modernity has come to be associated almost automatically with secularism, its main constitutive element is simply a sense of *unrepeatable time*," a view he affirms as "by no means incompatible" with Judeo-Christian eschatological views of history (Calinescu 13). The question of modernity, a historically minded attempt at periodization, is thus complicated from the outset by a set of temporal considerations that expand questions of "history" to include more far-reaching philosophical and theological notions. And it is important to note that Calinescu's conceptual framework establishes a continuity between modernity and Judeo-Christian notions of time through the category of the eschatological. This is the very continuity that Baudelaire's own vision will question by canceling the possibility of redemption.

An important step toward articulating an antimodern notion of time is the adaptation of theological discourse that Baudelaire accomplishes in both his poetry and the *Journaux intimes*. This is not, however, a simple transposition of terms from the theological to the secular realms. Hans Robert Jauss cautions against such a simplistic reading, claiming that if such were the case, "the modernity of the *Fleurs du Mal* would not be essentially different from the experience of 'empty transcendence' already discovered long before by the romantic poetry of solitude" (Jauss 177). Jauss underscores that Baudelaire instead "radicalized the Christian theology of original sin itself when he legitimated the antinaturalism of his aesthetics against the nature religion of romanticism," producing a "provocative secularization" that deepens Christian notions of the fall into original sin without retaining any notion of salvation or grace. This shift emerges quite explicitly in the *Journaux intimes* in passages such as the following:

> Une fois il fut demandé devant moi en quoi consistait le plus grand plaisir de l'amour. Quelqu'un répondit naturellement: à recevoir,—et un autre: à se donner.—Celui-ci dit: plaisir d'orgueil!—et celui-là: volupté d'humilité! Tous ces orduriers parlaient comme l'Imitation de J-C.—Enfin il se trouva un impudent utopiste qui affirma que le plus grand plaisir de l'amour était de former des citoyens pour la patrie. Moi, je dis: la volupté unique et suprême de l'amour gît dans la certitude de faire le *mal*.—Et l'homme et la femme savent de naissance que dans le mal se trouve toute volupté. (OC1: 651–2)

> [One time it was asked, in my presence, in what the greatest pleasure of love consisted. Someone naturally responded: in receiving,—and another: in giving oneself. The latter said: selfish pleasure of pride!—and the former: voluptuousness of humility! All these filthy people were speaking like the Imitation of Christ.—Finally there was an impudent utopian who affirmed that the greatest pleasure of love was to form citizens for the fatherland. As for me, I said: the only and supreme voluptuous pleasure of love lies in the certainty of doing evil.—And man and woman know from birth that it is in evil that all voluptuousness is to be found.]

Here, Baudelaire marks the passage from utopian political projects to a simultaneously wider and more pessimistic evaluation of the human condition in ways that go beyond narrow considerations of historical particularities to consider evil as the source of human motivation and pleasure. Such a discussion removes us from the specificity of the city while at the same time reminding us that it is only in a modern city that such an exchange of ideas among a variety of representatives of various kinds of human stupidity can occur.

The historical and geographical moment thus becomes the condition of the speaker's self-removal from that specificity; the modern and antimodern conjoin, as progress in the latter is facilitated by the conditions generated by the former. If there is no redemption from the depths of evil to which we are all condemned to descend, Baudelaire's vision nonetheless reinterprets theological discourse in political terms. In a fragment which resembles the prose poem "Assommons les pauvres!" ["Let's Beat up the Poor!"], the speaker imagines the following scenario:

> Si, quand un homme prend l'habitude de la paresse, de la rêverie, de la fainéantise, au point de renvoyer sans cesse au lendemain la chose importante, un autre homme le réveillait un matin à grands coups de fouet et le fouettait sans pitié jusqu'à ce que, ne pouvant travailler par plaisir, celui-ci travaillât par peur, cet homme,– le fouetteur,–ne serait-il pas vraiment son ami, son bienfaiteur? (655)

> [If, when a man takes on the habit of laziness, reverie, inaction, to the point of always putting the important thing off until the next day, another man would wake him one morning with big lashes of the whip and beat him pitilessly until, no longer able to work from pleasure, he would work from fear, that man—the one whipping-would he not truly be his friend and benefactor?]

The speaker concludes: "De même en politique, le vrai saint est celui qui fouette et tue le peuple pour le bien du peuple" ["The same goes in politics, the true saint is the one who whips and kills the people for the good of the people"] (655). One cannot speak, then, of a simple removal of theological vocabulary and notions of redemption nor of a simple turn away from politics. Baudelaire reintwines political and theological discourse here, even more so than in the prose poem which shares certain features of this anecdote, and which I shall analyze in the last chapter. Rather than secularizing sainthood by emphasizing a political utopia, the speaker imports religious discourse into the political by reinvesting violence with a kind of (negative) redemptive value and seeming to give moral value to tyranny.

If humanity is eternally the same, the speaker in the *Journaux intimes* demands that we change our perspective in order to remind ourselves that we have not in fact progressed beyond the savage state:

> Quoi de plus absurde que le Progrès, puisque l'homme [...] est toujours semblable et égal à l'homme, c'est-à-dire toujours à l'état sauvage. Qu'est-ce que les périls de la forêt et de la prairie auprès des chaos et des conflits quotidiens de la vie? Que l'homme enlace sa dupe sur le Boulevard, ou perce sa proie dans des forêts inconnues, n'est-il pas l'homme éternel, c'est-à-dire l'animal de proie le plus parfait? (663)

> [What is more absurd than Progress, since man [...] is always like and equal to man, that is, always in the savage state. What are the perils of the forest and prairie next to the everyday chaos and conflicts of life? Whether man embraces his dupe

on the Boulevard or skewers his prey in unknown forests, is he not the eternal man, that is, the most perfect animal of prey?]

If we have not progressed beyond the savage stage, then time and space can be compressed and flattened so that it no longer makes sense to conceive of them according to a linear model, and the modern city becomes not so much a copy of the wild forest as its eternally equivalent substitute, an eternal repetition of the same space wherever humanity finds itself. Seen in this light, I would argue that the form in which the *Journaux intimes* survives for us, as a de facto set of fragments and aphorisms, itself negates the notion of progress, inviting us to begin anew with each fragment and to see the work as a whole whose parts do not and cannot pretend to suggest progression, coherence, or systematic exposition. Baudelaire here carves out an antimodernist literary space of negation without redemption, the work of a speaker who could be any of us, representative of "l'homme, c'est-à-dire chacun" ["man, that is, every one"] *"naturellement* dépravé" [*"naturally* depraved"] (665).

Baudelaire's radicalization of original sin is at the heart of his antimodernism and catalyzes not only the removal from linear notions of time but also what he calls a "joie de descendre" ["joy of descending"] (683), an irremediable and eternal tendency to revel in evil. Such a reversal of the good is fully consonant with traditional theology, but Baudelaire pushes the boundaries of this assertion to arrive at new consequences of the logic of the fall:

La Théologie.
Qu'est-ce que la chute?
Si c'est l'unité devenue dualité, c'est Dieu qui a chuté. (688)

[Theology.
What is the fall?
If it is unity become duality, it is God who has fallen.]

This assertion blurs further distinctions, pressing the logic of duality which governs humanity (Baudelaire's famous "double postulation" toward God and Satan) and extending it to God himself who, with Satan's fall from grace, himself falls into duality and thus becomes the mirror of humanity and erases the distinction between divinity and humanity. Depravity is, for Baudelaire, inscribed in all of creation: "En d'autres termes, la création ne serait-elle pas la chute de Dieu?" ["In other terms, would creation not be the fall of God?"] (689). This realization then allows a reimagination of different notions of progress: "Theorie de la vraie civilisation./Elle n'est pas dans le gaz, ni dans la vapeur, ni dans les tables tournantes, elle est dans la diminution des traces du péché originel" ["Theory of true civilization./It is not in natural gas, nor steam, nor turbing tables, it is in the diminution of the traces of original sin"] (697). Baudelaire borrows and extends ideas of Joseph de Maistre, for whom history is synonymous with the Fall because human time is inaugurated by it.[2] Even the fall into time itself is double in structure, as Elissa Marder has argued: "The 'ancient fall' is conceived as a fall both *into* time and *out* of it. One falls into time by becoming conscious of it, but the moment one becomes conscious of time, one falls out of it because consciousness of time prevents one from being able to live in it" (20). This problem is at the heart of Baudelaire's supposed celebration of the modern, which canonical readings see in his call to represent the contemporary. But as Gérald Froidevaux has shown, representing the present implies just that kind of removal from the present that Marder signals, since one would have to be simultaneously in the present and outside it in order to represent it:

> The apparently tautological formula of the "representation of the present" expresses the Baudelairean desire to establish the present in an intemporal duration [...]. The modern beautiful liberates the present from its alienation from Time, gratifies it with a sort of ontological solidity and confirms it as a Same that escapes incessant chronological subversion. [...] Situated at the opposite of History, the Baudelairean idea of the present sets itself up in the negation of the historical present, of the present that defines itself by its place in temporal continuity. (Froidevaux 54)

Progress could only be attained by canceling duality, including the paradoxical duality of existing within and outside the present moment, and reestablishing lost Unity, but whereas the earlier Baudelaire held out the possibility of such unity at least at the level of esthetic perception, the later Baudelaire cancels any such hope and plants humanity firmly in the changelessness of duality and the fragmentation of which the *Journaux intimes* become an important illustration. The text performs the duality to which we are condemned by refusing efforts to order it or establish coherence or development within its structure, thus serving as a kind of refutation of the poetics of synaesthesia announced by poems like "Correspondances" or "Elévation."

What we have in the *Journaux intimes* as they come down to us is something that is not at all, of course, a personal journal or autobiography; the title *Journaux intimes* was imparted posthumously and never corresponded to anything Baudelaire had conceived as a journal. As such what we have is not merely a first-person subject. Far from a heart laid bare, that subject is a generalized persona, speaking from that no-time, that sort of eternal present that an antimodern modernity requires and seeks. In fact, often only the least developed fragments, segments which are not even full sentences, are the ones that evoke biographical elements of Baudelaire's life.[3] Most often, the speaking subject is removed from the specificity of a particular human person while, all the same, making reference to the particular times and places in which it was composed and thus serving as an illustration of the always only partial success of efforts to transcend the present by representing it.

In aphoristic writing the transitional and personal present become universalized, announced in an iterative present that solves the problem of representing the present by refraining from doing so, eschewing it in favor of a more generalized moment of utterance. Like the impossible present instant which is fragmented into ever smaller units, aphorisms ask us to leap over the gaps between them, assigning continuity or discontinuity to their fragments, imposing order even though such an order may only be a readerly construction.[4] In this sense each time the *Journaux intimes* are read as a collection, the reader takes on the same role as the editors who initially compiled the fragments into the order in which we read them now. Aphorisms thus perform two kinds of separation: from linear time and from other personal subjectivities and group identities, as Joshua Foa Dienstag remarks: "Rather than emphasizing community and identity, as a dialogue does, aphoristic wisdom tends to separate its reader from his or her self and from the group of which he or she is a part. The ironic and openly sarcastic aphorisms of the early masters of this form throw a cold light on various common social and political hypocrisies" (229).

This slippage between a general "I" and a particular "I" is in fact a crucial aspect of Baudelaire's aphoristic writing: "Ivresse religieuse des grandes villes.—Panthéisme. Moi, c'est tous; tous, c'est moi. Tourbillon" ["Religious intoxication of big cities.—Pantheism. I am all, and all are I. Whirlwind" (OC1: 651). The complexity of the blurred intersubjective relations here is revealed in affirmations such as the following: "Quand j'aurai inspiré le dégoût et l'horreur universels, j'aurai conquis la solitude" ["When I will have inspired universal horror and disgust, I will have conquered solitude"] (660). Baudelaire calls into question the very nature of the solitude he evokes here and provokes a fall into the undecidability of language in what initially seems like a straightforward assertion. Whose solitude is being conquered here? At first, it seems that the poet perversely conquers his own solitude by inspiring universal disgust as some kind of existential proof that he is not alone in the world, but it is also plausible that the poet helps others to conquer a more universal solitude, uniting everyone in their feelings of horror against the poet, in which case the poet takes on a kind of sacrificial role for universal benefit. Or perhaps awakening others to disgust and horror would inspire in them the same kinds of feeling already present in the poet and thus forge solidarity between them. This deceptively simple statement performs the kind of vertigo implied in "Moi, c'est tous; tous, c'est moi" and reinforces the move away from biography and toward a more generalized assessment of the workings of time and subjectivity, and with important political consequences as well, since Baudelaire calls the notion of an individualized subject into question and favors an older model of the human person playing a role as part of a more generalized humanity: "La peine de Mort n'a pas pour but de *sauver* la société, matériellement du moins. Elle a pour but de *sauver* (spirituellement) la société et le coupable" ["The goal of the death penalty is not to *save* society, at least in material terms. It is to (spiritually) *save* society and the guilty one"] (683). In this, too, Baudelaire calls into question the modernist philosophical and political project; indeed Robert Pippin identifies the question of "how there could be such a being that was both *in* the world and the subject *of* a world" as the "distinctive modern problem in any account of the subject-world relation" (xvi). Being as a subject and being in time are both called into question by Baudelaire in assertions that neither revert wholly to medieval models nor participate fully in the post-Kantian formulation of the subject.

This particular speaking subject, halfway between a specific individual and a more generalized voice, derives a certain authority precisely from that liminal status, a subject in the world but not of it and whose pronouncements can thus sometimes take the shape of prophecy:

> Quant à moi qui sens quelque fois en moi le ridicule d'un prophète, je sais que je n'y trouverai jamais la charité d'un médecin. Perdu dans ce vilain monde, coudoyé par les foules, je suis comme un homme lassé dont l'œil ne voit en arrière [...] que désabusement et amertume, et devant lui qu'un orage où rien de neuf n'est contenu, ni enseignements, ni douleur. (667)

> [As for me, who sometimes feel in myself the ridiculousness of a prophet, I know that I will never find there the charity of a doctor. Lost in this nasty world, bumped into by the crowds, I am like a weary man whose eye sees, behind him [...] only disillusionment and bitterness, and in front of him a storm where nothing new is contained, neither teachings nor pain.]

Baudelaire's prophet is stripped of the confidence or certainty that divine ordinance normally confers and is thus reduced to a self-doubt that calls the status of the prophecy into question. The prophet of antimodernity refuses progress and remains suspended in a present of intermittent lucidity alternating with a questioning of that very lucidity and of the value of announcing it. This observation comes in one of the longest but most tentative fragments of the *Journaux intimes*, and this entry is followed by a comment indicating that these remarks were off the mark, yet, even so, "je laisserai ces pages,—parce que je veux dater ma colère. [tristesse]" ["I will leave these pages,—because I want to date my anger. [sadness]"] (667). This statement puts in doubt the worth of the observations that precede it, claiming that their only value is biographical. But rather, we should reverse the claim and suggest that the remarks that Baudelaire undercuts by reducing them to a record of personal anger or sadness are in fact a key observation for the more generalized voice emerging from the *Journaux intimes*. The present moment barely exists for the speaker, who uses it only as a vantage point from which to see the present and future.

Moreover, the future is not even distinguishable from the present, since it contains "rien de neuf," a phrase that once again cancels linear time and returns us to the primacy of the atemporal, metaphysical experience of evil in Baudelaire's record of his contemporary urban experience. As Françoise Meltzer has argued:

> Obsessed with the concept of sin and a hyper-Augustinianism by way of Maistre, Baudelaire writes the city less as a theoretician of modernity than as a producer of texts that argue the inevitability, indeed the triumph, of evil in the new urban

world. Though he does (notoriously) revel in corruption and wickedness, Baudelaire's conviction that man is by definition irrevocably sinful is confirmed in his depictions of the modern, capitalist, industrial city. Baudelaire's pleasure then lies less in the escapism provided by debauchery than in the affirmation of his deepest belief: that man can never escape his sinful heritage. (15)

Acknowledging the primacy of Baudelaire's metaphysical vision over the poetics of representing the contemporary, as indeed the force determining the nature of that representation, allows us to avoid the temptation to see the "Tableaux parisiens" ["Parisian Tableaux"] and the prose poems of *Le Spleen de Paris* [*Paris Spleen*] as a progression on Baudelaire's part away from more abstract concerns and toward a representation of a more experiential lived reality. Besides the fact that there is not a sharp chronological divide between the compositon of lyric poems and prose poems, there is not a conceptual shift that would abandon the prototheological vision of "evil" for a more secularized vocabulary. While Baudelaire does certainly fulfill his role as one of the first to give poetic voice to urban alienation and shock, even that representation depends on the metaphysical vision which remains primary and operational simultaneously with the voice of the disenfranchised, temporally situated poet. To affirm the contrary would be to try to impose a linear development or progression on Baudelaire's work that his own musings on the nature of time would reject.

By now it should be clear that I am not suggesting a return to a "religious" or even post-secular reading of Baudelaire. As I have suggested, certain theological concepts retain their full force in Baudelaire while being divorced from the question of belief and removed from anything that we could recognize as an actually Christian framework. Baudelaire is not, like less remarkable antimoderns, suggesting we avoid science and return to a premodern Catholic worldview. While he suggests the limits of science, in texts such as "Le mauvais vitrier" ["The Bad Glazier"], which I shall analyze in the last chapter, and provides a warning about a misplaced faith in its methods and conclusions, he does not suggest that science be supplanted by a simple traditional Catholicism. In fact, in 1861, Baudelaire wrote in a letter to his mother: "Je désire de tout mon cœur (avec quelle sincérité, personne ne peut le savoir que moi!) croire qu'un être extérieur et invisible s'intéresse à ma destinée; mais comment faire pour le croire?" ["I desire with all my heart (with how much sincerity, no one but me can know!) to believe that an exterior and invisible being is interested in my destiny; but what to do in order to believe it?"] (*Corr* 2: 151).[5] No matter what valence the capacity to believe may have had for Baudelaire personally, lack of belief cannot reduce the impact of the theological concepts in his writing. Nowhere is such force more visible than in Baudelaire's engagement with original sin, which also evinces his distance from actual Christian frameworks not only in that it consists chiefly in knowledge rather than disobedience (an idea I explore in more depth in Chapter 2) but also in that it is never corrected by grace, eliminated by baptism, or triumphed over by redemption.

Original sin is far from a merely theological concept. As Simon Critchley has recently indicated:

> it is the conceptual expression of a fundamental experience of ontological defectiveness or lack which explains the human propensity towards error, malice, wickedness, violence, and extreme cruelty. Furthermore this defect is not something we can put right—which is why authoritarians think that human beings require the yoke of the state, God, law, and the police. Politics becomes the means for protecting human beings from themselves, that is, from their worst inclinations towards lust, cruelty, and violence. (108–9)

The high stakes of any modern or contemporary discussion of original sin immediately become apparent: quickly divorced from questions of belief, original sin becomes the base of a political theology that veers toward tyranny. The authoritarian conclusions fall back, however, into a logic of redemption, since beneath the concept of "protecting" human beings from themselves lies an implicit notion of redemption, in this case via the state, as Critchley goes on to note as he paraphrases proponents of original sin: "Because the human being is defined by original sin, authoritarianism—in the form of dictatorship, say—becomes necessary as the only means that might save human beings from themselves. Human beings require the hard rule of authority because they are essentially defective" (108). He will go on to defend anarchism as "the political expression of freedom from original sin" (108). Baudelaire's own position here is a more complicated one than is immediately apparent. While Baudelaire, in his most Maistrean moments, sometimes seems to affirm such a reactionary politics, as we saw in his defense of capital punishment above, such a view is ultimately inconsistent with his refusal of redemption. Here, Baudelaire is a more original thinker than de Maistre, who retains a logic of redemption by way of the notion of a sacrificial victim. While authoritarianism provides an (all too easy) answer to the "ontological defectiveness" at hand, Baudelaire cannot defend it in anything more than a halfhearted or temporary way. In other words, emphasis on original sin does not necessarily lead to reactionary politics; it does so only when we hold on, as de Maistre did but as Baudelaire ultimately refuses to do, to the logic of redemption. Trying to push beyond that logic is part of Baudelaire's crucial intellectual and literary project, and in this he might be better situated with thinkers like Freud and Schopenhauer than with overtly political reactionaries.[6]

United to this political problem is an epistemological one, the premise that knowledge, *pace* the Greek philosophical tradition, is a source of evil. We shall see below that the early Walter Benjamin returns to this idea, with important consequences that we can apply to the Baudelairean worldview as it emerges in his verse poetry. John Gray has noted the curious transformation, in the contemporary world, of the identification of knowledge and sin in Genesis:

> In modern times, nothing is more heretical than the idea that knowledge can be a sin [...]. The belief that humanity advances with the growth of knowledge is at the

heart of liberal humanism. In many ways humanism is not much more than secular Christianity; but it has suppressed the profound insights into the contradictions of human nature and the ambivalence of knowledge that were preserved in the Christian tradition. At the same time it has perpetuated Christianity's worst errors. (*Heresies* 6–7)

Chief among these errors is the anthropocentrism, more pronounced in Christianity than in other world religions according to Gray, that leads to an unreasonable and politically suspect humanism (hence the link that Gray establishes here between humanism and Christianity). As we shall see, Baudelaire's crucial revision of Christianity, which robs it of its core doctrine of redemption in a way that allows him to restore the full emphasis on knowledge as evil, also has the potential to serve as a corrective to a damaging anthropocentrism. This is so not because Baudelaire affirms the animal over the human but because his pessimism imposes limits on the untenable optimism of secular liberalism as Gray here describes it.

By such reference to a critique of secular liberalism I do not mean to imply that a full-fledged or clearly articulated politics emerges from Baudelaire's literary or nonliterary writings. Such was not his goal, and attempts to claim otherwise are destined to leave unexplained exceptions to any coherent political position unaccounted for. This is not to say that political conclusions cannot be drawn from his texts, but like any interpretive move in the case of Baudelaire, the conclusion can never be definitive on account of the very tensions and contradictions that characterize his texts. What I wish to trace is above all the metaphysics that ground the kinds of tentative political conclusions we may draw from Baudelaire's texts; on these grounds, the poet presents a more clearly delineable position that I have already begun to identify via the refusal of redemption and its consequences both for thought and lived experience. This latter consideration will come to the fore in later chapters, where I attempt to delineate the ethical implications of Baudelaire's metaphysics. While there are clearly political implications in many poems—one only needs to think of the caricatural violence of "Assommons les pauvres" or the implied argument against tyranny in "Une mort héroïque" ["A Heroic Death"]—the very uncertainty of Baudelaire's own political commitments mitigates against any overconfident reading of a positive political position in these texts. Indeed, while there are sure indications of a shift from revolutionary enthusiasm to conservative vituperation over the course of Baudelaire's life, his complex deployment of irony in his texts mitigates any definitive articulation of a political position. If Joseph de Maistre did indeed teach Baudelaire to reason, as the poet claims (I: 669), he does not ultimately follow him very far, since sacrificial violence in the name of the redemptive act is absolutely crucial to Maistrean thinking, lying at the very heart of his reactionary politics. By contrast, one of the few areas of Baudelaire's thought both untouched by irony and consistent throughout his writings is the refusal of redemption, which effectively closes down the possibility of a direct conceptual and political lineage from de Maistre to Baudelaire. This is not, of course, to say that it is easy to move past redemptive thinking. Is it in fact possible to think beyond the logic of redemption, whether by a god, or art, or politics, or something else altogether?[7]

Rethinking artistic creation in light of the logic of redemption or its impossibility has been the subject of some recent critical attention. Giorgio Agamben's essay "Creation and Salvation" explores the secularization of religious traditions related to the interdependent acts of creation and salvation, in the context of the work of the modern poet and the critic. Agamben's reflections can help us articulate what is at stake for Baudelaire's criticism and poetry in his attempt to think beyond salvation. In turn, the world of prophets, angels, creators, and redeemers that populates Agamben's essay can be illuminated by careful attention to the way in which Christian discourse functions in Baudelaire. While the theological framework in Agamben applies chiefly to the critic, in Baudelaire it is the poetry that abounds in reconceived religious structures. The enabling mechanism of religious discourse is thus transferred from poetry (in Baudelaire) to criticism (in Agamben) and serves as an interesting test case of the kinds of exchanges and mutual interdependence that Agamben theorizes between creation and salvation. Agamben (the critic-become-poet) and Baudelaire (the poet-become-critic) demonstrate the ways in which the critic's redemptive work also simulates, rather than merely reproduce or describe, the poet's creative work.

Several features of Agamben's essay invite questions about the best way to read it. While its nine pages can be read continuously, it is divided not so much into sections as into nine page-long propositions or theses that could also stand independently as variations on a theme. Another notable feature of the essay is its willful lack of contextualization within any larger critical conversation. In this essay that offers a meditation on the act of criticism, Agamben writes without footnotes, implicitly proposing an ahistorical intervention that blends well with the nonlinear temporality that his reflections on creation and redemption as perpetual and simultaneous acts imply. Agamben thus, by flattening critical time, demonstrating the interdependence of the creative and critical act and refraining from limiting the critical field by identifying fellow critical interlocutors, invites dialogue with creators and critics from other periods who have considered questions of the relationship of creation to salvation in the context of literary production and interpretation. My own attempt to read Agamben and Baudelaire together will pass through two other critics between Baudelaire's time and Agamben's, the early Benjamin and Paul de Man. What follows is an attempt to "interhistoricize" Agamben's essay in a way faithful to the kind of reading he suggests via his own ahistorical critical intervention in the "Creation and Salvation" essay.

After considering, in the first half of his essay, the role of the prophet in several world religious traditions, Agamben establishes what at first appears to be a straightforward secularization hypothesis whereby creation and salvation have been transformed into non-religious domains:

> In modern culture philosophy and criticism have inherited the prophetic work of salvation (that formerly [...] had been entrusted to exegesis); poetry, technology, and art are the inheritors of the angelic work of creation. Through the process of secularization of the religious tradition, however, these disciplines have progressively lost all memory of the relationship that had previously linked them. (*Nudities* 5)

Agamben's essay attempts to restore the memory of the link between creation and salvation by rethinking the relationship between literature and criticism, in ways I shall trace below, but from the outset I would inquire whether the secularization of these concepts was as complete as Agamben implies. If we are to take, for instance, the concept of political theology seriously, we need to rethink a simple secularization thesis whereby new concepts come to replace the old without remainder, leaving us with nostalgia for a time when criticism and poetry were interconnected in ways we find it difficult now to fathom.

Agamben goes on to attempt reading creation and salvation together, claiming that "inasmuch as they represent the two powers of a single God," they are "secretly conjoined" (6), and necessarily so, since "a critical or philosophical work that does not possess some sort of an essential relationship with creation is condemned to pointless idling, just as a work of art or poetry that does not contain within it a critical exigency is destined for oblivion" (6).[8] Agamben creates an altered myth of lost paradise, where "today" criticism and literature, just like their homologous pair salvation and creation, "search desperately for a meeting point […] where their lost unity can be rediscovered. They do this by exchanging their roles, which nevertheless remain implacably divided" (6). This is not restoration of lost primeval unity, then, but rather an exchange, where one becomes the other as they exchange roles. Later in the essay, however, Agamben asserts the ultimate impossibility of salvation. Since the created being "cannot but be lost" (8), turned into a memory or ultimately, as is the fate of all things, destroyed, it therefore cannot be saved, nor can the created being's "potentiality." Rather, creation and potentiality are rendered indistinguishable. The resulting consequence is that "the ultimate figure of human and divine action appears where creation and salvation coincide in the unsavable" (8). Following upon the logic of impossible salvation, Agamben asserts that salvation, unlike creation which is bound to be destroyed, is eternal, but, since it has survived creation, "its exigency is […] lost in the unsavable. Born from a creation that is left pending, it ends up as an inscrutable salvation that no longer has an objective" (9). Salvation remains as a pure but useless notion, given that it cannot have an object on which to act.

A crucial point of entry into the complex web of concepts that Agamben weaves is a consideration of time. What Agamben effects in his essay is a shift from eternity to simultaneity. He eliminates the possibility of creation's eternity, as we have seen, and retains salvation only as a potentiality: "Redemption is nothing other than a potentiality to create that remains pending, that turns on itself and 'saves' itself. But what is the meaning of 'saving' in this context? After all, there is nothing in creation that is not ultimately destined to be lost" (7). What remains, however, is the notion of simultaneity of creation and salvation; if they once were, as Agamben argues, indistinguishable and co-present, then it no longer makes sense to speak of creation preceding redemption. It is here that we need to ask an important question about Agamben's own temporal schema: he claims, as I have noted, that literature and criticism "have progressively lost all memory of the relationship that had previously linked them so intimately to one another" (5) but also claims that we have belated knowledge of the intimate connections between creation and redemption. In other words, Agamben's essay posits, simultaneously, the possibility and impossibility of perceiving creation and salvation together. This simultaneous postulation is rendered possible by the form of Agamben's essay itself, in its numbered sections that invite us to read them sequentially or cumulatively even though each can be read on its own terms, related to the other sections by its thematic concerns but not by the linear progression of a conventional argument.

Religious discourse operates here neither in a traditional Christian (or Jewish, or Islamic) frame nor as a source for ideas which will then be simply secularized, but rather as an enabling mechanism for rethinking the "modern," since it is at the very least implied that the separability of creation and salvation, and by extension literature and criticism, is a modern phenomenon. (Agamben cites Dante as an example of a writer for whom the literature/criticism distinction is not yet operable.) Religious discourse retains more than a simply haunting presence for writers like Agamben who draw on figures such as prophets and angels while clearly not carrying the same force of belief that this discourse may have had for pre-moderns. Here, Agamben operates in a line of poets and critics that goes far back within modernity; Baudelaire's poetry and criticism set the stage in important ways for a strain of critical discourse about redemption and modernity that recurs regularly throughout the twentieth century and beyond. Reading Baudelaire and Agamben together along with Benjamin and de Man highlights a simultaneity of thought among these writers, a notion that flattens time in a decidedly amodern way by collapsing conventional distinctions of historical time in order to focus on continuity. This notion of chronological simultaneity can be usefully expanded to analyze the coexistence of creation and salvation, and, by Agamben's further extension, of literature and criticism.

There are many fruitful points of intersection between Baudelaire and the Agamben of the "Creation and Salvation" essay, beginning with Baudelaire's formulation of the non-mutually exclusive relationship between poet and critic. In his essay on Richard Wagner, Baudelaire declares that "tous les grands poètes deviennent naturellement, fatalement, critiques" ["All great poets become naturally, fatally, critics"] and adds: "Je plains les poètes que guide le seul instinct; je les crois incomplets. [...] Il serait prodigieux qu'un critique devînt poète, et il est impossible qu'un poète ne contienne pas un critique" ["I pity the poets guided only by instinct; I think they are incomplete. [...] It would be prodigious if a critic were to become a poet, and it is impossible that a poet not contain a critic"] (OC2: 793). Baudelaire here defies Agamben's assertion that criticism and literature, once united, came to be perceived as distinct activities, for while Baudelaire affirms the unity of poet and critic, it is in a one-sided way, since the poet *contains* the critic whereas the critic cannot aspire to the status of the poet. In other words, Baudelaire's description depends on the dichotomy it calls into question in the case of the poet. In order for us to understand that the complete poet includes the critic but not vice versa, we need to have the kind of split between poet and critic that Agamben describes, without retaining his historical narrative of a move from unity to division. Agamben's link between the categories of poet/critic and creation/salvation proves fruitful here, since Baudelaire's assertion about the poet-as-critic remains ambiguous as to whether the poet acts as critic only when writing criticism or whether the poet is most effective as critic *by* writing poetry. If we follow a long strain of twentieth-century commentators stretching back at least as far as Heidegger, literature *qua* literature holds crucial insights into questions traditionally pursued by philosophy and that cannot be expressed any other way except as literature. Therefore the poet as Baudelaire describes him could very well be seen as acting as a critic (in the sense of interpreter) through the writing of poetry, thus participating in the simultaneous act of creation and redemption that Agamben describes, eliminating the temporal distance between those two acts at the same time as he eliminates the need for the role of critic and poet to be embodied by different individuals.

We recall Agamben's characterization of redemption as "nothing other than a potentiality to create that remains pending, that turns on itself and 'saves' itself" (7), even if there is nothing that can in fact be saved. Here there is resonance with Baudelaire's description of the modern artist as the one who is able to "tirer l'éternel du transitoire" ["to draw out the eternal from the transitory"] (OC2: 694). This formulation suspends the "modern" between the immediate present and the atemporal, in a way that allows us to make more of a link than is sometimes acknowledged between Baudelaire's theologically inflected poetry and his writing of the modern city in the "Tableaux parisiens" and the prose poems, which has captured the lion's share of recent critical attention to Baudelaire via the long legacy of Walter Benjamin's analysis of urban experience in Baudelaire. To complicate the picture by seeing more of a connection between the metaphysical and the urban Baudelaire is to pose important questions about the nature of time and modernity in Baudelaire's conception of artistic production and criticism. Given that his famous comments about the eternal and the transitory are offered almost in passing in an essay devoted to an analysis of the style and subjects of Constantin Guys, many critics have attempted to flesh out Baudelaire's theory of modernity, antimodernity, history, or theology as those are suggested in the tension between the eternal and the transitory. Among those critics is Paul de Man, in his essay "Literary History and Literary Modernity," which begins as a reading of Nietzsche but then turns to consider questions of modernity and history that are pertinent to our analysis.

De Man underscores the problem of temporality when addressing the "modern" precisely because of the impossibility of thinking the present moment as one is experiencing it: "The spontaneity of being modern conflicts with the claim to think and write about modernity; it is not at all certain that literature and modernity are in any way compatible concepts" (de Man 142). His elaboration of this idea questions the same split that Agamben evokes between the creative and the critical. Even though the term *modernity* would have appeared in manifestoes rather than learned articles, writes de Man, "this does not mean that we can divide the twentieth century into two parts: a 'creative' part that was actually modern, and a 'reflective' or 'critical' part that feeds on this modernity in the manner of a parasite" (143). De Man's reading of Nietzsche works through the opposition between the eternal and the transitory, establishing that "it is a temporal experience of human mutability, historical in the deepest sense of the term in that it implies the necessary experience of any present as a *passing* experience that makes the past irrevocable and unforgettable, because it is inseparable from any present or future" (148–9). The impossibility of stepping outside time in order to seize the present cancels the standard notion of linear time by showing the necessary connection among past, present, and future; Nietzsche's notion of the eternal return is one way of conceiving such an ahistorical sense of historicity. Agamben's notion of simultaneity of creation and redemption is another, along with Baudelaire's proposal that the artist, and presumably the critic as well, can draw the eternal from the transitory. On this view, the transitory disappears in the eternal because of the impossibility of accounting for the transitory in the immediacy of its moment, which is another way of expressing, perhaps *contra* Baudelaire, the necessity and impossibility of being both poet and critic except if we abandon a linear model of time. Agamben's interdependent and simultaneous relationship between creation and redemption is prefigured in de Man's comments on modernity and history, which "relate to each other in a curiously contradictory way that goes beyond antithesis or opposition. […] Modernity and history seem condemned to being linked together in a self-destroying union that threatens the survival of both" (151). We cannot view the present *as* present; thus we require an eternally recuperative act in order to save that which, as Agamben reminds us, is destined to be destroyed anyway, leaving the redemptive act without an object. De Man identifies a similar impasse in Baudelaire's own conception of the artist as critic: "As soon as Baudelaire has to replace the single instant of invention, conceived as an act, by a successive movement that involves at least two distinct moments, he enters into a world that assumes the depths and complications of an articulated time, an interdependence between past and future that prevents any present from ever coming into being" (161).[9] Recast in the theological language that Baudelaire prefers in his poetry, he has fallen into the unavoidable consequence of original sin, the fall into a linear time that renders impossible the very simultaneity that he wishes to establish. Paradoxically, this makes of original sin the origin of "modernity," if we take modernity to involve a shift from nonlinear to linear time, which is indeed necessary for the discourse of modernity as linked to a sense of "progress" is to hold.

In this scenario, the task of the critic is all the more urgent, since the impossibility of seizing the present reinforces the importance of the critical act, which is typically viewed as coming after the artistic/creative act, as a comment upon it. If there is no possibility of immediacy, the function of the critic becomes primary rather than secondary or rather it becomes simultaneous or even synonymous with the act of creation in ways that Agamben has suggested. While there is no creation to "save," it is the critical act itself that allows us to step out of the model of linear time that we saw Baudelaire forced to fall into. Criticism, inasmuch as it is creative rather than descriptive, is thus removed from sequential temporality, an idea de Man underscores:

> In describing literature, from the standpoint of modernity, as the steady fluctuation of an entity away from and toward its own mode of being, we have constantly stressed that this movement does not take place as an actual sequence

in time; to represent it as such is merely a metaphor making a sequence out of what occurs in fact as a synchronic juxtaposition. [...] Even in the discursive texts we have used [...] the three moments of flight, return, and the turning point at which flight changes into return or vice-versa, exist simultaneously on levels of meaning that are so intimately intertwined that they cannot be separated. When Baudelaire, for example, speaks of "représentation du présent," of "mémoire du présent," [...] his language names, at the same time, the flight, the turning point, and the return. (163)

De Man's formulation suggests that, when seeking an alternative model to linear time in Baudelaire, we may wish to abandon the concept of eternity in favor of the kind of simultaneity that I have been emphasizing from Agamben's analysis, and that Françoise Meltzer identifies as a key aspect of Baudelairean temporality: "Time in Baudelaire is precisely not the collapse of everything into one eternity of space. There are two times in Baudelaire: the past, which can serve as an antidote to the present, and the future, which poisons the present. [...] Thus the present is the place in which a double vision not only is made possible but is demanded" (237). These considerations of temporality in Baudelaire may seem to have taken us far from the question of redemption; a famous analyst of Baudelaire's work, Walter Benjamin, will help us establish the links among non-linear temporality, the critical act, and redemption but not by way of his writings on Baudelaire. Rather, two key passages from Benjamin's *Trauerspiel* book will not only further illuminate the links among these categories but also themselves serve as an illustration of the non-linearity of developments in literary criticism, as we go back in time from de Man to Benjamin by approximately the same forty-year period that separates de Man from Agamben. In the "Epistemo-Critical Prologue" to *The Origin of German Tragic Drama*, Benjamin writes: "Method is a digression. [...] Tirelessly the process of thinking makes new beginnings, returning in a roundabout way to its original object. This continual pausing for breath is the mode most proper to the process of contemplation" (28). Here Benjamin links the critical act with nonlinearity by identifying a return to the object of criticism which is not simply a temporal regression but rather a return with a renewed understanding, a new way in which artistic creation and criticism are conjoined. The stakes are much higher by the end of Benjamin's study, however, since the act of contemplation, here restricted for the most part to the critical act, is expanded and, most significantly for our purposes, infused with a theological impetus:

The Bible introduces evil in the concept of knowledge. The serpent's promise to the first men was to make them "knowing both good and evil." But it is said of God after the creation: "And God saw everything that he had made, and, behold it was very good." Knowledge of evil therefore has no object. There is no evil in the world. It arises in man himself, with the desire for knowledge, or rather for judgment. Knowledge of good, as knowledge, is secondary. It ensues from practice. Knowledge of evil—as knowledge this is primary. It ensues from contemplation.

Knowledge of good and evil is, then, the opposite of all factual knowledge. Related as it is to the depths of the subjective, it is basically only knowledge of evil. […] In the very fall of man the unity of guilt and signifying emerges as an abstraction. The allegorical has its existence in abstractions; as an abstraction, as a faculty of the spirit of language itself, it is at home in the Fall. (233–4)

Here a new significance is assigned to "contemplation," the concept which links this passage to the earlier one. It is now identified as the source of knowledge of evil, which Baudelaire in "L'irrémédiable" ["Beyond Redemption"] calls "la conscience dans le Mal" ["consciousness of doing Evil"] (OC1: 80). Identifying the fall with knowledge rather than primarily with an act of disobedience will be an important theme running through Baudelaire and some of his interpreters who will play an important role in my analysis, most notably Benjamin Fondane. If the word "contemplation" signifies the same kind of activity in both passages that I have quoted from Walter Benjamin, then the critical act is at the source of the knowledge of evil, and the conscience of evil is linked to the non-linear temporality that allows us to speak of literary creation and criticism as simultaneous rather than consecutive. It is notable that there is no reference to redemption here in Benjamin. Looking forward to Agamben, we recall that there can be no redemption on his account because it would be a redemption without an object, given that nothing, not even the artwork, can be eternally recuperated. Benjamin prefigures these austere visions of falling without redemption and knowledge of good and evil reduced to knowledge of evil alone. His theologically inflected reading of contemplation allows us to flesh out Agamben's analogy between literary creation/criticism and theological creation/redemption and to see that to set up a simple parallel between them is to miss a crucial point about the predominance of evil and some of the temporal consequences of this analogy.

We are now well positioned to see how evil, the fall, nonlinear time, creation, and criticism come together in Baudelaire's poetry; I would claim that we need to see the theological backdrop of Baudelaire's poetry not as a remnant of a poetic past which the more "modern" Baudelaire casts aside but rather as a crucial category for understanding Baudelaire's sense of modernity. Creatively and critically, it is most fruitful to see the theological concerns posed by *Les Fleurs du Mal* as primary and to consider the shock of the modern as a result of the impossibility of thinking the "modern" in the sense of a new form of the present. John Jackson has pointed to the links between time and the impossibility of redemption implied by Baudelaire's poetry. Analyzing "L'horloge" ["The Clock"] Jackson writes: "la conscience du temps qui passe, dans le poème, ne s'ouvre sur aucune possibilité de rédemption. […] Le « souviens-toi! » ne découvre, pour finir, qu'un désespoir" ["the consciousness of time that passes, in the poem, does not open onto any possibility of redemption. […] The 'remember!' only uncovers, finally, a despair"] (61). Going even further, Jackson acknowledges that the poem reveals a vision that "supprime la vision d'avenir, pourtant essentielle" ["cancels the ability to see the future, which is nonetheless essential"] (61). Similarly, Ian Alexander contends that in Baudelaire the future becomes merely the prospect of an endless recurrence of past sins. The result is that the present, isolated from past and future, is experienced as a mere point in an infinite succession of monotonously recurring and discontinuous instants. Time is not so much the passage as the substitution of identical and isolated moments, precluding both continuity and progress: behind, a load of sin, before, an endless recurrence of sin, and in the present, vain gnawing remorse, with at the end death as the final term. (4)

Whether the present in Baudelaire is nonexistent, as de Man had claimed, or a vantage point for double vision, as Meltzer maintains, or a moment isolated from past and future in order to become a torturous eternal return of monotony, it is clear that temporality in Baudelaire is inextricably linked to a vision that cannot be reduced to a mere secularization of Christian concepts. While Jackson does call Baudelaire's recuperation of death as the site of transcendence a "secularization" (55), he also offers the helpful concept of *resonance* of the theological in Baudelaire's metaphysical vision, a ghostly presence both absent and immediately present; this concept of the resonant presence of the past also underscores the alteration of temporality that allows us to think the modern as antimodern in Baudelaire and the act of criticism as an act of creation simultaneous with poetic creation.

A closer look at Baudelaire's poetry in conjunction with the early Benjamin will help us to articulate precisely why redemption is impossible in Baudelaire and what the consequences of this impossibility are. The most relevant poems form a cluster at the conclusion of the "Spleen et Idéal" ["Spleen and Ideal"] section of *Les Fleurs du Mal*. Of the seven final poems of that section, four are new to the 1861 edition. These additions recontextualize the other three poems and allow us to read this final cluster together as representing a move toward a more thorough thinking through of the logic and consequences of the impossibility of redemption. The poems together form an ending to "Spleen et Idéal" that closes in on itself and progresses toward its ending while at the same time introducing poems which, by their nonlinear development and the complex subjectivity that they construct, lead the reader into a vortex which cancels that forward momentum in ways that have theological as well as poetic implications. Evidence of a fall into stagnation appears in "L'irrémédiable," whose title unambiguously indicates the asoteriological logic that dominates the end of this section. The images in the poem are curiously devoid of any present-tense verb and remain frozen in a series of gerunds—"un malheureux […] cherchant la lumière" ["An unfortunate […] looking for the light"], "Un damné descendant sans lampe" ["A damned soul descending […] without light"], "Un navire pris dans le pôle/[…] Cherchant par quel détroit fatal/Il est tombé dans cette geôle" ["A ship caught in the polar sea/[…] Seeking the fatal strait through which/It came into that prison"]—are identified by the poet as

Emblèmes nets, tableau parfait
D'une fortune irrémédiable
Qui donne à penser que le Diable
Fait toujours bien tout ce qu'il fait! (I: 80)

[—Patent symbols, perfect picture
Of an irremediable fate
Which makes one think that the Devil
Always does well whatever he does! (269)]

All of these images frozen in time originate from a fall, as we see in the first stanza:

Une Idée, une Forme, un Etre
Parti de l'azur et tombé
Dans un Styx bourbeux et plombé
Où nul oeil du Ciel ne pénètre; (79)

[An Idea, a Form, a Being
Which left the azure sky and fell
Into a leaden, miry Styx
That no eye in Heaven can pierce; (267)]

Notably, it is not Satan's domain of hell but rather the path to a more neutral pagan underworld that is the destination of the fallen idea here, the kingdom not of revolt but of mere separation from the heavens of the kind that the Baudelaire of the first fall experiences as he is suspended in the contemplation of evil. If "the Devil always does well whatever he does" here, it is not the devil to which one can ally oneself by active revolt but one that paralyzes that revolt and who thus becomes an ally in the frozen contemplation with the promise neither of revolt nor redemption.

Contemplation figures in "L'irrémédiable" not only through the evocation of thinking in the stanza just quoted but also through the "tête-à-tête sombre" that the poet has with his own heart in the closing stanzas of the poem, which leads him, very much as Benjamin describes, to the "puits de vérité" that is consciousness of evil:

Tête-à-tête sombre et limpide
Qu'un coeur devenu son miroir!
Puits de Vérité, clair et noir
Où tremble une étoile livide,

Un phare ironique, infernal
Flambeau des grâces sataniques,
Soulagement et gloire uniques,
—La conscience dans le Mal! (80)

[Somber and limpid tête-à-tête—
A heart become its own mirror!
Well of Truth, clear and black,
Where a pale star flickers,

A hellish, ironic beacon,
Torch of satanical blessings,
Sole glory and only solace
—The consciousness of doing evil. (269)]

The beacon figured in this stanza is not ironic because it brings darkness rather than light, as would be the case in a more typical satanic scenario wrought by the Prince of Darkness. Rather, the beacon does in fact illuminate; the irony is to be found in the fact that the illumination is not projected out onto external reality but inward in order to produce the consciousness of evil that is rendered by contemplation, the autoreflexive mirror that once again, Narcissus-like, is reduced to actionless contemplation removed from temporality and thus from the possibility of action. This Baudelaire is different from the one Benjamin characterized in his later work on Baudelaire and who reveals, as Richard Wolin summarized, "the manner in which the always-the-same of prehistory manifests itself in the modern, insofar as the modern manifests itself as the always-the-same" of the "endless stream of consumer goods or 'fashion'" (129). The Baudelaire of the poem we have been considering is not even able to attain this eternal return of the same of modernity because he is suspended in a contemplation that precludes any kind of movement in time (and thus any kind of recurrence) and that results in nothing beyond the knowledge of evil untranslatable into any sense of history or temporal progression or regression.

The notion of the unredeemable and its consequences for a suspension of linear temporality as they are explored in "L'irrémédiable" sheds light, retrospectively, on a poem placed four spots back in the section and which also provides crucial insight into Baudelaire's asoteriological logic, "Le goût du néant" ["The Desire for Annihilation"] The poem begins by tracing a temporal scheme rooted in the "ne ... . plus," the source of the spirit's current restlessness:

Morne esprit, autrefois amoureux de la lutte,
L'Espoir, dont l'éperon attisait ton ardeur,
Ne veut plus t'enfourcher! (OC1: 76)

[Dejected soul, once anxious for the strife,
Hope, whose spur fanned your ardor into flame,
No longer wishes to mount you! (257)]

The poet enjoins his heart to resign itself to this fate, adding, "dors ton sommeil de brute" ["sleep your brutish sleep"] (OC1: 76). The poem has an unusual structure, with quatrains in *rime embrassée* followed by a single line whose rhyme is the same as the one that links the first and last lines of the stanza that precedes it, thus embodying in poetic form (the resonance of the rhyme) the kind of resonance of the theological that is an important part of Baudelaire's poetic universe. These three single lines of poetry that follow their respective stanzas sketch the general movement of the poem: "Résigne-toi, mon coeur; dors ton sommeil de brute" ["Resign yourself, my heart; sleep your brutish sleep"]; "Le Printemps adorable a perdu son odeur!" ["Adorable spring has lost its fragrance!"]; "Avalanche, veux-tu m'emporter dans ta chute?" ["Avalanche, will you sweep me along in your fall?"]. It is this final line that is of interest here, the culmination of a poem whose last stanza speaks of time swallowing up the poet:

> Et le Temps m'engloutit minute par minute,
> Comme la neige immense un corps pris de roideur;
> Je contemple d'en haut le globe en sa rondeur,
> Et je n'y cherche plus l'abri d'une cahute.
>
> Avalanche, veux-tu m'emporter dans ta chute? (I: 76)
>
> [And Time engulfs me minute by minute,
> As the immense snow a stiffening corpse;
> I survey from above the roundness of the globe
> And I no longer seek there the shelter of a hut.
>
> Avalanche, will you sweep me along in your fall? (257)]

The avalanche is given only in potential here; the poet is not even able to actualize his own damnation, clearly evoked by the "chute," but rather remains suspended in the impossibility of action, at one of those moments in Baudelaire where the past is visible but the present is ineffective and the future uncertain.[10] This final line sends the reader (and the poet, who is addressing himself) back to the concluding line of the first stanza: "Résigne-toi mon coeur." Since action is suspended in presumed impossibility, the only remaining option is resignation to inaction. The accomplishment of both redemption and damnation is blocked at the end of the poem, and a clue about the reason for this is available in the lines just quoted: "Je contemple d'en haut le globe en sa rondeur." While still existing, presumably, as a subject in the historical world, the poet identifies himself as removed from that world, engaged in contemplation. We recall that, for Benjamin, this is the very act that awakens our knowledge, not of good and evil but of evil alone. Here we have the poet engaged in the double role of creator and critic, if we extend the definition of the latter to include self-conscious reflection on the poem contained within the poem itself, so that the poet becomes simultaneously a critic and the reader becomes witness not just to the result of the poet's contemplation but to that very contemplation itself. The reluctance of the poet to follow his own advice to resign himself to the suspended action recalls a section of "De profundis clamavi" ["Out of the Depths Have I Cried"] from earlier in "Spleen et Idéal":

> Je jalouse le sort des plus vils animaux
> Qui peuvent se plonger dans un sommeil stupide,
> Tant l'écheveau du temps lentement se dévide! (OC1: 33)

[I envy the lot of the lowest animals
Who are able to sink into a stupid sleep,
So slowly does the skein of time unwind! (105)]

What is desirable about the animal state is that not only are animals unconcerned about salvation and damnation (because they cannot participate in it in the first place) but also that they are not endowed with the contemplative faculty. Here once again, consciousness, and the necessary faculty of contemplation that accompanies it, is the main source of suffering and cannot be corrected.

The poet's appeal to the avalanche at the end of "Le goût du néant" is an appeal either to damnation or oblivion, but both of these options have already, in the progression of the seven final poems of "Spleen et Idéal," been identified as impossible. The first of these final seven, "Obsession," plays a crucial structural role in conditioning the way we read the poems that follow it.

Grands bois, vous m'effrayez comme des cathédrales;
Vous hurlez comme l'orgue; et dans nos coeurs maudits,
Chambres d'éternel deuil où vibrent de vieux râles,
Répondent les échos de vos *De profundis*.

Je te hais, Océan! tes bonds et tes tumultes,
Mon esprit les retrouve en lui; ce rire amer
De l'homme vaincu, plein de sanglots et d'insultes,
Je l'entends dans le rire énorme de la mer.

Comme tu me plairais, ô nuit! sans ces étoiles
Dont la lumière parle un langage connu!
Car je cherche le vide, et le noir, et le nu!

Mais les ténèbres sont elles-mêmes des toiles
Où vivent, jaillissant de mon oeil par milliers,
Des êtres disparus aux regards familiers. (OC1: 75–6)

[Great woods, you frighten me like cathedrals;
You roar like the organ; and in our cursed hearts,
Rooms of endless mourning where old death-rattles sound,
Respond the echoes of your De profundis.

I hate you, Ocean! your bounding and your tumult,
My mind finds them within itself; that bitter laugh
Of the vanquished man, full of sobs and insults,
I hear it in the immense laughter of the sea.

How I would like you, Night! without those stars
Whose light speaks a language I know!
For I seek emptiness, darkness, and nudity!

But the darkness is itself a canvas
Upon which live, springing from my eyes by thousands,
Beings with understanding looks, who have vanished. (255)]

Here, we have the tormented consciousness that blurs the distinction between inside and outside so that the tumults of the Ocean recur within the mind of the subject, thus eliminating the need for an external world because the torment to be found there is already within the consciousness.[11] The first tercet is a straightforward wish for the *néant* [nothingness] that the poet evokes one poem later in "Le goût du néant," but the conclusion of "Obsession" provides an important insight as to why the wishes of the poet in "Le goût du néant" must go unfulfilled. This is because the desired *néant* is impossible: as long as the subject exists, he will continue to perceive sensations against the backdrop of the *néant*.[12]

The poem stages the kinds of reflection on nothingness which also figure in philosophical accounts such as those of Martin Heidegger, who in his 1929 essay "What is Metaphysics?" posed the question of how to think the nothing without transforming it into a something: "What is the nothing? […] Every answer to this question is also impossible from the start. For it necessarily assumes the form: the nothing 'is' this or that" (98–9). Heidegger goes on to argue that "anxiety reveals the nothing" and, as it does so, "robs us of speech" (103). For him, "Being held out into the nothing […] on the ground of concealed anxiety is its surpassing of beings as a whole. It is transcendence" (108). Yet, for Baudelaire, what serves as an answer to Heidegger's question about the nature of metaphysics only reinforces the impossibility of canceling existence, since what Baudelaire seeks is not a foundation for metaphysics but rather a way to move beyond it, which Heidegger effectively shows is impossible. For Baudelaire, the only escape from such a predicament is death, but an important consequence of the impossibility of redemption is that death would also mean the end of the subject altogether, not the freedom of the subject from the terror of the tumults and other disturbing sensations that the poet describes. If there is release from these sensations, there would no longer be a subject there to perceive this release, since the desired oblivion would abolish the subject as well. What remains is thus the poetic subject turned in on himself and condemned to suffer not only the torments he evokes but also the knowledge that there is no possibility of being able to perceive the state of nothingness where the torments would cease. "Obsession" provides the basic metaphysical framework for understanding the six poems that follow it at the conclusion of "Spleen et Idéal." It furnishes an endpoint because the position it exposes cannot be overcome by anything except a redemptive act, precisely the act that is consistently refused by Baudelaire. After "Obsession," then, we can go no further; we remain trapped in a cyclic subjectivity unable to transcend its situation or bring it to an end.

Georges Bataille's remarks on silence in *Inner Experience* resonate with Baudelaire's characterization of the necessarily frustrated desire to attain the nothing:

> But the difficulty is that one manages neither easily nor completely to silence oneself, that one must fight against onself, with precisely a mother's patience: we seek to grasp within us what subsists safe from verbal servilities and what we grasp is ourselves fighting the battle, stringing sentences together—perhaps about our effort (then about its failure)—but sentences all the same, powerless to grasp anything else. (15)

This inability to establish silence and condemnation to proliferate sentences endlessly echoes the image in "Obsession" of darkness being itself a canvas, and Bataille's use of a specifically linguistic conception of the impossibility of the nothing allows us to consider another of Baudelaire's poems, "Le soleil," in a new light. The battle that involves "stringing sentences together" suggests the famous image of the poet:

> Je vais m'exercer seul à ma fantasque escrime,
> Flairant dans tous les coins les hasards de la rime,
> Trébuchant sur les mots comme sur les pavés
> Heurtant parfois des vers depuis longtemps rêvés. (OC1: 83)

> [I go alone to try my fanciful fencing,
> Scenting in every corner the chance of a rhyme,
> Stumbling over words as over paving stones,
> Colliding at times with lines dreamed of long ago. (281)]

While this is in some sense an ennobling vision of the poet's task, and indeed the poet compares himself to the sun and claims that the latter "ennoblit le sort des choses les plus viles" ("ennobles the fate of the lowliest things" [281]) (83), we cannot help but see such ennobling as illusory, as an attempt at a redemption of sordid urban reality that may or may not attain a level of transfigured beauty. The fact that claims about the possibility of such transfiguration exist side-by-side with assertions of skepticism about that transformation must give us pause here, and in light of Bataille's comments about language and silence, we can see even the poet's creative attempts, as he portrays them here, as difficult attempts to cancel nothingness through the illusions of art, which in this context would be yet another unsuccessful attempt at maintaining "emptiness, darkness, and nudity." Rather than becoming distinct from everyday experience, artistic creation here joins with other aspects of life that interefere with, rather than help bring about, the desired nothingness.

The 1861 edition's inclusion of "Obsession" significantly mitigates the strangeness of "L'héautontimorouménos" ["The Man Who Tortures Himself"], which had been present in the 1857 edition couched between "Causerie" ["Conversation"] and "Franciscae meae laudes" ["In Praise of My Frances"], two poems that do not help to account for the self-torturing subjectivity of "L'Héautontimorouménos." By contrast, in its place in the 1861 edition as the fourth poem after "Obsession," the poem makes perfect metaphysical sense as a manifestation of the consciousness of the subject who, in "Obsession" and "Le goût du néant," had yearned for the *néant* but also established the condition of its impossibility and the reasons why such a condition is unredeemable. We are left, then, with the doubled subjectivity of a consciousness which is necessarily turned in upon itself by the act of contemplation to which we are condemned. Thus prepared by the poems that precede it, the speaking subject in "L'Héautontimorouménos" is not an exception but rather the rule in a humanity condemned to contemplation, which produces the doubleness incarnated in irony:

> Ne suis-je pas un faux accord
> Dans la divine symphonie,
> Grâce à la vorace Ironie
> Qui me secoue et qui me mord?
>
> Elle est dans ma voix, la criarde!
> C'est tout mon sang ce poison noir!
> Je suis le sinistre miroir
> Où la mégère se regarde.
>
> Je suis la plaie et le couteau!
> Je suis le soufflet et la joue!
> Je suis les membres et la roue,
> Et la victime et le bourreau!
>
> Je suis de mon coeur le vampire,
> —Un de ces grands abandonnés
> Au rire éternel condamnés
> Et qui ne peuvent plus sourire! (OC1: 78–9)
>
> [Am I not a discord
> In the heavenly symphony,
> Thanks to voracious Irony
> Who shakes me and who bites me?
>
> She's in my voice, the termagant!
> All my blood is her black poison!
> I am the sinister mirror
> In which the vixen looks.
>
> I am the wound and the dagger!
> I am the blow and the cheek!
> I am the members and the wheel,
> Victim and executioner!

I'm the vampire of my own heart
—One of those utter derelicts
Condemned to eternal laughter,
But who can no longer smile! (263–5)]

The opening at the conclusion of the poem, after the dash puts an abrupt end to the series of opposites into which the speaking subject falls and which could potentially continue on to infinity, removes the subject from the singular "I" and situates him in a larger group, "ces grands abandonnés" ["those utter derelicts"]. How are we to understand this group? The description of it as "au rire éternel condamnés" suggests the condition of those subjected to the kind of unredeemed and unredeemable experience that the poet has traced in the other poems we have been examining. The condemnation here is related to the impossibility of canceling experience through the *néant*, instead of which we are left with an eternal recurrence of the same, a stagnation that results in forever unrealized and unrealizable potential action. This is, for Baudelaire, the condition not just of a select few but everyone.[13] Belonging to the group of the "grands abandonnés" does not require anything more than the mere consciousness of what is always already the fact about human existence, that is, that we are condemned by knowledge to the kind of infernal and eternal repetition that the poem describes and which it would itself have enacted if not for the interruption of the series of opposites which brings the poem to its conclusion. That abrupt ending is itself an act of revelation of the condition of possibility of the eternal and unredeemable series of opposites. What this poem provides is, then, an illustration of "la conscience dans le Mal," which, as we have seen, is not the lot of a damned few but rather the generalized condition of unredeemable humanity, as that is revealed in the poem whose very title is "L'irrémédiable." And indeed "L'irrémédiable" follows "L'héautontimorouménos" in the 1861 edition, at a point in the text where the progression from "Obsession" to "Le goût du néant" and on through "L'héautontimorouménos" has made the conclusions of "L'irrémédiable" not surprising but inevitable and logical in light of the way Baudelaire has been painting the logic of anti-redemption through these final poems of "Spleen et Idéal." "L'irrémédiable" thus has much more metaphysical force in the 1861 edition as opposed to the 1857 edition, where it had been preceded not by "L'Héautontimorouménos" but by "Brumes et pluies" ["Mist and Rain"], which also suggests the delights of the *néant* but mitigates them in a more typically post-romantic possibility of sleeping off the desire for oblivion on a bed with a lover:

Rien n'est plus doux au coeur plein de choses funèbres,
Et sur qui dès longtemps descendent les frimas,
Ô blafardes saisons, reines de nos climats,

Que l'aspect permanent de vos pâles ténèbres,
—Si ce n'est, par un soir sans lune, deux à deux,
D'endormir la douleur sur un lit hasardeux. (OC1: 101)

[Nothing is sweeter to a gloomy heart
On which the hoar-frost has long been falling,
Than the permanent aspect of your pale shadows,

O wan seasons, queens of our clime
—Unless it be to deaden suffering, side by side
In a casual bed, on a moonless night. (339)]

In the 1861 edition, "Brumes et pluies" is situated far from "L'irrémédiable," appearing, incongruously perhaps, among the "Tableaux parisiens."

Baudelaire's desire to fall as it manifests itself in "Le goût du néant" ("Avalanche, veux-tu m'emporter dans ta chute?") seems at first to be a perverse one, a desire for damnation that one might identify as a symptom of the poet's already being in the grip of the devil, but, as Slavoj Žižek points out in his reading of Christianity, perversion is built into the story of redemption from the start:

> The hidden perverse core of Christianity: if it is prohibited to eat from the Tree of Knowledge in Paradise, why did God put it there in the first place? Is it not that this was a part of His perverse strategy first to seduce Adam and Eve into the Fall, in order then to save them? […]
>
> In all other religions, God demands that His followers remain faithful to Him—only Christ asked his followers to betray him in order to fulfill his mission. Here I am tempted to claim that the entire fate of Christianity, its innermost kernel, hinges on the possibility of interpreting this act in a nonperverse way. (*Puppet* 16–17)

This reading of Christianity takes its logic seriously but pushes the consequences of the original terms in which the fall and the subsequent salvific act are imagined to a point where the standard Christian reading of those events becomes untenable. If there is, as Žižek's reading suggests, a fundamental perversion embedded in the logic of Christian story itself, then idiosyncratic appropriations of Christianity such as Baudelaire's become far more comprehensible. Viewed in light of Žižek's analysis, Baudelaire's use of the Christian theological paradigm minus redemption is not a perverse misreading of Christianity, but, rather, is consistent with a Christianity that requires the fall in order for God to fulfill a preordained plan of redemption. The desire to fall, in Baudelaire, can now be seen as the betrayal that Christ, unique in this among the gods, asks for "in order to fulfill his mission."

On this reading, Baudelaire's desire is not perverse but rather necessary, since the desire for redemption is coextensive with the desire for condemnation, which is its precondition, or rather, its simultaneous condition: "The problem with the Fall is thus not that it is in itself a Fall, but, precisely that, *in itself, it is already a Salvation which we misrecognize as a Fall*. Consequently, Salvation consists not in our reversing the direction of the Fall, but in recognizing Salvation in the Fall itself" (*Puppet* 87). And here we have the answer to the question of why salvation is impossible for Baudelaire: contemplation, as knowledge of evil, blocks even our ability to fall, which is the necessary condition of salvation and may even be, on Žižek's reading, synonymous with it. Here the idea of the Baudelairean double fall becomes clear: the original fall, by virtue of the fact that it brings contemplative awareness of evil (as we saw through Benjamin's observation about the fall as knowledge of evil alone), reduces us to inaction, a stasis that calls for *another* fall, the fall into satanic revolt, which would cancel the stasis *and* be the necessary prelude to redemption. But, as we shall soon see, that second fall, into revolt, is impossible to accomplish, precisely *because* of the stasis from which we cannot ultimately escape. This is why the Satanism of the "Révolte" poems is ultimately ineffective: what Žižek calls the "perverse core" of Christianity cancels a simple God/Satan divide, as Baudelaire's poetry intuitively demonstrates by refusing to come to rest in the simple act of revolt, which fails to save the poet any more than drunkenness had in the section of *Les Fleurs du Mal* devoted to "Le vin."

In this light, I would like to offer a reading of the first of the "Révolte" poems, "Le reniement de Saint Pierre" ["The Denial of Saint Peter"] with reference not only to Žižek's reflections but also Agamben's analysis of glory and what he calls "inoperativity," to which I turn below. Baudelaire's poem resists any simple interpretation. On the surface, the affirmation, which comes at the very end of the poem's thirty-two lines, that Saint Peter was right to deny Jesus, can easily be labeled blasphemy, and indeed when the poem was published for the second time, it was accompanied by a note explicitly reaffirming Jesus as Savior.[14] But such simplicity disappears with any attempt to read that affirmation in the light of the poem as a whole. The devil, for instance, is never mentioned in the poem, which makes what transpires an affair between God and humanity. In the first two stanzas, God is portrayed as a despot, compared to "un tyran gorgé de viande et de vins" ["a tyrant gorged with food and wine"] falling asleep to the "doux bruit de nos affreux blasphèmes" ["sweet sound of our horrible blasphemies" (425)] (OC1: 121). Then, Jesus is directly addressed in five stanzas, where he is asked to remember the anguish of the Mount of Olives. This is a very human Jesus, trapped, as is all of humanity according to the poem, by the sadistic whims of the God evoked in the first two stanzas. While some have called attention to similar nineteenth-century poems set on the Mount of Olives such as Alfred de Vigny's "Le Mont des Oliviers" ["The Mount of Olives"] and Gérard de Nerval's "Le Christ aux Oliviers" ["Christ at the Mount of Olives"][15] an important difference here is that, while the heavens' silence in those two poems is indicative of God's potential non-existence, in Baudelaire, by contrast, God is very much present in order the better to punish Jesus and all of humanity; they are joined by the poet's evocation of Jesus' "crâne où vivait l'immense Humanité" ["skull where lived immense Humanity" (425)] (OC1: 121). After evoking the physical sufferings of the passion, Baudelaire asks the human Jesus:

Rêvais-tu de ces jours si brillants et si beaux
Où tu vins pour remplir l'éternelle promesse,
Où tu foulais, monté sur une douce ânesse,
Des chemins tout jonchés de fleurs et de rameaux,

Où, le coeur tout gonflé d'espoir et de vaillance,
Tu fouettais tous ces vils marchands à tour de bras,
Où tu fus maître enfin? Le remords n'a-t-il pas
Pénétré dans ton flanc plus avant que la lance? (OC1: 121–2)

[Did you dream of those days so brilliant and so fair
When you came to fulfill the eternal promise,
When the gentle donkey you were riding trampled
The branches and flowers strewn in your path,

When, your heart swollen with courage and hope,
You lashed those vile money-changers with all your might,
In a word, when you were master? Did not remorse
Penetrate your side deeper than the spear? (427)]

The incarnation here was a moment of hope for Jesus himself, and his greatest moment of glory is said to reside in the cleansing of the temple, the moment of Jesus' most forceful action. All the rest of the story, it turns out, involved suffering and torture, a crumbling of whatever hope had at first been present. In this, Jesus is very much human, condemned to live out the impossibility of the ideal which had filled him with a false and impossible hope.

This poem paints a cruel God, quite separate from the humanized Jesus, who orchestrates the suffering that Jesus undergoes once his hope is vanquished. If we return to Žižek's reading of the "perverse core of Christianity," the poem is not at all blasphemous but, rather, a faithful representation of the Christian notion of the *felix culpa*, the necessity of the fall, and thus of betrayal, in order to enact redemption. The fact that Baudelaire denies the possibility of redemption, not so much in this particular poem as in his works taken collectively, does not alter the fact that God's allowing the cruel suffering of his beloved son is perfectly in keeping with standard Christian theology. If there is blasphemy in the poem, it must lie in the conclusion: "Saint Pierre a renié Jésus … il a bien fait!" ["Saint Peter denied Jesus—he did well!" (427)] (OC1: 122). But given the thoroughly humanized Jesus that the poet presents in the poem, what does it mean to deny Jesus here? The fall into time was, for this Jesus, a fall from contemplation into action, and thus into suffering, which is the necessary companion of action as it is presented here. In the last stanza, separated by a dash from the section evoking Jesus' suffering and remorse, the poet explicitly addresses the question of action:

—Certes, je sortirai, quant à moi, satisfait
D'un monde où l'action n'est pas la soeur du rêve;
Puissé-je user du glaive et périr par le glaive!
Saint Pierre a renié Jésus … il a bien fait! (OC1: 122)

[—For my part, I shall indeed be content to leave
A world where action is not the sister of dreams;
Would that I could take up the sword and perish by the sword!
Saint Peter denied Jesus—he did well! (427)]

The poet reveals here that he is in the same state of potential but suspended action with which "Le goût du néant" closes ("Avalanche, veux-tu m'emporter dans ta chute?"). This is the poet who has made the first fall, into contemplation, and thus knowledge of evil, without the ability to make the second fall, into action, even satanic action, that would save him from the inoperativity of stasis. The remorse about which the poet speculates in Jesus' case is the same one that confronts the reader in the third line of the liminal poem of the collection, "Au lecteur," where the poet claims that "nous alimentons nos aimables remords,/Comme les mendiants nourrissent leur vermine" ["we feed our pleasant remorse/As beggars nourish their vermin" (3)] (OC1: 5). In that poem, it is not God but rather l'Ennui who is characterized as a tyrannical despot, dreaming of scaffolds "en fumant son houka" ["as he smokes his hookah pipe" (5)] (6). Remorse is represented more than once as impossible to transcend in *Les Fleurs du Mal*; in "L'irréparable" ["The Irreparable"], the poet asks rhetorically at the outset: "Pouvons-nous étouffer le vieux, le long Remords,/Qui vit, s'agite et se tortille" ["Can we stifle the old, the lingering Remorse,/That lives, quivers and writhes" (189)] (1: 54). This inability to triumph over remorse, presented in the section "Spleen et Idéal," returns near the very end of the collection, in the penultimate poem, "Le rêve d'un curieux" ["Dream of a Curious Man"], where the poet represents himself in a similar theatrical context, waiting for an action that never comes.[16]

Where, then, does that leave us in "Le reniement de Saint Pierre?" The answer is linked to Baudelaire's implied reading of the incarnation. Let us return to the passage I have cited from *Mon Coeur mis à nu*, where Baudelaire takes up the question of the fall:

La Théologie.
Qu'est-ce que la chute?
Si c'est l'unité devenue dualité, c'est Dieu qui a chuté […]
En d'autres termes, la création ne serait-elle pas la chute de Dieu? (1: 688–9)

[Theology.
What is the fall?
If it is unity become duality, it is God who has fallen.]

If Baudelaire highlights Jesus' fully human nature in "Le reniement de Saint Pierre," this implies that Jesus participates in creation, and his own launching into historical time, despite the Christian notion of Jesus' being "begotten, not made" (*genitum, non factum*), makes him share the fate of creation. Here once again it is helpful to read Baudelaire together with Žižek, who presents an initially counterintuitive reading of the incarnation:

> what does the becoming-man of God in the figure of Christ, His descent from eternity to the temporal realm of our reality, mean for God Himself? What if that which appears to us, finite mortals, as God's *descent* toward us, is, from the standpoint of God Himself, an *ascent*? What if […] eternity is less than temporality? What if eternity is a stertile, impotent, lifeless domain of pure potentialities, which, in order fully to actualize itself, has to pass through temporal existence? What if God's descent to man, far from being an act of grace toward humanity, is the only way for God to gain full actuality, and to liberate Himself from the suffocating constraints of Eternity? What if God actualizes Himself only through human recognition? What, however, if, […] eternity is the ultimate prison, a suffocating closure, and it is only the fall into time that introduces Opening into human experience? Is Time not *the* name for the ontological opening? The Event of "incarnation" is thus not so much the time when ordinary temporal reality touches Eternity, but, rather, the time when Eternity reaches into time. (*Puppet* 13–14)

This characterization corresponds at many points to the implied theology of Baudelaire's poem. It is easy to see the God that the poet presents at the beginning of the poem as suffering from the "suffocating constraints of Eternity"; this would be a God in the thralls of the same *ennui* that traps the poet in "Au lecteur," suggesting that, in heaven as on earth, the stasis of contemplation is unbearable. The comparison of God to a tyrant is followed by an indication that he "falls asleep" to the sound of human blasphemy. God is compared to a tyrant not on account of what he does but of what he cannot do; asleep, he is unable or unmotivated to react to suffering. On this reading, the vigorously active Jesus, whipping the temple merchants, is the effective antidote to the eternally inactive God, "la chute de Dieu," the attempt "to gain full actuality" described here by Žižek. All the more disappointing, then, that even as a fully incarnate human being, Jesus is unable fully to realize himself in action. He follows the same trajectory as any human being trapped in what I have been calling the "first fall," the fall into contemplation of evil that precludes action.

The poet unites himself to Jesus in the last stanza by rejecting a world where "l'action n'est pas la soeur du rêve"; if it is the suffering, inoperative, inactive Jesus of this poem that Saint Peter denies here, then the denial is at most ambiguous rather than fully blasphemous. For this Peter denies the fully human Jesus, the one reduced, like God himself, to inaction, the one who, like the poet of "Le goût du néant," is trapped in sterile contemplation (or, in the case of Jesus here, suffering). If the fall means abandoning eternity for the historical temporality of action, then the incarnation as the "chute de Dieu" has *not* been fully actualized in the life of Jesus. Or perhaps it has, inasmuch as this Jesus finds himself unable to complete the second fall, the fall into action that would cancel inoperativity. God and man, on this reading, both seek an Opening away from stasis, and both find it impossible. If this impotent

Jesus is the one Peter is said to deny here, it is difficult to see how this could *not* be a well chosen denial, since the Jesus that Peter denies, before Jesus' death, of course, is fully alive, and yet fully inoperative. This is precisely the human condition that awaits the second fall, into active rebellion, through which one would have to pass, on the logic that Baudelaire implies throughout these poems, in order finally to arrive at redemption. That next fall, however, is not fully realizable, and thus redemption is blocked. In that sense, Jesus' death redeems nothing, and the poem may well be considered blasphemous; taken, however, only at the level of Peter's denial as it is expressed at the moment when Jesus is alive but inactive, the denial can only be seen as a necessary refusal of Jesus' very *human* powerlessness, his impotence, like the poet's own, to get beyond "la conscience dans le Mal."[17]

This cosmological view does not simply deny the divinity of Jesus. Baudelaire offers instead a much more complicated scenario. As we have seen through reading Baudelaire and Žižek together, the distinction between God and man becomes blurred once we see stasis or inoperativity as a risk both in heaven and on earth, for both God and humanity. If creation is God's fall, a *felix culpa* [happy fault] in his case as for humanity's, Jesus' own status as both God and man is less crucial, since on this view God himself is capable of a fall. Confirmation of the blurred distinction comes at the end of the second of the three poems that comprise the "Révolte" section of *Les Fleurs du Mal*, "Abel et Caïn" ["Abel and Cain"]. In what appears to be a straightforward final couplet, Baudelaire seems to accomplish a simple reversal: "Race de Caïn, au ciel monte,/Et sur la terre jette Dieu!" ["Race of Cain, ascend to heaven,/And cast God down upon the earth!" (431)] (OC1: 123). If we redefine notions of fall and ascent, however, in a way that allows for the "chute de Dieu" as an actualization of God, this poem ends not with a call for God's dethronement but rather God's ennoblement through his sharing of temporally situated action, and Cain's subsequent "damnation" through ascent rather than descent, a condemnation to the stagnation of the heavens that can only create a tyrant insensitive to suffering, unable, like the poet, even to fall. Indeed, the spatial reference of the poem suggests the very opposite of that potentially salvific fall by its call for Cain to rise.

The last of the "Révolte" poems, "Les litanies de Satan" ["The Litanies of Satan"] is the only one specifically to mention the devil and the one that seems to be a straightforward and childish attempt at blasphemy, a simple reversal of God and Satan, a genuine act of revolt. But such a movement is ultimately a false path out of Ennui, an unsuccessful attempt to fall. This is made clear in the quasi-narrative structure of *Les Fleurs du Mal* itself, where "Révolte" gives way to "La Mort" ["Death"]. Given the fact that Baudelaire does not operate within the traditional Christian framework of redemption, however, it would be hasty and even inaccurate to assume that the blasphemy of "Révolte" leads to the damnation of the speaking subject.[18] First, there is no indication of such damnation, happy or otherwise, in the poems that comprise "La Mort." Rather, we are left with the poet suspended in eager but futile anticipation in the penultimate poem "Le rêve d'un curieux," followed by "Le voyage," which appeals to a personified Death for help in being able to "Plonger au fond du gouffre, Enfer ou Ciel, qu'importe?/Au fond de l'Inconnu pour trouver du *nouveau!*" ["to plunge/To the abyss' depths, Heaven or Hell, does it matter?/To the depths of the Unknown to find something new!" (463)] (OC1: 134). Why would heaven or hell be equivalent possibilities here? The answer lies in what we have already seen about the equivalence established between them, and, for that matter, between both of them and the earthly state as well.

If God in the eternal stasis of heaven is bound by the same sort of crippling Ennui that characterizes the poet's fallen state, then there is no reason to prefer heaven. This stasis, as we have seen, is already presented as a hellish state from which active revolt would be a release. But Baudelaire's hell as it is represented in the "Prière" that closes "Les Litanies de Satan" is a contemplative place rather than a site of rebellion:

> Gloire et louange à toi, Satan, dans les hauteurs
> Du Ciel, où tu régnas, et dans les profondeurs
> De l'Enfer, où, vaincu, tu rêves en silence!
> Fais que mon âme un jour, sous l'Arbre de Science,
> Près de toi se repose, à l'heure où sur ton front
> Comme un Temple nouveau ses rameaux s'épandront! (1: 125)

> [Glory and praise to you, O Satan, in the heights
> Of Heaven where you reigned and in the depths
> Of Hell where vanquished you dream in silence!
> Grant that my soul may someday repose near to you
> Under the Tree of Knowledge, when, over your brow,
> Its branches will spread like a new Temple! (437)]

Continuity between heaven and hell is established in the figure of Satan himself, who has inhabited both spaces in a similar way. If heaven is the site of the eternal changelessness of glory rather than the seat of action, then Satan's silent dreaming in hell is an apt equivalent. The poet's final wish for repose implies a different kind of rest than the contemplation we have seen operating in other poems, since rest is here figured as desirable rather than unbearable and irrevocable like the stasis of Ennui. The "Temple nouveau" suggests the kind of opening onto a transformation of experience that we see at the end of "Le voyage" and its "nouveau" that would be indifferent to heaven or hell. But the closing verses of the "Litanies" are situated solidly in a Satanism that would prohibit the poet from exclaiming "Enfer ou Ciel, qu'importe?"; this prayer is ineffective because the very status of the transfigured *nouveau* is called into question in both the "Litanies" and "Le voyage." Expressed as a wish or a prayer, there is no confirmation that such repose is possible and, again, even if it were, that it would be desirable. As we have seen, if the knowledge available to the descendents of Adam and Eve is knowledge of evil alone, it can only end in "la conscience dans le Mal" rather than repose. Satanism thus remains, here at the end of the "Révolte" section, a false escape. The poet remains trapped in the first fall, the one into stasis and contemplation but without rest. The same anti-redemptive logic that prevents death from being transformed into new life, and sin from being canceled by forgiveness, blocks the establishment of peace either in heaven or hell precisely because the new is shown to be impossible.

Baudelaire's notion of inoperativity is in some ways at odds with the way that concept is described by Giorgio Agamben, who links the function of "contemplative life and [...] inoperativity" with a corresponding entry into praxis by way of the opening of possibility:

> properly human praxis is sabbatism that, by rendering the specific functions of the living inoperative, opens them to possibility. Contemplation and inoperativity are, in this sense, the metaphysical operators of anthropogenesis, which, by liberating the living man from his biological or social destiny, assign him to that indefinable dimension that we are accustomed to call "politics." [...] *Zoe ainonios*, eternal life, is the name of this inoperative center of the human, of this political "substance" of the Occident that the machine of the economy and of glory ceaselessly attempts to capture within itself. (*Kingdom* 251)

Baudelaire refuses both the philosophical and Christian tradition, evoked here by Agamben, by the inability to pass from contemplation to action that marks his poetry. While Baudelairean contemplation brings lucidity about evil, it forecloses the chance of transcending that evil by its refusal of the possibility of redemption. Given that Baudelaire works through these ideas in his poetry, the relationship of literature to inoperativity becomes central; indeed, Agamben's own reflections about the potential action derived from inoperativity open onto questions of poetry in particular:

> A model of this operation that consists in making all human and divine works inoperative is the poem. Because poetry is precisely that linguistic operation that renders language inoperative—or, in Spinoza's terms, the point at which language, which has deactivated its communicative and informative functions, rests within itself, contemplates its power of saying [*potenza di dire*] and in this way opens itself to a new possible use. [...] And the poetic subject is not the individual who wrote these poems, but the subject that is produced at the point at which language has been rendered inoperative and, therefore, has becomes in him and for him, purely sayable.
>
> What the poem accomplishes for the power of saying, politics and philosophy must accomplish for the power of acting. By rendering economic and biological operations inoperative, they demonstrate what the human body *can* do; they open it to a new, possible use. (251–2)

At stake here is poetry's potential for conversion into action. While Agamben at first seems to offer poetry as the model of the kind of potential-filled inoperativity that he claims can be transformed into political praxis, there is a curious divide between poetry and praxis by the end of this passage. At first Agamben proposes the paradoxical situation of the act of (literary) creation as that which forecloses action by rendering language inoperative. One would therefore expect that from this inoperativity would spring, based on Agamben's earlier remarks, a new and active potential or possibility. But the rest of Agamben's analysis forfends the possibility of passing from saying to doing, since while poetry opens language to "a new possible use," that act of opening results here in nothing more than language becoming the "purely sayable," a curious and nearly autoreferential turn. While Agamben establishes a parallel between what poetry does for language and what politics does for acting, there is no interpenetration of the two worlds here, so that poetry can be said to contemplate itself, or, in other words, to give voice to the "conscience dans le Mal" that it itself creates via the poem, here seen as a contemplative act, involving a creative but not an active word.

In Baudelaire's world, then, art therefore carries no redemptive value. If, for Benjamin the task of the critic is, as Richard Wolin summarizes it, "that of rescuing the few unique visions of transcendence that grace the continuum of history, the now-times (*Jetztzeiten*), from the fate of oblivion which incessantly threatens to consume them" (48), we have seen that the very act of contemplation by which the poet becomes a critic renders that rescue impossible, since the poet is able to enter neither history nor a world of potential, but rather remains engulfed in the unfulfilled desire to fall, the negative potentiality of the poet of "Le goût du néant" calling for the avalanche to sweep him downward. Redemption is always either impossible, unwanted, or both. And this is where Baudelaire joins Agamben in an implicit commentary on Benjamin. We recall that for Agamben "redemption is nothing other than a potentiality to create that remains pending, that turns on itself and 'saves' itself" (*Nudities* 7). Agamben's "desire to create" joins Baudelaire's desire to fall in the realm of unfulfillable potential, a potential without potential. Herein lies the problem that comes with being both poet and critic, as Baudelaire would put it. Agamben writes: "That which the angel forms, produces, and caresses, the prophet brings back to an unformed state and contemplates. His eyes observe that which is saved but only inasmuch as it will be lost on the last day" (8). The unsavable remains, which Agamben defines as "that work in which creation and salvation, action and contemplation […] persist in every moment and […] in the same being" (8). The work of poetry, for Baudelaire, results paradoxically in his painting of the lyric subject suspended in contemplation, unable to fall; the poem is thus an active creation that is nonetheless unable to redeem the unproductive inoperativity it paints, the "purely sayable" remaining suspended in the space between contemplation and action.

The simultaneity of creation and salvation that Agamben describes in the passage just quoted calls into question our ability to preserve the distinction between the pairs of opposites he mentions, and at the same time challenges us to perform the kind of reading that I have attempted here, an "interhistorical" one that seeks to establish critical simultaneity among thinkers from several periods. Agamben's writing without footnotes helps to create the space for such dialogue across the history of criticism and even allows us to continue the critical conversation in a way that challenges Agamben's final assertion about "salvation that no longer has an objective" (9), a fact he considers belated knowledge and about which he affirms that we are ultimately left, in sharp contrast to the "purely sayable" that he evokes in *The Kingdom and the Glory*, with an awareness of what he calls in "Creation and Salvation" "our subsequent lack of anything else to say" (9). Both saying and salvation ultimately become divorced from their objects, so that what we are left with is a transformed saying, a pure iteration that was further explored in the "pure poetics" of Mallarmé and Valéry and, in the case of Baudelaire, a meaningless concept of salvation which cannot have value apart from its ability to take an object but, as Agamben demonstrates, which persists nonetheless. While we might not be able to get by without the category of salvation, the dialogue his essay can inspire when read in conjunction with Baudelaire's poetics of the unredeemable, suggests that it is from this belated knowledge that a new kind of alinear critical dialogue at the interstices of creation and salvation can spring.

A Veil Over the Abyss: From Benjamin to Fondane

The Baudelaire of Walter Benjamin has become iconic. His multifaceted portrait of the poet undergoing the traumatic shock of urban experience in the "capital of the nineteenth century" is intimately familiar, and even hauntingly so, to students and critics of Baudelaire in the age of cultural studies. Yet focusing on the Benjaminian Baudelaire exclusively as he emerges in essays such as "On Some Motifs in Baudelaire" and "The Paris of the Second Empire in Baudelaire" risks casting aside some of the most fundamental questions that ground the theologico-esthetic worldview that Baudelaire shapes in both *Les Fleurs du Mal* and *Le Spleen de Paris* while at the same time giving short shrift to crucial theological elements of Benjamin's earlier thought, which largely predates but arguably informs his later writings and their more explicit focus on Baudelaire. Common to Benjamin and Baudelaire is an idiosyncratic approach to the notion of redemption, and despite Benjamin's engagement with the messianic in his earlier thought, it will be my contention in this chapter that he ultimately gives insufficient attention to the removal of salvation from Baudelaire's cosmological worldview. My analysis in this chapter will continue the attempt in Chapter 1 to begin to draw all of the consequences from Baudelaire's asoteriological theology for his worldview and esthetics. Once again, the journey will take us back to Benjamin's earlier writings and in fact will involve an attempt to enrich a Benjaminian reading of Baudelaire with its complement, a Baudelairean reading of Benjamin which calls into question the space Benjamin makes, as small and fragile as that space may be, for the messianic. I will then turn, by contrast, to another figure, the poet and critic Benjamin Fondane, who engages with Baudelaire's asoteriological world in ways that I will suggest are more fruitful than Benjamin's when it comes to accounting for, and drawing the consequences of, Baudelaire's thinking outside and beyond redemption. Nearly exact contemporaries, the German critic who died fleeing the Nazis and the Romanian-French poet and essayist who perished at Auschwitz-Birkenau provide two different ways of coming to terms with Baudelaire's astoreiological vision at a particularly charged moment both for European history and for the reception and interpretation of Baudelaire's poetry and thought.

Given the tentative, interrogatory nature of some of Benjamin's fragmentary writings, it is worth remembering that his plan for the Baudelaire study was quite different from what has come down to us today, partly unfinished, partly never written. The plan of the book indicates a study where the experience of urban shock as it is portrayed primarily in the "Tableaux parisiens" was much less a central concern than it is in the writings that have come down to us in finished form and which have played such a defining role in the analysis of Baudelaire in the mode of cultural studies. Benjamin's book was to be in three parts, the first of which would "analyze the decisive significance of allegory for Baudelaire's *Fleurs du Mal* and reconstruct the foundations of Baudelaire's allegorical inclinations."[1] As Richard Wolin details, in the period when Benjamin was transitioning from his more theologically inflected work to the historical materialist writings that have held such strong sway in contemporary engagement with both Benjamin and Baudelaire, it was Theodor Adorno who

> strove desperately to bring Benjamin back to the conception of history of the Trauerspiel book, i.e. the idea of history as a continuum of disaster [...]. Yet, at this point in his intellectual development, Benjamin felt that the retention of the *equally undialectical* pessimistic philosophy of history of his theological phase would be incompatible with a genuinely materialistic perspective which emphasized the progressive emancipation of mankind through the mechanism of class struggle. (Wolin 178)

This is not, of course, to say that the later Benjamin simply accomplishes a clean break with his older modes of thought, as Benjamin himself acknowledges in a letter of March 1931: "I have never been able to think and research otherwise than, if I may say so, in a theological sense" (qtd in Wolin 248). Such remarks, along with a careful reading of Benjamin's critical texts themselves, easily confirm Uwe Steiner's contention that the division that some scholars of Benjamin would like to make between an "early period of metaphysical-theological interests, and a later period with a Marxist orientation" is "justified, while at the same time unjustified" (Steiner 7). Leo Bersani goes a step further, claiming that the "profound religious orientation" of Benjamin's thought in all periods is of such importance that "his thought makes no sense without it" and that it would be an error to "bracket his religious yearning as we admire and profit from his observations on Proust, Kafka, Baudelaire, and Goethe," because all of these insights stem from a consistent set of "assumptions of lost wholeness of fallen being" informing Benjamin's writings in all periods (Bersani 53).

What is true of Benjamin in this case is also true of Baudelaire, as I hope my argument thus far has begun to suggest. Baudelaire's work, like Benjamin's, can most profitably be understood only in the context of the idiosyncratic theology that informs Baudelaire's work throughout his career, and indeed, if anything, more rather than less so in his final period when he authored the prose poems, many of which present, along with the "Tableaux parisiens" inserted in the 1861 edition of *Les Fleurs du Mal*, his most incisive portrayal and analysis of life in the modern city—that supposedly increasingly secular space. This precedence and persistence of a theological vision is an often underacknowledged source of intellectual affinity between the late Baudelaire and the late Benjamin. As should be clear by now, in neither case do we have a simple or transparent transposition of an established or conventional theological view. Benjamin's transposition of messianism is in some ways as idiosyncratic to the Jewish tradition as Baudelaire's reinvention of a Christianity without redemption, and both of them consequently provide an intriguingly complex portrait of a secular world shot through with a theological impetus that calls traditional religious frameworks into question while at the same time questioning a thoroughly secularized worldview. But I will contend in this chapter that the fact that Benjamin retains some sort of focus on the messianic, in however an unconventional form that focus might take, compromises any similarity of vision we might establish between the theological orientations of Benjamin and Baudelaire, given that the latter's work unrelentingly seeks to think through the consequences of the elimination of redemption from his theological perspective.

In other words, nowhere is Benjamin simultaneously closer to and further from Baudelaire than in the former's earlier work, informed more closely and more directly by metaphysical and theological conceptions but retaining nonetheless an emphasis on redemption that Baudelaire would reject. If both the critic and the poet lean heavily on the primacy of the degraded condition of humanity as a consequence of the fall, Benjamin's retention of some kind of hope for redemption places him in a theological sphere markedly different from Baudelaire's right from the start. As Richard Wolin emphasizes in a reading of the prologue to Benjamin's Trauerspiel book:

> The concept of experience [Benjamin] strives to present seeks to approximate the fullness of theological experience, and thus the suspicion of dogmatism can never be entirely scotched. However, it is never a *positive* image of redemption that one finds reproduced in his writings; rather, by viewing the world from the standpoint of a hypothetical intelligible realm, it is his intention to set its degraded condition in relief all the more vividly. (Wolin 91)

I shall have more to say below about the notion of messianic time in Benjamin, but for now it is important to remember that his focus on redemption is not restricted to his earlier writings. As late as the "Central Park" fragments of 1938–9, just after the assertion that "the concept of progress must be grounded in the idea of catastrophe," we find this observation: "Redemption depends on the tiny fissure in the continuous catastrophe" (*Writer* 161). To hold out hope of redemption, even in hypothetical or even negative forms of expression, is to sustain a soteriological vision that Baudelaire's criticism and poetry show to be untenable. To be sure, there are moments of erotic and, especially, esthetic release from degradation and damnation in Baudelaire, but in the larger frame of his thought, and in the conceptual and narrative shapes of *Les Fleurs du Mal*, these moments are not capable of being sustained and must ultimately be dismissed as illusory, not unlike the artificial highs of drugs that mask truth rather than revealing it. In that sense, Baudelaire's vision is unrelenting and uncompromising, unwilling to grant any real status to the illusory forms of what might look like redemption or release. In that, he stands as a challenger both to Nietzsche's estheticism, as I shall explore in Chapter 4, and even to the theorist of "*weak* Messianic power" (*Illuminations* 254) who, as late as the "Theses on the Philosophy of History," transforms but does not completely reject a theology of redemption. Such holding on to the potential for salvation "in the midst of an iniquitous historical era that could only seem emphatically removed from all hope of salvation" (Wolin 107) is one of the main points of continuity of the early and late Benjamin, who shows himself as consistent in this paradoxical retention of the category of redemption as Baudelaire is over the course of his own career in its rejection and indeed ultimate elimination from his poetry and criticism.

Commentators on Benjamin's conception of redemption emphasize its relation to the idea of a return to origins or, more explicitly, the Kabbalistic notion of redemption as "the return to the condition of universal harmony represented by the Tree of Life usually envisioned in terms of a return to paradise or a restoration of the Davidic Kingdom" (Wolin 39). Reading Benjamin's essay on Proust along with "On Some Motifs in Baudelaire," Tomoko Masuzawa argues that Benjamin's notion of redemption "takes the form of memory and mimesis. A past is to be recognized and recovered; redemption refers to this recovery, or rather discovery for the first time, of the sentence of distance and depth of time" (Masuzawa 518). Redemption would signal not a mere recovery of origins but a transformation of historical experience in light of those origins. Benjamin's very first critical engagements with Baudelaire take up the question of origins but already in the context of knowledge and guilt to which, as we saw in Chapter 1, he pays critical attention in the Trauerspiel book. His first fragments on Baudelaire, which date from 1921 to 1922 and which thus predate the Trauerspiel study on which Benjamin began working in 1923 (the year in which he published his translations of Baudelaire's "Tableaux parisiens"), take up the question of guilt, remorse, and redemption explicitly:

> Underlying Baudelaire's writings is the old idea that knowledge is guilt. His soul is that of Adam, to whom Eve (the world) once upon a time offered the apple, from which he ate. Thereupon the spirit expelled him from the garden. Knowledge of the world had not been enough for him; he wanted to know its good and evil sides as well. And the possibility of this question, which he was never able to answer, is something he bought at the price of eternal remorse [Remord]. His soul has this mythical prehistory, of which he knows, and thanks to which he knows more than others about redemption. He teaches us above all to understand the literal meaning of the word "knowledge" in the story of Eden. (*Writer* 27–8)

There is no doubt that this "mythical prehistory" informs all of Baudelaire; what gives rise to question in this passage is the claim that Baudelaire "knows more than others about redemption." Without further elaboration, it is hard to know precisely what Benjamin means by this, but in light of Baudelaire's exclusion of redemption and refusal of the possibility of grace, we are compelled to read Benjamin's contention, despite Benjamin's own lingering engagement with redemption, as meaning that Baudelaire knows enough about redemption to reject it and to attempt to think beyond it. In the Trauerspiel book Benjamin would go on, we recall, to argue that knowledge of evil "has no object" because everything God made was good, and that knowledge of evil is "primary" and "ensues from contemplation" as "the opposite of all factual knowledge" (*Origin* 233–4). To dwell in knowledge and contemplation is to dwell in evil without the "tiny fissure" that would make room for the redemptive, even as a hypothetical possibility.

Commentators have highlighted the place he holds out for redemption. Beyond Richard Wolin's book-length study of the subject, Carol Jacobs reminds us of the mortification of the textual object involved in the act of criticism according to Benjamin: "The ruin and decay assigned to nature-history when staged by tragic drama reappears […] as critical writing. Transforming historical content into truth content, criticism 'saves' the work of art only at the price of its 'mortification.' […] It is as though criticism were already in the work of art as its potential" (Jacobs 6–7). It is not hard to see traces, and more than traces, of a Christian redemptive logic of transformation by death after a suffering that brings to actuality a potential for an afterlife that was present but not yet actualized by the work.[2] Sometimes, among critics writing in English, this redemptive move is the result of a translation of Benjamin's notion of *Rettung* as "redemption," an interpretation that adds a theological resonance to a German concept generally bereft of religious overtones and that might be better rendered as "rescue." Such is the case of Michael Jennings' reading of the dialectical image in "The Paris of the Second Empire in Baudelaire," the "key" to which is, according to Jennings, "Benjamin's much-discussed notion of the 'redemption' (*Rettung*) of certain moments of the past" (Jennings 38). We need not, however, lean heavily on the notion of *Rettung* with its tenuous connections to religious salvation in order to see a logic of redemption in Benjamin. Benjamin's redemption could "occur *only* as an extrahistorical event" (Jennings 62), thus bringing it more in line with a Jewish concept of messianism rather than the Christian salvific intervention *in* history (the death and resurrection of Christ) in addition to the moment *beyond* history. Nevertheless, whether under the sign of the hypothetical or the actual, the immanent or extrahistorical, the polito-historical or the critico-literary, redemption continues to govern Benjamin's thought in ways that make it incompatible with Baudelaire's. Even if Benjamin's "antirevolutionary conception of history […] judges with a profound pessimism the chances that the punctual breakthroughs that undermine the always-the-same will combine into a tradition and not be forgotten," as Jürgen Habermas wrote, it is nonetheless true that that conception of history "is not rendered utterly blind toward steps forward in the emancipation of the human race" (Habermas 101).

Given Benjamin's early reflection on Baudelaire and the related ideas developed, without reference to the poet, in the Trauerspiel book, it is surprising to consider the quite different turn that Benjamin's writings on Baudelaire were to take later; these represent almost an abnegation of his earlier thoughts even as the theological impetus that informs them persists in Benjamin's latest writings. By the time of "The Paris of the Second Empire in Baudelaire" (1938), a fully materialist reading of Baudelaire comes to the fore in this comment on the poem "Abel et Caïn": "Cain, the ancestor of the disinherited, appears as the founder of a race, and this race can be none other than the proletariat" (*Writer* 55). This remark stands in stark contrast to a note in the *Arcades* project where Benjamin resists Ernest Seillière's reading of

"Le reniement de Saint Pierre," a poem from the same section of *Les Fleurs du Mal* as "Abel et Caïn," which sees Christ's remorse as stemming from "having let pass so fine an opportunity for proclaiming the dictatorship of the proletariat," a reading Benjamin dismisses as "inane" (*Arcades* 266). Similarly, in the "Paris of the Second Empire" essay, Benjamin asserts that "Baudelaire's Satanism must not be taken too seriously. If it has some significance, it is as the only attitude in which Baudelaire was able to sustain a nonconformist position for any length of time" (*Writer* 56). Here Benjamin prefigures Fredric Jameson's dismissal of "the Baudelaire of diabolism and of cheap *frisson*" (Jameson 223), but to dismiss Satanism as an uninteresting or irrelevant aspect of Baudelaire's work is to misunderstand its role, for it is not simply an adolescent reversal of conventional virtue or a simple desire to generate scandal that motivates the "Révolte" poems. Rather, Satanism is a powerful but ultimately futile attempt to resolve the implications of Baudelaire's asoteriological theology; depending as it does on the logic of redemption, it remains thoroughly tied to traditional Christian theology and thus must be rejected under Baudelaire's radical revision of it. To say that we should take Baudelaire's Satanism seriously is not to claim that we should consider him an active Satanist; in that respect Benjamin's assertion is correct. But it would be wrong to conclude that we should dismiss the poems of "Révolte" in favor of other supposedly more pertinent "modern" poems located in other sections of *Les Fleurs du Mal*, since that would deny the primacy of the theological in Baudelaire, as Benjamin seems to do at this point in his own engagement with the poet, when he goes on to comment that "it is merely a different view of the problem if one asks what impelled Baudelaire to give a radical theological form to his radical rejection of those in power" (56).

This period in Benjamin's work sees a tension, then, between a chiefly politically inflected reading of Baudelaire and a more nuanced interpretation that would emphasize some continuity with his earlier and more explicitly metaphysical or theological work. Benjamin wrote the "Paris of the Second Empire" essay in the summer and fall of 1938, a period which overlaps with the time of composition of the "Central Park" fragments, on which Benjamin was at work from April 1938 to February 1939. In the latter, Benjamin takes up theological considerations more explicitly and more seriously and with a vocabulary that also echoes his earlier work on Trauerspiel. Benjamin traces the transformation of the Catholic notion of *taedium vitae* into spleen and notes that "in Baudelaire's melancholy [*Trauer*], all that is left of the infinite regress of reflection […] is the 'somber and lucid tête-à-tête' of the subject with itself. The specific 'seriousness' of Baudelaire's work is located here. It prevented the poet from truly assimilating the Catholic worldview, which could be reconciled with allegory only under the aegis of play" (*Writer* 136). This remark contains the seed of an important insight about Baudelaire's relation to traditional Catholicism because it shifts the question from one of adopting or abandoning that view to one of the impossibility of assimilating it. The latter formula is strongly indicative of the kind of theological engagement, disengaged from both belief and religious practice but persisting in more than merely metaphorical form, that I have been attempting to demonstrate in Baudelaire. The silent term of the dialogue as Benjamin presents it here is the idea of redemption, the other major stumbling block to Baudelaire's ability to assimilate the Catholic worldview, which depends in its entirety on not just the possibility but the actual assurance of redemption. Benjamin begins to hint at the fact that what is at stake in Baudelaire is neither a surpassing of the theological nor a simple reversal of Christianity in favor of Satanism but rather a coming to terms with the elimination of redemption and whether or not that ultimately culminates, as Benjamin implies here, in the solipsism of a self in an endless loop of dialogue with only itself.

Benjamin advances tentatively in the terrain of redemption's translation into the world of the modern, inquiring, for instance, about the status of fashion: "Fashion is the eternal recurrence of the new. — Yet can motifs of redemption be found specifically in fashion?" (*Writer* 155). The question remains open, unanswered, an invitation to (uncompleted) further reflection rather than a definitive statement that there can in fact be a modernity infused with the remnants of a redemptive theology, a question to which Baudelaire seems to answer a more definitive "no" than Benjamin is willing to grant.[3] And indeed the question about fashion precedes by only a few pages the aphorism I have already cited that asserts that "redemption depends on the tiny fissure in the continuous catastrophe" (161). Much is at stake in the tiny fissure, since it is clear from the paragraph that precedes this contention that Benjamin is thinking of redemption not only in a theological but also a political sense: "The concept of progress must be grounded in the idea of catastrophe. That things are 'status quo' *is* the catastrophe" (161). The fissure, then, is the interruption of the ever-the-same, the time that is, according to the "Theses on the Philosophy of History," "shot through with chips of Messianic time" (*Illuminations* 263). Benjamin's political theology is clearly skeptical about the possibility of the redemption that is evoked here only hypothetically, under the sign of "dependence" on a fissure whose existence is not asserted categorically by Benjamin. Nevertheless, even that tentative, hypothetical redemption would not hold when tested against Baudelaire's more categorical refusal of redemption.

In the fragments of the *Arcades* project, there are traces of theological investment in Baudelaire but never a direct intervention in the question of redemption. Given the incomplete nature of the project, we should resist the urge to impose a unity on the assembled notes that form the project as it has come down to us. I will therefore look to a few key moments that illustrate the tension between Benjamin's earlier theological orientation and his later materialist one, to examine the degree to which he takes into account the full consequences of Baudelaire's asoteriological vision. At certain times, Benjamin seems to be working to banish the theological from his own thinking on Baudelaire by radically secularizing the poet himself. Thus we read the following remark on the abyss, which will, as we shall see later in this chapter, be essential for Benjamin Fondane in his own reading of Baudelaire: "With Blanqui, the cosmos has become an abyss. Baudelaire's abyss is starless; it should not be defined as cosmic space. But even less is it the exotic space of theology. It is a secularized space: the abyss of knowledge and of meanings" (*Arcades* 271). Given the highly theological nature of Benjamin's speculations about knowledge and the fall that we explored in the last chapter, and given the immediate relevance of the fall to Baudelaire's poetry, it is surprising to see the abyss of knowledge equated here to a secularized space. While the space of knowledge is certainly not theologically *traditional*, it would be difficult to justify a reading of Baudelaire's abyss as thoroughly secular. Yet at another moment Benjamin cites without comment the following assessment by Gonzague de Reynold from 1920, comparing François Villon to Baudelaire: "In the one, we find the mystical and macabre Christianity of an age in the process of losing its faith; in the other the more or less secularized Christianity of an age seeking to recover its faith" (cited in *Arcades* 311). One might object that what many early twentieth-century critics of Baudelaire had trouble articulating is the fact that Baudelaire's view can be said to be neither secular nor Christian, for while it is steeped in the more than metaphorical vocabulary of God and Satan, its refusal of some of the most basic tenets of Christianity make it very difficult to apply that label, even with the qualification of an unconventional Christianity.

Further evidence of Benjamin's struggle to articulate Baudelaire's point of view, and of further grappling with the categories of secularization and Christianity with regard to Baudelaire, can be seen in this comment, which renews the theological imperative that the fragments I have quoted above seem to want to reject:

> To interrupt the course of the world—that was Baudelaire's deepest intention. The intention of Joshua. […] From this intention sprang his violence, his impatience, and his anger; from it, too, sprang the ever-renewed attempts to cut the world to the heart [or sing it to sleep]. In this intention he provided death with an accompaniment: his encouragement of its work. (*Arcades* 318, words in brackets in original)

In contrast to the dismissals of the theological evident in other fragments, this one returns to that realm in ways that bring us round once more to Benjamin's ever-present notion of redemption, visible here in the interruption of the world, which echoes the "ever-the-same" which Benjamin labels catastrophe and which messianic time would interrupt. We remember that messianic time is extrahistorical, thus representing an interruption rather than an immanent moment within time. In this fragment Benjamin comes closest to the idiosyncratic theology we have been tracing in Baudelaire, most notably in the emphasis on the impossibility of any redemptive action on the part of the poet: intentionality here does not translate to possibility, and thus death is the only effective solution. Baudelaire's interruption of the course of the world would be not a redemptive political act but rather a reduction to nothingness, which carries the label "death" only if death is understood to lead to no afterlife.

In this sense, Benjamin's notion of "petrified unrest" is pertinent to Baudelaire. In the *Arcades* fragments, he returns at several points to his study of Trauerspiel to sketch points of connection between that earlier work and his thought on Baudelaire. He refers to the image of petrified unrest as "the bleak confusion of Golgotha" (*Arcades* 326) and attempts to historicize it:

"In the final analysis, the image of petrified unrest called up by allegory is a historical image. It shows the forces of antiquity and of Christianity suddenly arrested in their content, turned to stone amid unalloyed hostilities" (*Arcades* 366). At this point we need to raise a crucial question about the possibility of historicizing petrified unrest. A brief detour through Theodor Adorno's work will give some context to this question. Adorno famously writes in *Minima Moralia* that "the only philosophy which can be responsibly practiced in face of despair is the attempt to contemplate all things as they would present themselves from the standpoint of redemption" (Adorno 246). Retaining a notion of redemption, as Benjamin does, would require stepping outside of history, via the messianic moment, in order to be able to contemplate things from that standpoint. Leo Bersani points out that Adorno affirms "the 'utterly impossible' nature of any such philosophy because 'it presupposes a standpoint removed, even though by a hair's breadth, from the scope of existence, whereas we well know that any possible knowledge must not only be first wrested from what is, if it shall hold good, but is also marked, for this reason, by the same distortion and indigence it seeks to escape'" (Adorno 247, quoted in Bersani 54). Bersani goes on to critique the persistence of the redemptive not only in Benjamin but also in the culture of contemporary criticism, which is drawn so strongly to Benjamin, according to Bersani, because of its own attachment to a logic of redemption:

> The disease of modernity (more profoundly, of history) that Benjamin analyzes is first of all (and perhaps last of all) the disease of his perception of modernity. The redemptive need in Benjamin's critique of the moderns condemns that critique to a kind of mystified morbidity; it always has to be a question of "truth" breaking in on, or being made to emerge from, degraded phenomena—degraded by virtue of their very phenomenality. It is tempting to see Benjamin's great popularity today as a sign of our complicity in such mystifications. It is perhaps, more pointedly, a sign of the extraordinary hold on our thought of the culture of redemption. For in Benjamin we find the traits most deeply characteristic of the culture: the scrupulous registering of experience in order to annihilate it, and the magical and nihilistic belief that immersion in the most minute details of a material content will not only reduce that content but simultaneously unveil its hidden redemptive double. (Bersani 54)

Here again, the persistence of categories such as annihilation and resurrection cannot but echo a secularized Christian logic of redemption, precisely the logic that Baudelaire rejects.

Françoise Meltzer has also pointed to differences between Benjamin's and Baudelaire's approaches to questions of history and especially the possibility of historical perspective. Meltzer identifies a "double vision" in Baudelaire that sees before and behind but is incapable of seizing, and therefore of conceptualizing, the present moment. This double vision "not only prevents an overview, panoramic discernment, or perspective, but puts him into a solipsism that sees in historical events, and in capitalist culture, more fodder for his conviction that progress will eventually atrophy 'the spiritual part'" (Meltzer 224). The prophetic here cancels the possibility of a historical vision in ways not unlike those that we identified with Adorno's comments on "the standpoint of redemption." In both cases, the missing and impossible stance (the present moment for Meltzer, the extratemporal messianic point for Adorno) calls into question the ability to think historically in ways on which Benjamin depends. As I have been attempting to show, Benjamin thus also depends on a messianic viewpoint that is adamantly refused in Baudelaire when the poet cancels the possibility of redemption and invites reflection on how we might think beyond and without it. Meltzer develops her comparison between the two in terms of "exhaustion":

> Benjamin comes from an era in which nostalgia has lost both its purpose and the luxury necessary for its indulgence. If anything, poetry and the poetic serve for him as vehicles to the disaster of human events. So Benjamin himself resembles the angel of history in that he can see things (in horror) from something like an aerial perspective; he sees accumulation, not depth. Baudelaire's man is exhausted, not horrified. He sees his own life, not "history." (Meltzer 225)

A Baudelairean reading of Benjamin, then, would challenge the messianic viewpoint that would allow Benjamin to play the role of angel of history and would give priority to the metaphysical conditions enumerated by Baudelaire which, to be sure, manifest themselves historically but could not definitively be shown to be defined by that history. The philosophical stakes of Baudelaire's writings cannot be reduced to a historical approach, paradoxically perhaps, because such an approach seems to depend on a messianic vision, thus suggesting the priority of theological considerations. Baudelaire's writings shift the terrain back to the primacy of the theological by radically redefining what it might mean to think theologically without a notion of redemption from, and hence also removal from, history.

Benjamin's reflections on Baudelaire sometimes hint at the problem of time and its non-linear manifestations, especially in Benjamin's comments on the poet as "brooder," which Benjamin opposes to the "philosopher": "Baudelaire was a bad philosopher, a better theorist in matters of art; but only as a brooder was he incomparable" (*Arcades* 328). The difference between a thinker and brooder is that the former

> not only meditates a thing but also meditates this meditation of the thing. The case of the brooder is that of the man who has arrived at the solution of a great problem but has then forgotten it. And now he broods—not so much over the matter itself as over his past reflections on it. The brooder's thinking, therefore, bears the imprint of memory. Brooder and allegorist are cut from the same cloth. (*Arcades* 367)

Here we are close once again to the notion of contemplation, and contemplation of evil, that reinforced the importance of original sin in Baudelaire. Brooding removes the subject not only from action but also from historical progression by becoming a metacognitive act wherein the subject is trapped and forced to turn in on himself. While the thought bears the imprint of memory, it is not simply an act *of* memory but rather a cyclical back and forth between past and present from which there can be no escape, no removal, no forward-directed thought or action. In the completed writings on Baudelaire, Benjamin does not push these reflections to their full theological consequences, even though in the *Arcades* fragments he has his eye on the theological stakes:

> Though Baudelaire likes to appeal to Catholicism, his historical experience is nonetheless that which Nietzsche fixed in the phrase "God is dead." In Nietzsche's case, this experience is projected cosmologically in the thesis that nothing new occurs any more. In Nietzsche, the accent lies on eternal recurrence, which the human being has to face with heroic composure. For Baudelaire, it is more a matter of "the new," which must be wrested heroically from what is always again the same. (*Arcades* 337)

Benjamin intriguingly suggests the possibility not of the full-blown atheology that the phrase "God is dead" may imply but rather of the remainder of the Catholic God who, for Baudelaire, does not save. On this reading, we can see Baudelaire proposing, *avant la lettre*, a reading of the rest of Nietzsche's famous utterance, which goes on to assert: "and we have killed him" (*Gay* 181) since along with that death our possibility for redemption is canceled as well. Under Baudelaire's asoteriological logic, the effort to wrest the new from the always the same is bound to fail, insofar as the new is always pulled back to the same without the messianic moment that would endow the new with value and distinguish it from the rest. Benjamin here assimilates Baudelaire to his own salvific vision of the role of the critic, summarized thus by Richard Wolin: "For Benjamin, the philosophy of history becomes *Heilgeschichte*, the history of redemption, and the task of the critic—or later, that of the historical materialist—is that of rescuing the few unique visions of transcendence that grace the continuum of history, the now-times (*Jetztzeiten*), from the fate of oblivion which incessantly threatens to consume them [...]. To preserve a record of such now-times, the function of historical remembrance, is the ultimate end of the method of redemptive criticism" (Wolin 48). Baudelaire's thought refuses the possibility of the poet or critic playing this role, not least because the role of brooder which Benjamin assigns to Baudelaire precludes the possibility of the heroic action he might hope to accomplish.

There is another reader of Baudelaire in the 1930s and early 1940s whose life, like Benjamin's, was cut short by Nazi barbarism. Romanian-born French literary critic and poet Benjamin Fondane's last book, *Baudelaire et l'expérience du gouffre* [*Baudelaire and the Experience of the Abyss*], on which he was at work from 1941 to 1944, was completed but not revised by the author before he was deported from France and exterminated at Auschwitz-Birkenau on October 2, 1944. His lengthy and complex study of Baudelaire, eclipsed by the debate around Jean-Paul Sartre's existentialist/biographical reading of the poet published shortly after Fondane's study appeared posthumously (Sartre's *Baudelaire* was published in January 1947 and Fondane's book a few months later), is informed by a complex network of philosophical and theological thinkers and writers including Pascal, Kierkegaard, Nietzsche, and Kafka. It provides an important counterpoint to Benjamin's reading of Baudelaire, one that accounts in ways that Benjamin's does not for Baudelaire's asoteriology and its consequences for his worldview as it emerges in his writings. Fondane's study of Baudelaire is, like Benjamin's writings on the poet, the culmination of a long engagement with the relationship of literature to philosophical questions. Despite this long-standing investment in Baudelaire over approximately the same time period, Fondane and Benjamin did not know each other, nor did they refer to each other's works (Teboul 85). While both thinkers engage with the theological stakes in Baudelaire in order to illuminate larger questions of the significance of the poet's works, there are important differences between the two:

> Walter Benjamin considers that the "illusory theological halo" of the "legend" of the author of the *Fleurs du Mal* must be "totally dissipated" whereas Benjamin Fondane makes Baudelaire's religious experience a central stake in his analytical discourse, even if the emphasis is often on the Satanic diverting of Christianity. [...] In Benjamin, the poet never seems important as an individuality, and his "flâneur" is an anonymous face emerging for a brief moment from the wave of the crowd in order to signify that the modern artist draws the essential aspect of his vocation from the streets of the great capitals. In Fondane, to the contrary, the street and urban modernity are absent and his Baudelaire is rather a poet of the depths of the self than a poet of the exteriors of the city. (Pop-Curseu 149–50)

The critics' differing emphases generate two quite different lists of touchstone poems to which each critic returns again and again and which acquire a kind of emblematic status. As Ioan Pop-Curseu has indicated, while Benjamin's Baudelaire is the poet of "Le cygne," "A une passante," "Perte d'auréole," "Le vin des chiffonniers," "Les sept vieillards," and "Le soleil," ["The Swan," "To a Woman Passing By," "Loss of Halo," "The Rag-Pickers' Wine," "The Seven Old Men," and "The Sun"] Fondane's poet comes to us through poems such as "L'irréparable," "L'irrémédiable," "De profundis," "Le gouffre," "Une charogne," and "Un voyage à Cythère" ["The Irreparable," "The Irremediable," "De profundis," "The Abyss," "A Carcass," and "A Voyage to Cythera"].

This is not to say that Benjamin succeeds in finding the true "modernity" of Baudelaire the poet of urban experience while Fondane seeks to perpetuate the poet as a practitioner of art removed from his historical context. Quite to the contrary, Fondane argues against Paul Valéry's and T.S. Eliot's influential readings of the poet in order to situate him in a philosophical context that engages with important voices in anti-systematic philosophical approaches to literature in the 1930s and 1940s. Fondane does not ignore the poet's situation in the urban nightmare of his time; his reading, however, gives precedence to metaphysical concerns that manifest themselves in, but are not determined by, the poet's historical context.[4] I turn below to Fondane's work on Baudelaire in order to illustrate the way it engages with Baudelaire's asoteriology and provides an important counterpoint to Benjamin's approach. Since Fondane is a less well-known thinker than Benjamin, I would like to begin by situating his work on Baudelaire in the context of an earlier collection of essays, *La conscience malheureuse* [*The Unhappy Consciousness*] (1936), which outlines key aspects of his approach.

Fondane's is an eclectic approach that defies simple categorization. While influenced by Lev Chestov, his work, like Benjamin's, cannot be said to fall neatly into a philosophical school, nor does it attempt to be systematic in its approach. In *La conscience malheureuse* he argues against Marx but not from what could be labeled a politically conservative stance. Rather, he groups Marx together with Hegel as thinkers who place too much stock in reason as the force of historical progress. Fondane's project is to rejuvenate a metaphysical approach to conceptualizing both art and history at a time when political forces were rendering visions of historical progress less tenable, while giving credence to thinkers of anguish, nothingness, and the *gouffre*, all of which go on to inform his reading of Baudelaire some eight years later. This is not to say that Fondane defends antihistorical thinking: "Combien évanescente et précaire que soit le trame des événments historiques, politiques et économiques, force nous est de lui consentir une *présence redoutable*. Et sommes-nous *libres* de n'en pas tenir compte? [...] Nous sommes à la fois, en tant que citoyens du malheur social, des êtres poltiques, et en tant que citoyens du malheur humain, des êtres métaphysiques" ["However evanescent and precarious the web of historical, political, and economic events may be, we must grant it a *formidable presence*. And are we *free* to not take it into account? [...] We are, as citizens of social discontent, political beings, and as citizens of human unhappiness, metaphysical beings"] (*Conscience* x). It is not, for Fondane, a question of opposing metaphysical or historical approaches to art or philosophy but rather of refusing to grant priority to the historical in such a way that the metaphysical would be seen as a mere historical category, generating a set of historically determined questions and disappearing given the appropriate historical conditions:

> Il est même vraisemblable qu'une société absolument débarassée de tout souci matériel—si jamais cela arrive—soit autrement plus propre que la nôtre à se livrer totalement et sans arrière-pensée à l'angoisse métaphysique. [...] Tant que la réalité sera telle qu'elle est, de manière ou d'autre—par le poème, par le cri, par la foi ou par le suicide—l'homme témoignera de son irrésignation, dût cette irrésignation être—ou paraître—absurdité et folie. Il n'est pas dit, en effet, que la folie ne doive jamais finir par avoir raison de la raison. (xvii)

> [It is even plausible that a society absolutely freed of all material worry—if ever that were to happen—would be better suited, in a different way, than ours to hand

itself over totally and without a backward glance to metaphysical anguish. […] As long as reality remains what it is, in one way or another—by the poem, the shout, by faith or suicide—man will testify to his refusal to surrender, even if this refusal have to be—or seem—absurdity and folly. It is not established, in effect, that folly must not end up triumphing over reason.]

In his interrogation of the way historical and larger metaphysical concerns overlap, and in his granting to poetry a privileged status in terms of the insight it provides into those concerns, Fondane's approach is akin to that Benjamin, but with significant differences that give full import to the metaphysico-theological considerations that determine Baudelaire's relationship to history: "Je ne nierai pas que la dialectique historique n'épuise une partie importante de notre réel; mais encore: enveloppe-t-elle *toutes* nos questions? ne laisse-t-elle *rien* de côté?" ["I will not deny that historical dialectic exhausts an important part of our real; but still: does it envelop *all* our questions? Does it not leave *anything* aside?"] (xii).

Fondane offers a critique of Hegel, Marx, and then Husserl on similar grounds of seeking "un édifice de certitude qui soit hors d'atteinte" ["an edifice of certainty that would be invincible"] (xviii), an impossible and falsifying ideal for philosophy. This philosophical move is itself, Fondane argues, based in these philosophers' own awareness of the impossibility of certitude and a reaction inspired by fear of anguish, absurdity and madness, the presence of which systematic philosophers recognize but attempt to conceal by means of the philosophical system, thereby creating a reliance on reason which itself becomes a kind of madness (xviii). He affirms the need to think religiously and philosophically at the same time in order to generate a full picture of human subjectivity in a way that resists reason's potential for reductionism. It is important to specify that, like Baudelaire's, Fondane's reference to the religious or theological has nothing of an orthodox affirmation of faith in a God and certainly not of the redemptive God. In fact, Benedetto Croce identified the lack of hope of redemption as one of the key characteristics of Fondane's thought as it is revealed in his study of Baudelaire. Croce wrote in 1948 that Fondane's book is exemplary of what Croce calls "the new *Weltzschmerz* of our time" whose characteristics he identifies as "pain without the light of moral faith and without hope of redemption" (cited in de Lussy 40–1). Like Baudelaire, Fondane adopts the vocabulary and structures of religious thought in ways that bracket questions of belief or practice but retain the full force of theology as a mode of thought, compensating, in Fondane's case, for the excesses of reason that led to the positivism of the nineteenth century that Baudelaire deplores and, in a conceptual framework that has much in common with Horkheimer and Adorno's dialectic of Enlightenment, the catastrophe of the mid-twentieth century that Fondane lived and which he attempted to theorize in its full metaphysical force.[5] An important source of theoretical kinship between Baudelaire and Fondane is their refusal of redemption even as they work within the semantic framework of Judeo-Christianity. One of Fondane's criticisms of Hegel is, tellingly, what Fondane perceives as a messianic spirit in his thought that tends toward what Fondane views as an impossible reconciliation of the contradictions of consciousness:

> L'Esprit de Hegel prétend avoir supprimé cet « au-delà »; il prétend avoir résolu les contradictions de la conscience; sa *notion*, qui est « pleine raison », a commencé ses effets bienfaisants. Voici l'époque annoncée, messianique, de l' « apaisement infini après une contradiction infinie » ... L'homme est devenu grand, a trouvé sa propre unité, il se reconnaît fils de Dieu—que dis-je, Dieu lui-même! ... (51)

> [The Spirit of Hegel claims to have canceled this "beyond"; it claims to have resolved the contradictions of consciousness; its *notion*, which is "full reason," has begun its beneficent effects. Here is the announced messianic era of the "infinite calming after an infinite contradiction" ... Man has become great, has found his own unity, he recognizes himself as son of God—what am I saying, God himself! ...]

Fondane identifies Kierkegaard, Dostoyevski and Nietzsche as reacting against Hegel's "religion du bonheur" ["religion of happiness"], which obliges us to adopt reason as our master even though it proves itself to be "méchant, coercitif, indifférent à l'homme" ["mean, coercive, indifferent to man"] (51). Using Hegel's own notion of the master/slave dialectic which prevents happiness so long as it exists, Fondane argues that Hegel's approach to reason as master assures the persistence of the dialectic. This is not to say that happiness can be found by renouncing the systematic philosophical tradition but rather that the combination of theological and philosophical reflection that Fondane promotes yields a more lucid understanding of human subjectivity which cannot be redeemed by faith, reason, art, or any other potentially saving force.

Like Baudelaire, Fondane is led to the narrative of original sin as an important indicator of our relation not only to divinity but to knowledge, mortality, and redemption. Fondane's reading emphasizes the absurd, even as the story itself is given as an account of the desire for knowledge. Drawing on Kierkegaard, Fondane asks, "comment pourrait-on *comprendre* une chose aussi absurde que le péché?" ["How could one *understand* a thing as absurd as sin?"] (190). Kierkegaard affirms that God would not tempt humanity, and thus we need to assume that Adam was speaking to himself. This reading begins to resemble Žižek's "perverse" reading of Christianity that wonders why, if the tree of knowledge is forbidden, God put it there in the first place. Fondane affirms that "le récit de la Genèse est en effet fondé sur plusieurs non-sens" ["the Genesis story is in fact founded on several non-sensical aspects"]:

> D'une part, Dieu demande à l'homme, posé dans un état d'innocence, d'éviter la connaissance—ce qui est contradictoire; d'autre part, l'homme agit sous le coup d'une menace—celle de mourir—mais il ne peut savoir ce qu'est la mort; ici Dieu

menace et là, le serpent—qui est encore Dieu—le tente; où serait donc le péché? Il faut—pour que tout puisse s'expliquer—que menace et tentation aient lieu dans le seul homme; mais où trouver une catégorie psychologique qui nous donne une tentation qui ne serait que la tentation d'un *rien*, puisque l'innocence *exclut* le savoir? (191)

[On one hand, God asks man, posed in a state of innocence, to avoid knowledge—which is contradictory; on the other hand, man acts under a threat—that of death—but he cannot know what death is; here God threatens and there, the serpent—who is still God—tempts him; where then would the sin be? For everything to be explained, it is necessary that threat and temptation happen in the same man; but where to find a psychological category that would give us a temptation that would only be the temptation of a *nothing*, since innocence *excludes* knowledge?]

Sin is redefined on this account as synonymous with knowledge and removed from the arena of choice to that of necessity.[6] Or, rather, Fondane translates the concept of original sin back to its relation to knowledge. He affirms:

Il fallut donc définir à nouveau le péché originel, car au Savoir il était évident que l'on ne pouvait renoncer. C'est ainsi qu'insensiblement, on déserta la vérité: l'Eglise logea son péché orighinel dans l'acte de chair, du moins en pratique; un philosophe catholique, comme Gilson, soutient aujourd'hui encore, avec l'autorité de l'Eglise, que le péché n'était que de *désobéissance*, que Dieu, qui avait tout donné, n'avait refusé à l'homme qu'une toute petite chose, un fruit de rien du tout. Et un théologien juif, comme Martin Buber, ira plus loin et dira que le péché originel n'était rien d'autre que le meurtre d'Abel par Caïn. (266–7)

[It was thus necessary to define original sin once again, since it was evident that one could not renounce Knowledge. It was thus that, without realizing it, we deserted truth: the Church located its original site in the carnal act, at least practically speaking; a Catholic philosopher, like Gilson, still maintains today, with the authority of the Church, that sin was only *disobedience*, that God, who had given all, had refused to man only one very little thing, a little fruit of no importance. And a Jewish theologian, like Martin Buber, will go further and say that original sin is nothing other than the murder of Abel by Cain.]

Since knowledge is irrevocable and unredeemable, we are condemned to unhappiness by our very nature as knowing beings. Given that the desire to know, and the fact of knowing, are part of what it means to be a human subject, there is no choice but to know, and thus no choice but to sin. At the same time, that sin is unredeemable since an elimination of knowledge would also alter the fundamental character of our humanity, making the human into something else altogether rather than redeeming the human itself. The temptation, once we are conscious of knowledge as synonymous with sin, is not *toward* sin but *away* from sin, since "L'homme est tenté, avec le concours de l'angoisse, par le Rien" ["Man is tempted, with the aid of anguish, by the Nothing"] (191). This is where Fondane's thought intersects in important ways with Baudelaire's, since the poet is ultimately tempted not by Satanism but by the possibility of the Nothing, which reveals itself, in poems such as "Obsession," to be an impossibility, an inconceivable category on account of our condition as knowing beings, which Fondane helps us to define as synonymous with unredeemable original sin. "Dieu a vu juste qui disait que nous allions mourir, mais le serpent a vu juste aussi qui disait que nous deviendrions pareils aux dieux. Il ressort donc de là cette conséquence effrayante que, pour qu'il y ait Esprit, il faut qu'il y ait le péché. Notre liberté n'est que de mourir. Et « le courage pour l'angoisse devant la mort » est la suprême sagesse de l'être authentique" ["God saw correctly when he said that we were going to die, but the serpent saw correctly when he said that we would become like gods. What comes from this, then, is the frightening consequence that, for there to be Spirit, there must be sin. Our freedom is only freedom to die. And 'the courage for anguish in the face of death' is the supreme wisdom of authentic being"] (192).

It is in this way that Fondane revitalizes and justifies his intellectual engagement with the myth of the fall, now effectively removed from its traditional Judeo-Christian context and introduced as a way to enact the introduction of theological thinking into an otherwise secular philosophy. This allows him to avoid the danger of an overreliance on reason that fails to give an adequate account of the persistence of metaphysical problems manifested in, but not limited by and certainly never resolved by, history:

> Chaque fois que la philosophie entreperend de fonder, de légitimer ou de justifier ses sources, ses pouvoirs, ses droits *autonomes*, elle se heurte à quelque écueil […]; l'Urgrund irrationnel, irréductible, de Schelling réapparait; et ce n'est pas seulement un fragment rébarabatif de réel qui refuse de se laisser penser; c'est le réel en sa totalité qui ne se laisse pas penser. Que l'on se soit résolu l'evanouissement de ce réel au profit de la seule raison, –et que cela ait effectivement eu lieu, tout le long de l'histoire de la philosophie—ne supprime pas la contradtiction, comme il le semble. (193)

> [Each time that philosophy undertakes to found, legitimate, or justify its sources, its powers, its *autonomous* rights, it bumps up against some stumbling block […] the irrational, irreductible Urgrund of Schelling reappears; and it is not only a rebarbarative fragment of the real that refuses to let itself be thought; it is the real in its totality that does not let itself be thought. That one has resolved the fainting of this real to the advantage of reason alone,—and that that would in fact take place, all through the history of philosophy—does not cancel the contradiction as it would seem to.]

This reassignment of the theological allows Fondane to critique systematic philosophy and its ultimate optimism, inadequate to the task of accounting for metaphysical anguish, while refusing at the same time to resort to traditional antimodern theological accounts of human sinfulness, equally inadequate in their reliance on God, transcendence, and redemption for the coherence of that explanation.[7] What Fondane admires in Kierkegaard and Heidegger alike is the aspect of their thinking that he calls "une théologie sans Dieu" ["a theology without God"] (193), a label he applies to any adequate metaphysics.

It is the task of metaphysics properly understood to theorize, without attempting to resolve, unredeemed mortality under whatever labels varying modes of thought may apply to it:

> la finitude, la mort, le malheur, continuellement matés, ne cessent de faire leur réapparition; nous sommes dans un monde de gâchis, et ce gâchis, appelé ou non: faute, péché, conscience malheureuse, Urgrund, illusion, continue néanmoins d'être la grande affaire philosophique. Que l'on se constitue comme Kierkegaard « l'avocat général du divin », ou comme Freud « l'avocat général du renoncement » nous tournons également en rond autour d'une théologie *positive* ou *négative*. (194)

> [finitude, death, hardship, continually suppressed, never cease to reappear; we are in a mess of a world, and this mess, whether or not it is called fault, sin, unhappy consciousness, Urgrund, illusion, nonetheless continues to be the grand philosophical matter. Whether one constitutes oneself like Kierkegaard as "the general advocate of the divine" or like Freud as "the general advocate of renunciation" we turn round in circles around a *positive* or *negative* theology.]

These are the complex parameters in which Fondane is operating in his study of Baudelaire. Mircea Martin has described the difficulty a reader initially has in placing Fondane's Baudelaire book within an established genre: while the title might indicate a biography, there is also the exploration of literary history as well as its social context, both of which, along with certain biographical elements, "are put in relation with the stages of its creation" (Martin 236). Martin goes on to ask: "Do we have here studies or essays? [...] Is it the critique of a professional or of a poet? Is it a critique of Baudelaire's poetry or his philosophy? [...] Does this critique come from a poet or a philosopher?" (Martin 236). Martin's rhetorical questions set the stage for Fondane's analysis, which does in fact situate itself at the intersection of the literary criticism, philosophy, and poetry. Fondane's book differs substantially from Sartre's, where Baudelaire's biography is taken for a kind of case study of bad faith by which Baudelaire had in fact "deserved" his suffering.[8] As Olivier Salazar-Ferrer indicates, nothingness and the related concept of the *gouffre* function quite differently in Fondane and Sartre:

> Fondane's nothingness, as opposed to Sartre's which is engendered by the ontological structure of the for-itself, designates the inconsistency of rational, cognitive, ethical or esthetic representations of idealism. The abyss is thus

the apperception—the "vision"—of the inconsistency of rational and idealist convictions, accompanied by the idea that the totality of rational representations only constitute a set of appearances. ("L'ambivalence" 50)

In what follows, I seek to revitalize Fondane's philosophically inflected reading of Baudelaire by demonstrating the ways in which it accounts for his refusal of redemption. More specifically, Fondane does this by coming to terms with the poet's unprecedented use of the category of the *néant* as a state toward which to aspire as a corrective to the ultimately fruitless gesture of satanic revolt and as the only alternative in a world bereft of anything we could recognize as the Christian God. Such a philosophical approach does not negate a historical one; both implicitly and explicitly, Fondane's reading of Baudelaire (in the context of a France occupied by the Nazi forces that would exterminate Fondane himself) engages with the political stakes of the metaphysical vision he traces.

Fondane's *Baudelaire et l'expérience du gouffre* is, as I have suggested, an unclassifiable book. Monique Jutrin describes the experience of reading it this way:

From his first approach, the reader finds himself plunged into a thick and dense work: 34 chapters without titles or epigraphs, where thought develops in a spiral, returning indefatigably to itself. He does not know what Minotaur awaits him or what Ariane guides him. Everything seems aimed at losing him and misleading him, even though he senses that he is being led somewhere. Certain leitmotifs are perceived as signals: citations from Dante, Baudelaire, insistent citations, as are the recurrent motifs of the monad "without doors or windows," the allegory of the live rat, or the opposition between "thinking and feeling." (« Relecture » 16)

Fondane does not seek to transform Baudelaire the poet into a philosopher but rather identifies the necessity of the move toward and through philosophy in order to emerge as a poet once more: "C'est précisément *pour pouvoir demeurer poète—* et non pas philosophe—qu'il fallait devenir philosophe et combattre, afin d'arracher la poésie à la définition qui en faisait une expérience 'fausse' et lui restituer le droit (que Pascal demandait pour la philosophie pure) d'être une 'recherche en gémissant' " ["It is precisely in order to *be able to remain a poet*—and not a philosopher—that it was necessary to become a philosopher and do battle, in order to tear poetry away from the definition that made of it a 'fake' experience and to restore to it the right (that Pascal claimed for pure philosophy) to be a 'seach while moaning' "] (BEG 228). Poetry helps establish a corrective to an approach to philosophy as a commitment to progress through reason. At the same time, Baudelaire's particular approach removes the danger of poetry coming to serve, like systematic philosophy, as an attempt to cover up the abyss rather than revealing it. Baudelaire's art has a disclosive function for Fondane, and this in spite of the epigraph, slightly misquoted from Baudelaire's "Une mort héroïque," that affirms art's role as throwing a veil over the abyss: "L'ivresse de l'art est plus propre que toute autre, à jeter un voile sur les terreurs du gouffre"

["The intoxication of art is more proper than any other to throwing a veil over the terrors of the abyss"] (BEG 11).[9] Paradoxically, even art's attempt to veil the abyss acknowledges its reality in ways that systematic philosophy refuses to do: "Ni Hegel, ni Kant, ni Schopenhauer ne nous ont parlé d'un gouffre et qui subsiterait *après* la conciliation du vrai et du reel […]; la philosophie est incapable d'admettre l'existence du Gouffre […]; et le poète, lui, est incapable, malgre sa « bonne volonté », de les écarter de son drame" ["Neither Hegel, nor Kant, nor Schopenhauer spoke to us of an abyss that would subsist *after* the conciliation of the true and the real […] philosophy is incapable of admitting the existence of the Abyss […]; and the poet is incapable, despite his 'good will,' to cast them aside from his drama"] (BEG 43). In lieu of consoling fictions or proto-Stoic removal from reality, Baudelaire is forced to confront "un réel qui n'entend pas céder" ["a real that does not intend to cede its place"] (BEG 93). The laying bare of the impossibility of happiness, as we shall see, relates back to Fondane's earlier reflections on knowledge itself as both original sin and necessary condition of our human being. A double will emerges in Baudelaire, both to continue and rebel against the fundamental unhappiness that accompanies knowledge and to remove himself from the fight in an equally impossible desire for nothingness.

By wishing to be removed from the progression of an individual or collective life, Baudelaire also strives to exist outside time, both as a metaphysical subject and as a poet:

> Il n'est pas, comme le dira Eliot, « en avance sur son temps »; il est à côté de son temps, il est en dehors de n'importe quel temps, passé ou à venir; sa pensée n'est ni en retard, ni en avance, elle est tout simplement « extrême ». […] Il lui faut employer de vastes resources pour devenir de *son temps*, pour se situer, pour avoir l'*air banal*; il lui faut un malentendu. Et, tout de suite, avec une tension inouïe, il s'applique à forger de toutes pièces ce malentendu nécessaire. Il le forge d'autant mieux qu'il est le premier à avoir peur de sa propre pensée, qu'il est le premier à en être à la fois terrifié, honteux et fasciné, le premier aussi à juger correctement des réactions qu'elle est susceptible de provoquer. (BEG 56)

> [He is not, as Eliot will say, "ahead of his time"; he is next to his time, he is outside any time at all, past or future; his thought is neither behind nor ahead, it is very simply "extreme". […] He needs to employ vast resources in order to become of *his time*, to situate himself, to *seem banal*; he needs a misunderstanding. And, right away, with unheard of tension, he tries to create all of a piece this necessary misunderstanding. He creates it all the better since he is the first to be afraid of his own thought, the first to be at once terrified, ashamed and fascinated, the first also to judge correctly the reactions that it is liable to provoke.]

Fondane argues against a reading of Baudelaire that would see him as a product of his historical moment, namely, a decadence that seeks "l'originalité à tout prix" ["originality at all costs"] (BEG 60). For, such an originality would remain at the level of the individual, the eccentric. Art is a hopeless enterprise, because there cannot be said to be any salvific value in illusion, even in an illusion, such as art, that knows itself to be illusory.

Thus the stakes are high in Baudelaire's attempt to pursue art for art's sake. Fondane reads this not as an evasion of historical (or any other) reality but rather as a latent attempt to react against hopelessness, even in the full knowledge that the attempt itself is hopeless.

> Le culte de l'art pour l'art n'est pas, pour Baudelaire, une évasion, une fuite facile […]; il est une terrible lutte entreprise sans espoir, sans illusions, mais entreprise tout de même, déspérément, pour une réalité qu'il sait *fausse*, afin d'écarter la seule chose qu'il exècre, mais qu'il tient pour réelle: le Gouffre. De la réussite ou de l'échec de cette lutte dépendent, non seulement l'idée que Baudelaire se fait de l'art, mais aussi celle qu'il se fait de la vie, de Dieu. (BEG 105)

> [The cult of art for art's sake is not, for Baudelaire, an evasion, an easy escape […]; it is a terrible fight undertaken without hope, without illusions, but undertaken nonetheless, desperately, for a reality that he knows to be *false*, in order to cast aside the one thing he hates but that he holds to be real: the Abyss. On the success or failure of this fight depend, not only the idea that Baudelaire makes for himself of art, but also the one he has about life, and God.]

This sense of desperation in the pursuit of art for art's sake as an impossible and illusion-free enterprise is key to Fondane's approach to Baudelaire, where the stakes are high for Baudelaire, as they were for Fondane as well as he struggled, years before, with questions of the persistence of meaning or value in the face of God's non-existence. In notes Fondane took in the 1920s, he states he no longer believes in God and articulates the full force of such a rejection:

> Dieu lui-même n'est qu'une hypothèse, cela s'entend. Mais c'est l'hypothèse fondamentale dont toutes les autres dépendent. […] Supprimez Dieu—et […] à quoi bon? se demande l'homme, à quoi bon l'art, à quoi bon la patrie, à quoi bon la vie? Dieu est l'hypothèse unique qui supprime toutes les questions de ce genre: il les condamne; les déclare des péchés; désormais aucune question n'est plus possible. (qtd in *Avec Benjamin Fondane* 17)

> [God himself is only a hypothesis, that is understood. But it is the fundamental hypothesis on which all the others depend. […] Cancel God—and […] what's the use? wonders man, what's the use of art, fatherland, life? God is the single hypothesis that cancels all questions of this sort. He condemns them, declares them sins; henceforth no question is possible any longer.]

God exists more as a category than as a living being, that is, as the justification of law and the origin of sin. Given that Fondane had by the 1930s identified under the conventional label "sin" the necessary human capacity for knowledge itself, the category "God" remains thoroughly empty of traditional Judeo-Christian characterizations in order to become, as it did for Baudelaire, a function whose necessary absence causes anguish but whose necessary presence generates law, sin, and punishment. As he writes in a personal notebook:

> Nous sommes à une époque (ou peut-être est-elle en train de finir) dominée par cette absence de Dieu. Mais je n'entends pas par absence, privation. J'entends par absence un trou, un inachèvement, une nostalgie, une présence d'absence, quelque chose comme un rien solide, substantiel, créateur d'actes. Tout ce que nous avons écrit, pensé, édifié, ne s'était proposé qu'un seul but: combler un fossé, combler le trou que l'absence de Dieu avait ouvert dans notre univers. (qtd in *Avec Benjamin Fondane* 133)

> [We are in an era (or maybe it is about to finish) dominated by this absence of God. But by "absence" I do not mean deprivation. By absence I mean a hole, an unfinished quality, a nostalgia, a presence of absence, something like a solid, substantial nothing, creator of actions. Everything that we have written, thought, built, had proposed for itself only one goal: to fill in a gap, to fill the hole that the absence of God had opened in our universe.]

Fondane's mature writings on Baudelaire continue to draw the consequences of the knowledge that God as a personal, loving, and saving concept has met a definitive end, for both Baudelaire and Fondane. As Olivier Salazar-Ferrer has suggested, "Fondane envisages poetry as the expression of an existential disarray, haunted by nostalgia for God" (*Fondane* 99). In the *Faux traité d'esthétique* [*Fake Treatise of Esthetics*], Fondane links poetry to a nostalgia for an older spiritual vision which, nonetheless, we can no longer find tenable:

> La poésie est le lieu même—spirituel—où le péché a la nostalgie de la foi; ou, en d'autres termes, le lieu même où la conscience rêve de la possibilité d'un acte pur, libre, puissant, qui transporterait les montagnes, ou créerait le poème—en se jouant. Rêve légitime! En effet, la perfection serait de commander à la réalité et non de s'y soumettre passivement. […] Mais, écrit Gérard de Nerval dans *Aurélia* […] « L'ignorance ne s'apprend pas ». (*Faux traité* 135)

> [Poetry is the very place—a spiritual one—where sin has nostalgia for faith; or, in other words, the very place where consciousness dream of the possibility of the pure, free, powerful act, which would move mountains, or would create the poem—by deceiving. Legitimate dream! In fact, perfection would be to command reality and not to submit oneself passively. […] But, as Gérard de Nerval writes in *Aurélia* […] "Ignorance cannot be learned."]

Baudelaire's works negate the nostalgic vision of faith in all but its most ghostly traces while retaining the full force of the notion of irredeemable sin. As we have seen, one consequence of this shift in perspective is to rob satanic revolt of any power as an effective action. Such revolt belongs now to the dream of a "pure, free" act that Fondane relegates here to world of nostalgia, precisely because of the problem of knowledge, which for Fondane is always knowledge-as-sin.

The *néant* emerges in Baudelaire and Fondane as third space, beyond heaven and hell, an attempt to see damnation as a dead end without trying to affirm the possibility of redemption:

> Mais le Néant est une des deux seules issues ouvertes dans l'univers de Baudelaire; aussi horrifique que soit l'Enfer, il *est*; aussi peu digne qu'il soit de la miséricorde, ce n'est que là cependant qu'on la trouve encore; c'est sur l'autre porte, sur celle du Néant qui mène à la vertu et à la connaissance « autonomes », qu'il est écrit: Lasciate ogni speranza voi ch'entrate! C'est là que vont les « complimenteurs de l'humanité » trouver la fausse paix, la fausse vertu et la fausse connaissance! C'est là qu'ils s'échapperont par la mort à la douleur, et par le néant à l'Enfer! (BEG 242)

> [But Nothingness is one of the only two open exits in Baudelaire's universe; as horrifying as Hell is, it *is*; as little worthy as he may be of mercy, it is nevertheless only there that one still finds it; it is on the other door, on that of the Nothingness that leads to "autonomous" virtue and knowledge that it is written: "Abandon all hope, you who enter here!" It is there that the "complimenters of humanity" go to find false peace, false virtue and false knowledge! It is there that they will escape from pain by death, and from Hell by nothingness!]

Despite the hopelessness of the *néant*, it is the preferable choice for Baudelaire, since it cancels the problem of knowledge and anguish that existence necessarily brings; no other stance is tenable if knowledge is affirmed as the unredeemable original sin. Not even damnation is capable of canceling the nefarious effects of existence, and damnation becomes a threat only because it prolongs existence rather than canceling it.

Still, there is a tension, in Fondane and Baudelaire alike, between affirming the (unfruitful and hopeless) revolt of Satanism (as a rebellion against the *néant*) and affirming the (impossible) desire to come to rest in nothingness, a rest which a conscious subject could never experience, precisely because it is impossible for consciousness to experience nothingness. On one hand:

> En un univers où le néant commence aux portes de la pensée, il n'est d'affirmation que celle qui nie; en un univers sans paradis, il faut en toute hâte opposer *quelque chose* au triomphe du Néant; et l'Enfer, qui était le dernier échelon de l'être dans le monde du Dante, devient le premier dans celui de Baudelaire. Le « je ne veux pas » de son rebelle est un acte plus dangereux, plus noble que l'obéissance, et en regard de ce que le damné accepte de perdre (vertu, paix, connaissance), Baudelaire refuse d'y voir un lâche consentement à ses plaisirs, à sa pente. (BEG 243)

[In a universe where nothingness begins at the gates of thought, the only affirmation is one that negates; in a universe without paradise, one must in all haste oppose *something* to the triumph of the Nothing; and Hell, which was the last level of being in Dante's world, becomes the first in Baudelaire's. The "I do not want to" of his rebel is a more dangerous, nobler act than obedience, and with regard to what the damned one accepts to lose (virtue, peace, knowledge), Baudelaire refuses to see there a cowardly consent to one's pleasures, one's inclination.]

But on the other hand, "Les valeurs ont changé de place. La non-activité, l'obéissance, la recherche de la paix, du repos, le renoncement ne sont plus, à présent, les caractéristiques du Sage, mais celle de la « brute »; ce sont l'activité, le courage, le goût du risque et « l'Expansion infinie ». Vertus du « rebelle », qui caractérisent le héros, ce héros devenu, pour cette raison même, un sacrifié de la vie et un paria de l'intellect" ["Values have changed places. Non-activity, obedience, the search for peace and rest, renunciation are no longer, at present, the characteristics of the Sage, but of the 'brute'; they are rather activity, courage, the taste for risk and 'infinite Expansion.' Virtues of the 'rebel,' which characterize the hero, this hero become, for this very reason, a sacrificial victim of life and a pariah of the intellect"] (BEG 243). It is harder to make the case for renunciation as a heroic characteristic, and rebellion is more frequently figured in Fondane by the active revolt of the Satanist, even if that revolt is known in advance to be impossible. Still, Fondane recognizes the temporary character of the desire for active revolt and affirms, along with Baudelaire, the *néant* as the only viable if equally impossible solution

The fact that any action is doomed to failure is brought into poignant relief by the historical circumstances in which Fondane was writing his *Baudelaire*. While contemporary politics seldom plays a significant role in his analysis, it is undeniably and forcefully present at certain moments:

Un jour viendra, peut-être, où l'historien consentira à jeter un regard dans l'Histoire sur les formes de l'ennui les plus basses. C'est l'ennui qui est la source des changements soudains, des guerres sans motifs, des révolutions meurtrières; il n'est pas de cause plus opérante que lui. Un besoin se fait jour de se sentir *exister*, de rompre la *monotonie* de l'être, du pur pensable; le meurtre, la vengeance, la joie de détruire pour détruire, se donnent librement cours chez un peuple qui, il y a un instant, semblait tranquille et sage, suprême fleur d'une civilisaton consommée. (BEG 331)

[A day will come, perhaps, when the historian will consent to cast a glance in History on the basest forms of ennui. It is ennui that is the source of sudden changes, war without motive, murderous revolutions; there is no more operative cause than that. A need to *exist*, to break the *monotony* of being and of the thinkable pure, is coming to light; murder, vengeance, the joy of destroying for destruction's sake, are having their way in a people who, an instant ago, seemed tranquil and wise, the supreme flower of a consummated civilization.]

Given that the kind of revolt against *ennui* that we might be tempted at first to label heroic can in fact lead to murderous destruction, there are no grounds to affirm satanic rebellion as an effective countermeasure to the knowledge of the necessary insatisfaction of existence ushered in with knowledge. Hence the temptation to nothingness is, on this account, a more genuinely attractive option even though it refuses being and, on the surface, can even resemble *ennui* in that both lead the subject toward inactivity. The two kinds of inoperativity are, however, quite different, in that the desire for nothingness is still an act of will. Insofar as it is an act of will, though, it dooms itself to impossibility, since the willing subject is condemned, like the poet in "Obsession," never to achieve the willed-for nothingness without ceasing to be and thus ceasing to be able to perceive the desired nothingness. The traditional Christian view of good vs evil is significantly complicated by Fondane, who recognizes that "il n'y a plus de paradis dans la Comédie de Baudelaire; la route du paradis est fermée, barrée; le choix est restreint; il n'y a plus que le Néant et l'Enfer" ["there is no longer any paradise in Baudelaire's Comedy; the route to paradise is closed, barricaded; choice is restricted; there is only Nothingness and Hell"] (BEG 244). By removing redemption, Baudelaire eliminates the choice of fidelity to a loving God, leaving a choice between satanic revolt and nothingness. But by identifying the drive to exist with cruelty, he makes it impossible to affirm revolt, given the dangerous political risks it necessarily implies. The choice is then not one of cruelty or non-cruelty but the appropriate victim of the cruelty. Via the path of revolt, what results is what Fondane calls "exterior cruelty": "inquisitions, buchers, massacres d'hérétiques, croisades" ["inquisitions, stakes, massacres of heretics, crusades"] which will be the choice of "les âmes simples, les masses" ["simple souls, the masses"] whereas "les âmes fines se tourneront contre elles-mêmes" ["fine souls will turn against themselves"] (BEG 331). The self-torturing subject resembles Baudelaire's "L'héautontimorouménos," although Fondane does not make this connection explicit. Rather, he highlights the cyclic character of the internal revolt, which leads from *ennui* to attempted revolt and back to what Fondane labels, following medieval Christian tradition, *acedia*: "C'est sur un vaste canevas d'ennui que l'on brodera les cruautés, les crucifixions, que l'on terrassera l'ennemi, le diable, le néant, et quand la torture elle-même deviendra impuissante, quand l'imagination sera épuisée, le tissu primitif reparaîtra à la surface et ce sera … l'*acedia*" ["It is on a vast canvas of ennui that we will embroider cruelties and crucifixions, that we will take down the enemy, the devil, nothingness, and when torture itself becomes powerless, when imagination is exhausted, the primitive fabric will reappear at the surface and it will be … *acedia*"] (BEG 332). Fondane emphasizes that this is not just the mystics' "absence of God" but is also the absence of the devil as well, "car il n'y a plus rien là où règne l'ennui, l'immuable, l'immobile" ["since there is no longer anything there where ennui, the unchangeable, the immobile reigns"] (BEG 332). Here the boundaries of Fondane's terms become blurred, since, while there is nothing (*rien*) where there is *ennui*, this cannot be the same nothing as the *néant*, which is precisely the desired but impossible state that the subject would hope to reach in order to be free of the circular self-torturing Fondane has just described.

To be is to suffer according to Fondane, and not just in a clichéd romantic sense. Rather, suffering is the very proof of existence not only of the human subject but of the divinity, and Fondane reads Christianity's emphasis on the crucified Christ as its attempt to establish a valid basis for belief in a divinity, whose existence can only be guaranteed if it is witnessed as suffering:

> Il faut exister pour croire; il faut que ce à quoi l'on croit soit existant, non pas pensé seulement mais *senti*, et non pas pensant seulement mais *sentant!* De là peut-être, la foi du moyen-âge au seul Dieu crucifié. Il fallait faire souffrir jusqu'à la mort le moteur immobile d'Aristote, pour lui rendre un semblant de vie. Il fallait tuer l'Ennui—et donc le Logique [sic], jusqu'en Dieu. (BEG 332)[10]

> [One must exist in order to believe; it is necessary that that in which one believes exist, not only thought but *felt*, and not only thinking but *feeling*! From there perhaps come the Middle Ages' faith in the one God crucified. It was necessary to make Aristotle's unmoved mover suffer unto death, in order to give him back a semblance of life. It was necessary to kill Ennui—and thus the Logical, even all the way to God.]

If the distance between God and humanity is leveled, both beings operate by a similar logic motivated by *ennui*, which we can see in the tyrannical God of "Le reniement de saint Pierre," described as like "un tyran gorgé de viande et de vins, [qui] s'endort au doux bruit de nos affreux blasphèmes" ["a tyrant gorged with food and wine, [who] falls asleep to the sweet sound of our horrible blasphemies" (425)] (OC 1: 121) as well as in the figure of Ennui itself in "Au lecteur," famously dreaming of the scaffolds "en fumant son houka" ["as he smokes his hookah pipe" (5)] (1: 6). Fondane acknowledges, after this provocative exposition, that to illustrate his thesis about the eruption of violence and cruelty as a misguided attempt at rebellion against *ennui*, he has chosen "un exemple extrêmement compliqué et sujet à de multiples interprétations" ["an extremely complicated example that is subject to multiple interpretations"] (BEG 332), a danger he would have avoided by focusing on the descent of the Roman empire and the cruelty of figures such as Caligula and Nero. What Fondane leaves unsaid is that such an example would fail to map onto the political situation under which he was crafting these ideas, with all of the secular theological implications of the metaphysical tradition with which he is engaging and for which he is attempting to account. We cannot help but be tempted sometimes to affirm being over nothingness, but we are repulsed by the necessary affirmation of cruelty that must accompany it as the only alternative unless we accept the task of desiring nothing and the self-torture of its impossible accomplishment.

Given the expressly nonsystematic nature of Fondane's thought, there is no simple answer about whether there is a redemptive vision in his analysis, but I contend that he goes further than most commentators on Baudelaire toward accounting for the poet's lack of redemption. Fondane only rarely appeals explicitly to the vocabulary of redemption. One such instance comes fairly early in his study of Baudelaire:

> La haine qu'il a pour son moi n'est pas seulement philosophique, elle est *sainte*— aborrecimiento santo de si mismo—tout comme pour saint Jean de la Croix. Vaincre et nier son moi, le salut est à ce prix! Dans sa passon idéaliste, il apporte *aussi* la passion moyenageuse, dantesque, catholique, mystique; le bien, le mal ont pour lui encore un contenu, une épaisseur; le vide qu'il cherche n'est pas un vide pur, mais les « ténèbres »; son esprit aussi bien que son corps. (BEG 92)

> [The hatred that he has for his self is not only philosophical, it is *holy*—holy hatred of oneself—as it was for Saint John of the Cross. Salvation comes at the price of vanquishing and negating one's self! In his idealist passion, he brings *also* the medieval, Dantesque, Catholic, mystical passion; good and evil still have content and thickness for him; the void that he seeks is not a pure void, but "darkness"; his spirit as well as his body.]

Seeking is not the same as finding, and the affinity that Fondane highlights between the Catholic mystical tradition and Baudelaire's thought is a starting point rather than an ending. If dark emptiness is the goal, we have seen that it is impossible to fulfill, as the "darkness" in "Obsession," for instance, is also "canvases" (1: 76), to the poet's horror. And once again we encounter the paradoxical situation whereby the pure void would be imperceivable because there would no longer be a subject there to perceive it. The fact that we can imagine such a redemption, without being able to achieve it, turns it into a temptation and a source of anguish, thereby removing its salvific quality.

Still, Fondane seems to struggle with the implications of this vision he elucidates in Baudelaire. Even as he enumerates Baudelaire's position, there is a certain anxiety as to how to avoid despair in the face of an impossible belief in grace:

> Il n'est pas toujours certain que Baudelaire croit autant qu'il le dit au péché originel et à la grâce qui peut nous en sauver, mais ce qui est certain, c'est qu'il voit dans le péché originel *la seule cause possible* de la misère humaine et, dans la Grâce, la seule issue possible de cette impasse. On peut, certes, n'y pas croire—Baudelaire lui-même n'y croit pas toujours—mais comment peut-on n'y pas croire sans désespérer? (BEG 155)

> [It is not always certain that Baudelaire believes as much as he says he does in original sin and in the grace that can save us from it, but what is certain is that he sees in original sin *the only possible cause* of human misery and, in Grace, the only possible exit from this impasse. One can, certainly, not believe in it—Baudelaire himself does not always believe in it—but how can one not believe in it without despairing?]

The question is left open, for Baudelaire and Fondane alike, and at any rate, Fondane does not present evidence of where Baudelaire makes room for grace, even if it be a grace in which one cannot believe. Fondane rightly goes on to link the impossibility of redemption to Baudelaire's contempt for those "complimenters of humanity" who affirm that human beings are born good, a contempt that Fondane sees as both a "réminiscence maistrienne" ["Maistrean echo"] and a "souvenir de son éducation catholique" ["memory of his Catholic education"] and a "sentiment original, personnel, embrassé avec haine et violence, vécu" ["original, personal sentiment, embraced with hatred and violence, lived"] by Baudelaire (BEG 155). While at first glance it is difficult to see how this idea could be both derivative and original, this line of thought brings us back to the difficulty inherent in describing Baudelaire's engagement with theology. As I have tried to make clear, Baudelaire is certainly not drawing on conventional Catholicism but nor is he simply borrowing terminology from theology in order to subvert it. Likewise, the question of belief is equally thorny here: while Baudelaire uses theological terminology in more than a metaphorical way, the essential question is not whether Baudelaire could be said to "believe" in God. What matters most is, rather, that he uses such terms for their conceptual and explanatory value in his reflections on broader metaphysical questions relating to issues such as evil, knowledge, and progress. It is on account of that particular usage of the theological register that problems at the foundations of traditional theology can be said to be of secondary importance to Baudelaire. As Fondane notes:

> C'était peu de chose à ses yeux, que le paradis fût perdu; ce qu'il voulait c'est qu'il fût perdu *à jamais*; que l'on renonçât à y penser. Et c'est le consentement à cette perte qui se donnait pour la grande vertu et l'unique moyen de rédemption. Bien entendu, en lieu et place du paradis *perdu*, le penser logique permettrait un état où le conflit qu'il enegendre serait aboli; un paradis *futur* mais […] non plus sacré, mais profane. Ce paradis est fait de résignation, d'indifférence, de détachement du fruit; il est payé de l'abandon non de le pensée aberrante et subversive, mais de la pensée innocente et libre; ce n'est que le triomphe final de ce *rien* précisément qui s'est introduit, on ne sait comment, dans le monde de la pureté et en a pourri l'essence. (BEG 185–6)

> [It is of little importance in his eyes that paradise was lost; what he wanted was that it be lost *forever*; that we renounce thinking about it. And it is the consent to this loss that offered itself as the greatest virtue and the only means of redemption. Of course, in place of the *lost* paradise, logical thought would permit a state where the conflict it engenders would be abolished; a *future* paradise but no longer sacred but profane. This paradise is made of resignation, indifference, and detachment from the fruit; it is bought by the abandoning not of aberrant and subversive thought, but of innocent and free thought; it is only precisely the final triumph of this *nothing* that worked its way, we do not know how, into the world of purity and rotted its essence.]

Here once again, redemption is evoked only under the sign of its ultimate impossibility, because it depends on an impossible forgetting of lost paradise, the same kind of oblivion that Fondane and Baudelaire elsewhere label nothingness. Such radical renouncement would require the elimination of knowledge *tout court*, and the result is, according to Fondane, anything but a paradise:

> Pour que ce triomphe fût assuré, il nous fallait désormais « surveiller » jusqu'à nos moindres démarches, nous faire constamment une sorte de violence, […] bref bannir jusqu'à la nostalgie, jusqu'au « regret » de ce que, par le péché originel, l'humanité avait rejeté de son sein. C'est, on le voit, le contraire d'un paradis—un état d'extrême tension, d'effort exaspéré, de maximum de conscience, vivant dans la terreur perpétuelle de voir s'écrouler sa fragile construction, à la merci d'un « regret » […]. C'est en cette terreur que la pensée spéculative, la théologie et jusqu'à la psychanalyse et la critique poétique s'entêtent à voir le *souverain bien*. Mais que ce souverain Bien fût un *rien*, un effort héroïque dans le vide, un effort inhumain et non ontologique, cela évidement ne tombait pas sous les sens. Ne pouvaient le voir que ceux-là seuls qui se souvenaient d'un monde non seulement perdu, mais trahi et souillé. (BEG 186)

> [For this triumph to be assured, we had from then on to be vigilant over even our most insignificant moves, constantly to do a sort of violence to ourselves, in short to ban even nostalgia and the "regret" for that which, by original sin, humanity had rejected from its breast. It is, we see, the opposite of a paradise—a state of extreme tension, of exasperated effort, of a maximum of consciousness, living in the perpetual terror of seeing crumble one's fragile construction, at the mercy of a "regret" […]. It is in this terror that speculative thought, theology and even psychoanalysis and poetic criticism stubbornly insist on seeing the *sovereign good*. But that this sovereign Good be a *nothing*, a heroic effort in the void, an inhuman and non-ontological effort, that evidently was not perceivable. The only ones who could see it were those who remembered a world not only lost, but betrayed and sullied.]

Baudelaire's insight is, then, to be able to see the *néant* as a good, but without postulating it as an attainable ideal. The question remains as to how such thought is sustainable without falling into despair or becoming tempted by what turns out to be the false redemptive option of revolt. Thought's lucidity about its own condition of possibility, that is, knowledge, precludes its satisfaction through anything but an impossible abolishing of itself. What Fondane theorizes as "terror" here becomes the link among philosophy, theology, and poetry, and marks or categorizes the "extreme tension" that, in the condition of lucidity, replaces paradise.

What for Baudelaire is a solution, however, becomes for Fondane another kind of temptation: "Car le diable n'est plus un sophiste, […] ce n'est plus la chair qu'il tente, mais l'esprit, et à l'esprit ce n'est pas l'orgueil qu'il propose et la désobéissance, mais le refus de participer à l'être" ["For the devil is no longer a sophist, […] it is no longer the flesh he tempts, but the mind, and to the mind it is not pride and disobedience that proposes, but the refusal to participate in being" (BEG 328). While Fondane does not openly advocate revolt against the desire for the *néant*, passages such as this one suggest his reticence to affirm the desirability of seeking it. If it were a demonic temptation to seek the nothing, then there would no longer be anything distinguishing that temptation from the more conventional kinds of demonic temptations to blasphemy, lust for power, and so on. As Fondane goes on to highlight, the problem is, once again, one of intelligibility:

> Le péché originel envisagé comme désobéissance, cela était intelligible […]. Envisagé comme sexualité, il est encore intelligible; Schopenhauer, disciple de l'Inde, se déclare en ceci d'accord avec le christianisme; mais il ne fait guère bon pour nous de regarder « la-dessous » et de conserver le mythe du péché originel comme une chose « pensable », s'il proclame, avec Nietzsche, que la connaissance est douleur et qu'il ne nous reste que les vérités salutaires des *homini religiosi*. (BEG 328–9)[11]

> [Original sin envisaged as disobedience, such a thing was intelligible […]. Envisaged as sexuality, it was still intelligible; Schopenhauer, disciple of India, declares himself in agreement on this with Christianity; but it is hardly good for us to look "underneath" and conserve the myth of original sin and a "thinkable" thing, if he proclaims, with Nietzsche, that knowledge is suffering and that all that remains for us are the salutary truths of the *religious men*.]

The problem becomes one of how to conceive of original sin if it is defined as knowledge itself, since such a characterization would allow no move beyond itself, no redemptive conceptual moment, by which to characterize that which serves as the motor of our desire to characterize it in the first place. Any attempt to move beyond this impasse only further implicates us within it. This is where violence becomes a tempting option, because it is definitive in a way that thought cannot be:

> [Baudelaire] ne supporte pas que les réponses manquent aux questions les plus claires et les plus distinctes de l'homme, et il en arrive à haïr l'homme justement parce que son existence, par le seul fait d'être, pose de telles questions! Il est des questions qu'on ne peut étouffer qu'en étouffant celui qui les pose! En politique comme ailleurs, dit-il, « le vrai saint est celui qui fouette le peuple, pour le bien du peuple ». […] Baudelaire souhaite au peuple ce même fouetteur que nous l'avons vu se souhaiter à lui-même, et pour les mêmes raisons; il s'agit de supprimer cette chose *inintellgible*: la disproportion entre la faculté et la volonté, entre l'idée adéquate et la confuse « cause extérieure ». Il ne doute pas, et nous n'avons garde d'en douter, que le bourreau fera son *devoir*, fouettera et tuera […]. Quant à verifier si cet emploi de la force, assurément *inintelligible* et fort souvent efficace, constitue véritablement une *réponse* aux questions de l'homme, Baudelaire ne s'y arrête pas, il est fatigué, il est las. (BEG 144)

[[Baudelaire] does not tolerate that answers are lacking to the clearest and most distinct questions of man, and he comes to hate man exactly because his existence, by the simple fact of being, poses such questions! There are questions that one cannot stifle without stifling the one who asks them! In politics as elsewhere, he says, "the true saint is the one who whips the people, for the good of the people." […] Baudelaire wishes for the people the same thrasher that we have seen him wish for himself, and for the same reasons; it is a question of suppressing this *unintelligible* thing: the disproportion between the faculty and the will, between the adequate idea and the "exterior cause." He does not doubt, and we take care not to doubt, that the executioner will do his *duty*, will whip and kill […]. As for verifying whether this use of force, assuredly *unintelligible* and very often effective, truly constitutes a *response* to the questions of man, Baudelaire does not linger over that, he is tired and weary.]

Fondane's reading of Baudelaire's impulse to violence is anchored not in a simple taste for evil, nor in a facile political conservatism inspired by Joseph de Maistre but rather in the epistemological and theological ground of the intelligible. Fondane's criterion allows him to collapse the distinction between violence toward the self and violence inflicted on others (and, for that matter, metaphorical and literal violence), since the violent act in both cases is accomplished in the name of repairing the unintelligible. Fondane's crucial move here is in the final comment quoted above, namely, that Baudelaire remains silent on whether such violence constitutes a true response to the questions it intends to answer. The implied answer is that such violence belongs to the ultimately unfruitful domain of satanic revolt, and thus political action, for good or for evil, can only perpetuate and never solve, or even approach, the problem of intelligibility. In fact, insofar as violence calls out for interpretation, it implicates us further in the realm of the intelligible:

Mais si, après l'echec du bourreau et la carence de l'idéal il sent se renforcer en lui sa haine contre les hommes et les idées, qu'est-ce que ça peut lui faire qu'il rende « furieux » les gens équilibrés que nous sommes, à qui tout réussit, avec ou sans bourreau? […] Il se pourrait que le triste moi, incapable de travailler, et trop capable de rêver, hélas! fût le siège d'une vérité plus profonde, quoique inadéquate et obscure! Et dans ce cas, justement parce que tiraillé, troublé par l'envie, l'impuissance et la haine, Baudelaire verrait plus clair qu'avec ses yeux ouverts et sa tête lucide. (BEG 145)

[But if, after the failure of the executioner and the inadequacy of the ideal he feels reinforced in him his hatred for men and ideas, what can it matter to him that he renders "furious" the balanced people that we are, for whom everything succeeds, with or without executioner? […] It is possible that the sad self, incapable of working, and too capable of dreaming, alas!, was the seat of a more profound truth, even if inadequate and obscure! And in this case, precisely because tugged

at and troubled by desire, impotence and hatred, Baudelaire would see more
clearly than with his eyes open and his head lucid.]

It is at this point that Fondane's metaphysical reading can begin to take account of
the political violence at play in Europe in the years during which he was writing his
Baudelaire. Clearly, the stakes of the ideas that Fondane is exploring are high, and his
metaphysical orientation in no way seeks to avoid political implications but rather to
inform them and attempt to account for them.

Fondane directly confronts the most potentially troubling passage in Baudelaire
with reference to the historical events of the 1940s. Among the fragments of Baudelaire's
autobiographical notes, we find the following: "Belle conspiration à organiser pour
l'extermination de la race juive" ["A fine conspiracy to organize for the extermination
of the Jewish race"] (1: 706), which Fondane, in an effort to "mieux comprendre la
pensée qui a agité si terriblement notre âge" ["better understand the thought that has
so terribly agitated our age"] quotes and about which he adds:

> Belle conspiration *motivée*? Non, puisque Baudelaire ajoute immédiatement:
> "Les Juifs, bibliothécaires et témoins de la Rédemption." Mais quelle belle cruauté
> *inutile*! Pas même lâche! Car Baudelaire ne demande pas mieux, on l'a vu, que
> d'être, alternativement, victime et bourreau; il lui importe peu d'exterminer—ou
> d'être exterminé. Ce qu'il veut, c'est une belle flambée pour détruire, oublier son
> ennui, et on ne peut, hélas! incendier tous les jours Rome. (BEG 335)[12]

> [Fine *motivated* conspiracy? No, since Baudelaire immediately adds: "The Jews,
> librarians and witnesses of Redemption." But what a fine *useless* cruelty! Not even
> cowardly! For Baudelaire asks no better, we have seen, than to be, alternately, victim
> and executioner; it matters little to him to exterminate—or to be exterminated.
> What he wants is a beautiful blaze to destroy and forget his ennui, and one cannot,
> alas, set Rome on fire everyday.]

Since Fondane's reading of Baudelaire situates the metaphysical as primary, and
thus as determining other areas of his thought that move into ethics and politics,
Baudelaire's violence, while to be taken seriously, is also to be taken as ineffective, and
known by the poet to be so. Here we have to distinguish, in ways that it is not clear
that Fondane always does, between two kinds of *néant*. On the one hand, the *néant*
is, as we have seen, the condition that would put an end to the suffering necessarily
caused by knowledge, which is the way Baudelaire and Fondane have framed original
sin. Fondane, near the end of his *Baudelaire*, seems to use the *néant* as a different
kind of term, more associated with what is often referred to as nihilism in terms of
a politics bereft of ethical considerations. This is a more typically diabolical kind of
néant, which, like other kinds of diabolical temptations, encourages us to take it for
something which it is not:

> Tel est le drame qui se noue entre le Néant, dont la suprême ruse est de nous
> persuader qu'il est l'Etre—et l'existant qui, pour se sentir vivre […], pour appeler

à lui l'Etre aux ailes de gaze […], ne sait que recourir à la cruauté. Le malheur *vague* est entré dans le monde; le Dieu d'Aristote, *primum movens* immobile, n'a engendré que l'Ennui. Et alors, comme dit Baudelaire: « A quoi bon ceci? A quoi bon cela? » Si l'idéal, si l'ennui existent, que ferons-nous de notre moi? (BEG 337)

[Such is the drama that is formed between Nothingness, whose supreme ruse is to persuade us that it is Being—and the existent which, in order to feel itself live […], to call to itself Being with its wings of gauze […], can only have recourse to cruelty. The *vague* misfortune has entered the world; the God of Aristotle, immobile prime mover, has engendered only Ennui. And so, as Baudelaire says: "What good is this? What good is that?" If the idea and ennui exist, what will we do with our self?]

This *néant* finds its outlet in the kind of cruelty that would cut short Fondane's life, senseless, unredemptive, and ineffective in canceling the metaphysical condition against which it is supposedly attempting to combat. Nazi cruelty becomes yet another manifestation of the tempting yet ultimately ineffective satanic revolt that Baudelaire practices in his poems singing the praises of the devil.

If Fondane has rightly observed that for Baudelaire the choice is no longer between paradise and hell but rather between hell and nothingness, the kind of political violence Fondane evokes here is more aligned with hell, even though he affiliated it with the *néant* here than with the nothingness which would be the only effective cancellation of the *ennui* brought on by knowledge:

Seule, la cruauté semble témoigner encore du refus absolu de l'homme du XXe siècle à supporter l'*intelligere* « autonome » qui a supprimé le soleil, et la voie lactée, et le triste moi, qui a forcé l'homme de crever dans son trou, comme un rat empoisonné: « Si Dieu n'existe pas, alors, tout est permis », crie le vieux Karamazoff; si Dieu n'existe pas, alors, *homo homini lupus*: brûlons Rome, exterminons les Juifs, sacrifions les types les plus élevés de note humanité! Dieu, le péché, ne recouvrent rien de *pensable*; l'*intelligere* n'a pas fini de nous dire qu'il n'y a rien de bon pour nous là-dessous. C'est la preuve de Dieu par l'absurde et nous y sommes tous engagés. Le règne de la cruauté ne fait que commencer. Telle est, me semble-t-il, l'apocalypse de l'Ennui. (BEG 337)

[Alone, cruelty seems still to bear witness to twentieth-century man's absolute refusal to tolerate the "autonomous" knowledge that has suppressed the sun, and the Milky Way, and the sad self, that has forced man to die in his hole, like a poisoned rat: "If God does not exist, then all is permitted," cries the old Karamazoff; if God does not exist, then, a man is a wolf for man: let's burn Rome, exterminate the Jews, sacrifice the most elevated types of our humanity! God and sin do not cover anything *thinkable*; the intelligence has not ceased telling us that there is nothing good for us underneath. It is the proof of God by the absurd and we are all engaged in it. The reign of cruelty has only just begun. Such is, it seems to me, the apocalypse of Ennui.]

It is important to emphasize that Fondane is not enumerating a conservative critique that would have us turn back toward a God on account of the absurdity of meaningless cruelty that ensues from claiming his nonexistence. He leaves open the question of what could ground ethics in God's absence, a question admittedly far afield from his main subject in the Baudelaire book. But Baudelaire does take on the role of a kind of prophet here for having articulated the potential consequences of the *ennui* which he associates, from the very beginning of *Les Fleurs du Mal*, with the diabolical. It is through Baudelaire that we are invited to draw the consequences of a lack of redemption; first among those consequences is any sort of recuperative meaning that could be found in the eruptions of violence that Fondane calls "l'apocalypse de l'Ennui." The question of God's existence is secondary to the fact of the nonexistence of redemption, and on this reading the apocalypse cannot redeem but only destroy, since it cannot but affiliate itself with satanic revolt rather than the true *néant* that would be the only way out of the problem of knowledge as sin.

Fondane's own poetry functions simultaneously on both the historical and metaphysical levels, further enhancing the inextricable link between them that he develops in his philosophical writings. Neither register is reducible to the other, even in the latest poetry that addresses the horror of the deportation and extermination of the Jews. Some of his poetry is eerily prophetic, especially the work *L'Exode: Super Flumina Babylonis* [*Exodus: By the Waters of Babylon*], begun in 1934 and subsequently revised throughout the next several years in light of the Shoah. At the beginning and conclusion of the work, he borrows the biblical form of lamentations, each one introduced by a letter of the Hebrew alphabet, while the large middle consists of a dramatic poem featuring a reciter, a chorus, and three other speakers. The speaking subject in the preface that Fondane added in 1942 cannot be said to function exclusively as a historical subject nor a metaphysical one. Rather, the historical and transhistorical come together to inform and influence each other, giving metaphysical but not necessarily comforting religious import to suffering:

> Oui, j'ai été un homme comme les autres hommes,
> nourri de pain, de rêve, de désespoir. Eh oui,
> j'ai aimé, j'ai pleuré, j'ai haï, j'ai souffert,
> j'ai acheté des fleurs et je n'ai pas toujours
> payé mon terme. Le dimanche j'allais à la campagne
> pêcher, sous l'œil de Dieu, des poissons irréels,
> je me baignais dans la rivière […]
> Après, après, je rentrais me coucher […]
> cherchant, cherchant en vain sur un ventre de femme
> cette paix impossible que nous avions perdue
> naguère, dans un grand verger où fleurissait
> au centre, l'arbre de la vie. (*Mal* 152)

> [Yes, I was a man like other men,
> nourished by bread, dream, despair. Oh yes,
> I loved, I cried, I hated, I suffered,

I bought flowers and I did not always
pay my rent. On Sundays I would go to the country
to fish, under God's eye, for unreal fish,
I bathed in the river […]
After, after, I would go home and lie down […]
looking, looking in vain on the belly of a woman
for this impossible peace which we had lost
long ago, in a great orchard where
in the center, the tree of life was flowering.]

As in Baudelaire's poetry, God is operative but not necessarily existent in a conventional sense in these poems, a reflection of Fondane's ambiguity as to the question of the existence of God which I outlined above. The representation of the speaking subject as thoroughly ordinary here in the preface not only throws into relief the horror of the Jewish subject's exclusion in the poems to follow but also gestures toward collapsing the distinction between Jew and non-Jew by identifying a metaphysical anguish which, as we have seen, is common to all humanity in all historical and economic conditions according to Fondane. He reiterates this position late in his career, in a projected preface to a revised version of his poem "Ulysse," dating from 1941:

Le lecteur naïf pourra croire que le poète a puisé sa poésie à même le vécu imminent—comme si cela était possible. Mais il est vrai qu'un traumatisme actuel—qui, par essence est destructeur d'affectivité créatrice—peut réveiller des traumatismes déjà anciens, déjà guéris, mais analogues—faire jaillir la poésie dans une autre couche, plus loin. (*Mal* 263–4)

[A naïve reader could believe that the poet drew his poetry from imminent lived experience—as if that were possible. But it is true that a present trauma—which, in its essence, is a destroyer of creative affectivity—can awaken former traumas, already healed, but analogous—and make poetry spring up in another layer, further on.]

With these words, Fondane pleads for a reading that resists the urge to reduce the poetry to the particulars of its historical moment, and he seems conscious of the danger of that kind of reductive historical interpretation in light of the extreme historical circumstances in which he was revising his work.

The doubled interpretation that figures in the prologue, then, hovers between the particular and universal, the historical and metaphysical, and it conditions our reading of the entire long poem that follows. The second of the three men who speak in the poem recounts an episode of physical flight from those chasing him, laden with more abstract implications:

J'ai quitté ma chemise et j'ai marché tout nu
les pieds ensanglantés par les torrents de pierre […]

mais quelquefois le gouffre prenait la voix d'un
    homme
    il criait au secours:
« PLUS HAUT, PLUS HAUT QUE L'HOMME! »
et cette solitude me donnait la nausée […]
Le doute commença à ronger ma chair
qui donc avait voulu nous tromper de la sorte?
        à qui profitait notre perte?
pendant que l'on montait quelle était donc la chose
        que l'on voulait nous voir quitter?
        qui donc nous a trompés de soif
        afin de nous voler la vie
et nous jeter, transis, aux pays de la mort? (*Mal* 174)

[I took off my shirt and I walked naked
my feet bleeding from the torrents of stone […]
but sometimes the abyss took on the voice of a
    man
    it cried for help:
"HIGHER, HIGHER THAN MAN!"
and this solitude made me nauseous […]
Doubt began to eat at my flesh
who had thus wanted to trick us that way?
        Who was profiting from our loss?
while we were climbing what was then the thing
        that they wanted to see us abandon?
        who thus tricked us with thirst
        in order to steal our life from us
and to throw us, chilled with fear, to the land of death?]

Transcendence is the temptation here, the impossible attempt to go beyond the human. Fondane's lyric subject does not, like Baudelaire's, seek death and the consequent reduction to nothingness but rather wants to resist it, to perform the impossible by resisting death and maintaining immortality. And yet we can see an important parallel with Baudelaire here in the way God could be said to be playing the role typically ascribed to the devil here, that of the tempter. While forcing man on to higher and higher ground, the outside force which would, presumably, be the divinity, all the while destines him for death and profits, as the poet says, from his loss. This is not inconsistent with Baudelaire's wish for oblivion in order to avoid the tragicomedy of human existence.

The parallel with the Baudelairean worldview becomes more pronounced by the end of the poem, where Fondane enumerates a series of four-line poems in the form of lamentations. In these, he returns more explicitly than before in this poem to the question of knowledge as the unredeemable source of human suffering:

SAMECH
Suprême ivresse de connaître!
Voici les ventres d'océans:
Vagins ouverts qui forcent l'Etre
Au sperme auguste de Néant!

PHÉ
De quel côté chercher l'Issue?
Quelle île suspendue au Rien?
Déjà, soleil, ta viande crue
Saignait aux portes du matin. […]

SHIN
J'ai vu la mort compter les morts.
Elle leur enlevait la graisse.
Et j'ai crié: Heureux les Morts!
Qu'avaient-ils donc besoin de graisse?

THAV
Etait-ce bien le dernier jour?
Pourquoi appelais-je au secours?
Et de quel œil, dans mon attente,
Tombait cette larme brûlante? (206–7)

[SAMECH
Supreme intoxication of knowing!
Here are the bellies of the oceans:
Open vaginas that force Being
To the august Sperm of Nothingness!

PHE
In which direction to look for the Exit?
What island suspended upon the Nothing?
Already, sun, your raw meat
Was bleeding at the gates of morning. […]

SHIN
I saw death counting the dead.
It was removing the fat from them.

And I cried: Happy are the Dead!
What need did they have then of fat?

THAV
Was it really the last day?
Why was I calling for help?
And from which eye, in my wait,
Was this burning tear falling?]

The first of these quatrains evokes the eagerness of the Baudelairean subject at the end of "Le voyage" (and hence the end of *Les Fleurs du Mal*) who urges death to take him "au fond de l'Inconnu pour trouver du *nouveau!*" ["to the depths of the Unknown to find something *new!*" (463)] (OC1:134). As I shall show in the next chapter, this ending is a false lead, since it is contradicted by the necessary disappointment that experience brings, as that is portrayed in the penultimate poem "Le rêve d'un curieux." Given that the elimination of consciousness altogether would be the only way to cancel the suffering induced by human knowledge, the "intoxication of knowing" must be, for Fondane, an illusion that feeds human discontent. And yet this reading, while consistent with Fondane's own philosophy, is in tension with the way that death is represented in *L'Exode*. In the section "Samech" quoted above, death appears, rather conventionally, as a threat rather than a release. But by the end of the poem, in the final quatrain "Thav," consciousness persists, thus marking the (at least temporary) victory over the threat of the *néant* but not for the benefit of the speaking consciousness, who is now represented as alien to himself and, presumably, trapped in this state of tormented consciousness, the anguish of knowledge, with which the poem ends.

This kind of poetic and philosophical vision does not lend itself to tidy conclusions, either for Baudelaire or for Fondane, for whom an attempt at definitive conclusion would just sink us deeper into a logic that will not provide answers and in fact exacerbates the desire to know that leads us to negative revolt in the first place. It is in that sense that neither God nor sin is *thinkable* for Fondane. Is there, then, any kind of redemptive vision in Fondane?

Commentators on his *Baudelaire* are divided on this, which is unsurprising given Fondane's refusal of systematic thought. By affirming the importance of poetry and the poetic in the elaboration of his vision, Fondane invites ambiguity and the participation of the reader in struggling with, rather than trying to reduce, the questions posed by his thought. Mircea Martin emphasizes the disclosive function of art according to Fondane, which precludes the redemptive function:

Art, Poetry can no longer be for [Fondane] solutions of comfort or salvation. For him, their role is not to cover, to throw a veil over the terrors of the Abyss but, on the contrary, to remove this veil. And the Abyss is the Irrational, the Absurd, Evil, the Impasse, the Dead End, the Unanswered, the bewitched silence. (Martin 246)[13]

The function of art for Fondane is clearer than the function of God, about which there is certainly ambiguity in Fondane's reading. While we have seen that he declares unbelief in the 1920s, and while there is no statement of belief to be found in his later works, the role of God in Fondane is, as it is in Baudelaire, difficult to assign either to the category of existence or to the category of metaphor. Olivier Salazar-Ferrer makes room for a saving God in Fondane:

> Fondane supposes in effect that Baudelaire's God transcends the limits of his theological essence. He is thus liable to transgress the principle of non-contradiction and to save and even love the damned. [...] It is a merciful God who transcends the binary logic of salvation and damnation. ("D'un Baudelaire" 296)

Fondane does not offer evidence for the prominence of such a loving God in Baudelaire's poems, an omission made all the more visible by the indifferent or even tyrannical God that plays a role in so many of the poems that Fondane features in his analysis. Salazar-Ferrer offers a clue as to how to account for the merciful God that appears in Fondane:

> We find here of curse the God of Chestov, all powerful, who defines himself only by an absolute reign over the possible. The fideist attitude resulting from the negative theology of Chestov and Fondane assumes the idea of a merciful God capable of making man participate in his powers and his infinity. ("D'un Baudelaire" 296)

The mention of Lev Chestov reminds us of the formative influence of that philosopher on Fondane and suggests that a God who surpasses binary logic in order to love the human being may have more in common with a Chetsovian or Kierkegaardian view than with the one being worked out in the late Fondane. Given the degree to which Fondane follows Baudelaire closely on metaphysical questions, it is unlikely that he could affirm a theology, even a negative one, that resembles the Christian mystics more than it does Baudelaire's idiosyncratic God. And indeed this ultimate impossibility of salvation for Fondane is what Salazar-Ferrer goes on to indicate:

> Fondane never accepted the linearity of Christian history, marked by a time of a fall from the originary paradise [...]. In his *Baudelaire*, he wanted and demanded the fundamental return to innocence, by the grace of poetry or by a magical thought which restored lost childhood to us. This is not a Redemption that is on the horizon of this metaphysics, but a restitution. ("D'un Baudelaire" 316)

As Salazar-Ferrer notes, Fondane quotes Jacques Maritain in order to affirm that we must regard the state of innocence as "definitively lost" (qtd 316). For the Catholic Maritain, this loss would be redeemed by the divine sacrifice, but since Fondane rejects this possibility, he is left to affirm the impossibility of the very state of restitution he theorizes here.

What remains is the possibility of "the grace of poetry," a redemptive value not simply revealed by poetry but effected by it. This is the salvific function of the artwork that we have already addressed through Agamben's reading of redemption in the work of art and of criticism, and to which we shall have occasion to return in a consideration of Friedrich Nietzsche. While Fondane claims that Baudelaire's poetry reveals the *gouffre* rather than throwing a veil over it, revelation is quite separate from redemption, and it is not at all clear that poetry, which remains complicit in the production of knowledge which is at the root of our unredeemed original sin, can play any role in restoring a state of innocence. This is not to say that poetry plays a merely descriptive role by revealing to us the conditions of the *gouffre*; such a conception is totally at odds with Fondane's conception of poetry's link to lived experience. Rather, poetry participates in the suffering inextricably allied with the human experience and is one of the best expressions of that suffering. In that sense, poetry both discloses and expresses that suffering. Dominique Guedj reads a kind of redemptive value in that function of poetry for Fondane:

> Truth demands that we do not fear letting misfortune speak without regard for "the objective value of judgment […] brought on the real" […] and it is poïetic poetry that can do it; beyond the anguish generated by misfortune, it restores to man a freedom and a way out. (Guedj 116)

Poetry undoubtedly brings insight according to Fondane as well as active creation, but given Fondane's reservations about even a restitution of innocence, not to mention a redemption of experience, it is not clear that there is a full-fledged version of hope in this claim that poetry represents a way out of our metaphysical predicament. As Fondane had argued in his earlier works, history cannot progress because it cannot solve the fundamental metaphysical problems that Fondane claims transcend the particulars of any given historical situation. While he allots far greater power to poetry than to reason, there is at best a tension between his remarks about the restitution of freedom and the larger direction of his argument about the *gouffre*.

While Naziism is for Fondane the absurd fullest extent of a reason informed by a misguided humanism, he gives little evidence of believing that simply choosing a different path will allow a way out of the metaphysical predicament he traces. Such is the interpretation he offers in one of his last works, "Le Lundi existentiel et le dimanche de l'histoire" ["The Existential Monday and the Sunday of History"]:

> La faute est peut-être à cet humanisme même, qui avait trop manqué de pessimisme, qui avait trop misé sur l'intelligence séparée et divine, et négligé plus qu'il ne fallait l'homme *réel* que l'on avait traité en ange pour finalement le ravaler au-dessous de la bête … […] Un humanisme qui n'aurait pas *sur-estimé* la raison n'eût certainement pas mis tous les atouts de la science entre les mains de ceux à qui on refuse aujourd'hui jusqu'au don de la raison! (« *Lundi* » 139–40)

[The blame belongs perhaps to this very humanism, which had lacked pessimism, which had counted too much on the separate and divine intelligence, and neglected more than it should have the *real* man that one had treated as an angel in order, in the end, to lower him below the beasts … […] A humanism that will not have *overestimated* reason would certainly not have put all the advantages of science in the hands of those in whom we do not see today the gift of reason!]

Baudelaire's thought unquestionably tempers humanism with pessimism in order to paint a more lucid picture of the human condition than the traditional story of redemption would allow. Whether this results in a way out of unhappiness, as opposed simply to lucidity about its nature and causes, remains ambiguous in Fondane.

The struggle against despair that is visible in Fondane's analysis of Baudelaire and his poetry suggests that Baudelaire's work serves him as a reminder of the reality of the impossibility of a redemptive vision, a possibility that Fondane more successfully and consistently holds in view than Benjamin does. While Fondane's poetry gives evidence of a struggle against the realization of that impossibility or a reluctance to accept it, his account of Baudelaire's work provides an illustration, via such thinkers as Kierkegaard, of the way we can transform Baudelaire's asoteriology into a livable vision that neither succumbs to despair and inactivity nor relies on illusion or the traces of a messianic glimmer of hope. In that sense, I have argued that Fondane accounts better than Benjamin does for Baudelaire's unrelenting insistence on the impossibility of redemption. Rather than mourning that impossibility, both Baudelaire and Fondane seek a form of thought and action that allows us to come to terms with it. With their emphases on different corners of Baudelaire's oeuvre, so to speak, Benjamin's portrait of the poet as urban prowler and Fondane's exposition of the poet as metaphysical subject illuminate different but complementary aspects of the Baudelaire's work. An important question to consider, however, is the primacy of the historical or the metaphysical in Baudelaire's own vision. Given the importance Baudelaire accords those theological notions which he revises radically but never abandons, and on which so much of his oeuvre depends, Fondane's account allows us to give full weight to Baudelaire's notion of original sin in ways that Benjamin's does not. While never losing sight of historical considerations at play in Baudelaire's thought, Fondane's analysis grants metaphysical considerations their full weight in Baudelaire, whereas, as we have seen, Benjamin's often subordinates them while never fully eradicating a theological perspective, one that, in important contrast to Baudelaire's, retains soteriological notions that Baudelaire cannot entertain.

If Baudelaire preserves the notion of original sin even while harboring serious doubts about the very existence of God, it is because it has the potential to render human experience intelligible. As we will see in the last chapter, in the prose poem "Le mauvais vitrier" ["The Bad Glazier"] Baudelaire prefers theological accounts to medical ones when it comes to attempting to explain otherwise unexplainable human actions, but even those explanations do not fully account for or explain the behavior in question, operating rather as one hypothesis among others, albeit for

Baudelaire a more plausible one. As I have demonstrated above, Fondane highlights Baudelaire's intolerance of unintelligibility and locates Baudelaire's temptation to violence in an impossible attempt to cancel that unintelligibility. Benjamin's notion of shock can be considered in this same light, but Fondane's account takes us beyond the level of everyday lived experience in order to infuse those experiences with their full metaphysical weight in ways that do justice to Baudelaire's frequent meditation on questions of violence, subjectivity, evil, and intelligibility outside the specific context of modern urban experience. In our own attempts to render Baudelaire's words intelligible, Fondane provides an essential perspective that allows us to take a step beyond shock experience while at the same time refusing tidy answers that are content to remain at the level of traditional theological certainty. The tension between certainty and uncertainty, and between intelligibility and its opposite, along with the way that Baudelaire's doubled ironic subjectivity negotiates that terrain, are a vital part of what makes his poetry continually worth revisiting in our own attempts at rendering modern experience intelligible.

Coming to an End: Agamben and Baudelaire

In the last chapter, Fondane helped us articulate the relationship of a philosophically inflected lived experience to Baudelaire's poetry and to see a dynamic relationship between the two that neither depends on a simple biographical reading of the poet nor sees the poetry as a mere illustration of a worldview. Rather, a more complex model emerges that involves the poetic working out of a worldview, a back and forth between a poetic metaphysics and a metaphysical poetry that refuses systematic approaches and that can therefore be difficult to summarize or even articulate precisely. In this chapter, I would like to develop the ways in which the theological and the poetic are intertwined in Baudelaire, drawing not only on the foundation that Fondane helped us establish but also the work of Giorgio Agamben, particularly his notion of the "end of the poem." Endings are common ground between theology and poetry, both of which give shape to experience by defining an end point, an observation which brings us back to the notion of the messianic. In continuing to draw conclusions from Baudelaire's refusal of a logic of redemption, I will examine the ways Baudelaire confirms, challenges, or extends Agamben's analysis of the end of the poem, which Agamben anchors in poetics and theology and which allows him to put forward the ways in which they influence each other.

Agamben's discussion of ends is informed by his notion of messianic time, which is not the end of time but rather "the time that time takes to come to an end, or, more precisely, the time we take to bring to an end, to achieve our representation of time" (*Time* 67). This is derived from Paul's notion of living in the end times, the final days *before*, rather than the time *of*, the coming of the messiah. What is crucial for our purposes here is that such a notion does not depend on the actual arrival of the messiah, and thus it is compatible with the asoteriological vision we have been tracing. Like Baudelaire's conceptions, it borrows from Christian theology without reproducing its essential element and thus widens the application of that new perspective on theology far away from Christianity but not toward a fully realized secularism. Furthermore, Agamben's own work on the philosophy and theology of messianic time is never divorced from esthetic considerations and, most often, explicitly poetic considerations: "The poem is therefore an organism or a temporal machine that, from the very start, strains toward its end. A kind of eschatology occurs within the poem itself. But for the more or less brief time that the poem lasts, it has a specific and unmistakable temporality, it has its own *time*" (*Time* 79). Poems become a sort of microcosm of messianic time in that they both are meant to drive on toward their end while at the same time resisting that end, hence the "straining" toward the end. Dante's preferred rhyme scheme of *terza rima*, a favorite example of Agamben's, illustrates this well, with rhyme in general calling for a next line with which to rhyme while the end of the poem necessitates breaking the pattern in order to be able to end. Agamben enlists Baudelaire as another example of the difficulties a poem can have in coming to an end, citing "Le Cygne" and its sudden interruption via the "bien d'autres encor!" ["many others too!" (293)] of the last line (OC 1: 87):

> The disorder of the last verse is an index of the structural relevance to the economy of the poem of the event I have called "the end of the poem." As if the poem as a formal structure would not and could not end, as if the possibility of the end were radically withdrawn from it, since the end would imply a poetic impossibility. (*End* 113)

Poetry must go on in order to remain poetry; otherwise, it falls into prose or into silence. Thus the very condition of its existence precludes its own ending even as it is driven toward that ending from the beginning of the poem. The end of the poem is thus catastrophic for Agamben in that the reversion to prose brings about the end of the coming-to-an-end that was the poem. If there is a parallel to be drawn with messianic time (as the time of coming to an end) and the poem (as a structure destined from the beginning to find its end), prose then comes to mark the moment of annihilation of messianic time as it is conceived in the poetic event.[1]

The defining feature of poetry for Agamben is thus enjambment, which calls into question the stability of the single line of verse as a unit of meaning by displacing the end of the unit in which sense is to be found:

> For what is enjambment, if not the opposition of a metrical limit to a syntactical limit, of a prosodic pause to a semantic pause? "Poetry" will then be the name given to the discourse in which this opposition is, at least virtually possible; "prose" will be the name for the discourse in which this opposition cannot take pace. (*End* 109)

The concept of the end has rich implications for the relation between poetry and metaphysics that we have been tracing in Baudelaire via Fondane, especially in the ways in which it discourages an opposition between esthetic or poetic concerns and larger philosophical matters or between form and content. Rather, on this view, poetic form would be the actualization of ideas of the end that the poetry puts into play. Agamben poses the question "Why does poetry matter to us?" (*End* 93) and claims that, typically, responses to this question are "divided between those who affirm the significance of poetry only on condition of altogether confusing it with life and those for whom the significance of poetry is instead exclusively a function of its isolation from life" (*End* 93). Agamben wishes to think beyond this opposition in ways that resonate with the analysis that Fondane develops and which, as we saw when first introducing it, defies easy classification as literary analysis, philosophy, biography, and so on as it draws on Baudelaire's poetry as, we might say, a tool to think with. Agamben, for his part, appeals to what he calls the experience of the poet, who affirms that if poetry and life remain infinitely divergent on the level of the biography and psychology of the individual, they nevertheless become absolutely indistinct at the point of their reciprocal desubjectivization. And—at that point—they are united not immediately but in a medium. This medium is language. The poet is he who, in the word, produces life. Life, which the poet produces in the poem, withdraws from both the lived experience of the psychosomatic individual and the biological unsayability of the species. (*End* 93)

Thus it is important to underscore that, for Agamben as for Fondane, it is not a question of producing what is typically labeled "biographical criticism." There is in fact scant reference to the events of Baudelaire's life in either critic's analysis. Rather, both seek to redefine "lived experience" in light of its direct relationship to the poetic act, and in the relation of that act to the creation of a philosophical worldview with theological implications that will underwrite and inform anything we would like to say about the poet's relation to lived experience, historical events, or political participation.

All of these, it is important to note, pass through the experience of poetic creation and the metaphysical implications it creates by its own status as an event.[2] Agamben underscores the priority accorded to the poem over the life that on first glance seemed to generate it by appeal to a historical example:

It is good not to forget that in Romance literature, narrative (at least in the sense of short story) is born as the *razo* [an explanatory note at beginning of some medieval poetry relating it to the poet's life] of lyric poetry. It is thanks to the poetic word's unspeakable dwelling *in the beginning* that something like lived experience is made for the narrator. This is the "novella" that he limits himself to exemplifying. (*End* 81)

Lived experience is thus not prior to but co-existent with, and to a large extent determined by, the poet's dwelling in language, a condition that is laden, as language itself is, with theological concerns, as Agamben indicates just prior to the passage I have quoted by a reference to the opening of the prologue of John's gospel, "In the beginning was the word." The language of the poem and the experience embodied in and created by that language emerge from nothingness at the start of the poem, an observation Walter Benjamin makes about Baudelaire in particular near the opening of the *Central Park* fragments, where he observes, without further elaboration: "The special beauty of so many of the openings of Baudelaire's poems lies in this: a rising up from the abyss" (*Writer* 134). The question shifts, with Agamben, from the beginning to the end. If Baudelaire's poems arise from the abyss for Benjamin, and if for Fondane they are an exploration of the abyss itself, with Agamben we can pose the question of what it means to ask about the possibility of the end of the abyss. Do Baudelaire's poems return to the abyss from which they emerged, from silence to silence? If a poem strives toward its own end, are Baudelaire's poems carried along by the desire to seek the abyss once more, as if language were a curse and a return to silence the most desirable alternative? The same kinds of questions that we have asked in earlier chapters about the status of the *néant* in Baudelaire return here under the more specific guise of the poem itself, which we can now read as intimately linked to the metaphysical vision that we have been discussing. Baudelaire's poetic subject actively seeks the *néant* in a system where existence can only be seen as a temptation, a source of torment that can only be corrected by being brought to an end, not by being redeemed by art or anything else. On this view, the poetic act itself participates in the fall by its use of language, which does not give voice to but actually helps to further the effects of the fall and to plunge us deeper into our unredeemable experience. And yet, Baudelaire's subject is still sometimes tempted by the lure of the new, as the end of "Le voyage" enacts. There is, then, for the poet, both as subject and as poet (i.e. as the subject speaking in the poem and as the creator of that subject's voice), the same ambivalence as the one at play in Agamben's characterization of the poem as that which both strives toward and resists its own end. What the poet who wishes to affirm the poetic act at some level ultimately expresses, then, is not so much the desire to write, which implicates the poet in furthering the consequences of the fall, as the desire *to have written*, to have passed through the stage of creation in order then to be freed of it, and to achieve the desired *néant* from which no poetic discourse could truly spring.

Now the theological consequences of writing for Baudelaire are beginning to become clearer. Theology does not simply provide the poet's raw materials, a tradition ripe for variation, but rather is intimately wrapped up in the poet's characterization of the act of creation itself. The way Baudelaire ends his poems will thus be of central importance for the full elaboration of the worldview we have been tracing. And indeed, important commentators on Baudelaire's poetry have noted the peculiar quality of his endings and particularly those of some of his masterpieces. Marcel Proust, for one, claimed that "Le voyage," like "Le cygne," "stops short, almost falls flat" (quoted in *End* 113), which Agamben notes as his main example of the problematics of the ending of the poem as he conceives it. On the heels of this modern example, Agamben looks back to Dante's *De vulgari eloquentia* [*On Eloquence in the Vernacular*] and its comment on the final verses of a poem: "The endings of the last verses are most beautiful if they fall into silence together with the rhymes." Agamben asks: "What is this falling into silence of the poem? What is beauty that falls? And what is left of the poem after its ruin?" (*End* 114). With these questions, we are solidly back on Baudelaire's territory, which Agamben leaves unpursued beyond the passing reference to the endings of "Le voyage" and "Le cygne." Theorizing silence in terms of a fall allows us to continue to probe the relation of the poetic and the theological as it is manifest in Baudelaire, for whom all of our reality is conditioned by the fall. What would be the theological consequences of falling, now not into language but into silence? What would it mean to come to a cadence, to come to rest? And would that rest be an abyss or an escape from that abyss?

Agamben takes great care to emphasize that the questions he is pursuing force us to avoid separating what he calls "the semantic and the semiotic current" (*End* 114), or what we might also term the form and content of the poem. These two systems work jointly in Agamben's theology of the poem, according to which the poem functions as "something that slows and delays the advent of the Messiah, that is, of him who, fulfilling the time of poetry and uniting its two eons, would destroy the poetic machine by hurtling it into silence" (*End* 114). Agamben goes on to inquire:

> But what could be the aim of this theological conspiracy about language? Why so much ostentation to maintain, at any cost, a difference that succeeds in guaranteeing the space of the poem only on condition of depriving it of the possibility of a lasting accord between sound and sense? (*End* 114)

The space of the poem is thus a space of tension between sound and sense, two elements which should present a unity but cannot help but be perceived in duality. There are strong echoes here of Baudelaire's divided poetic subjectivity, of the *homo duplex*, the person divided, by virtue of the fall, against himself by simultaneous postulations toward God and Satan, a contradiction that cannot be resolved by a redemptive act but must remain in tension so long as the poem continues. The falling of the poem into silence, in what we could call a theology of poetic form, in the double sense of the genitive "of," would thus not bring about the desired reconciliation of the tension but, like the onset of the *néant*, merely obliterate the contradiction by obliterating all of existence. By classifying the end of the poem as a fall into silence, the fall itself is doubled, since we have not a falling and a rising but rather an initial fall into language followed by a second fall into silence, the cancelation of which could only be another manifestation of the fall into language, or what we otherwise call the beginning of another poem. Even the falling into silence of a single poem is not, for Agamben, a gesture of finality. In a remark on the continued tension between the semiotic and the semantic which is consistent with Baudelaire's theory and poetic practice, Agamben notes that

> the double intensity animating language does not die away in a final comprehension; instead it collapses into silence, so to speak, in an endless falling. The poem thus reveals the goal of its proud strategy: to let language finally communicate itself, without remaining unsaid in what is said. (*End* 115)

The key poetic techniques by which language communicates itself as poetry are enjambment, as we have already seen, and rhyme, to which Agamben also attributes a theological status:

> Rhyme, understood in the broad sense of the term as the articulation of a difference between semiotic series and semantic series, is the messianic heritage Paul leaves to modern poetry, and the history and fate of rhyme coincide in poetry with the history and fate of the messianic announcement. (*Time* 87)

Agamben provides the example of Hölderlin's reflections on the leave-taking of the gods, which corresponds to the breakdown of closed metrical form in his poetry.

Baudelaire's case is different in that, while he begins to write in prose poetry, he never definitively abandons verse and does not significantly alter patterns of rhyme and meter in his late verse. This is consistent with Baudelaire's theology which, unlike Hölderlin's, does not announce God's death or departure but rather rewrites theology to exclude redemption. The messianic moment never arrives in Baudelaire not because he shifts from theology to atheology, but because redemption is simply not possible.

Thus, for all of the affinities we have seen between Agamben's conception of theological poetics and Baudelaire's poetic practice, there are some differences. In addition to the one just noted, Agamben's insistence on the goal of poetry as being, as cited above, to "let language finally communicate itself" is in tension with Baudelaire's poetry, which always retains, and indeed depends on, the possibility of a poetic subjectivity that is not merely the pure agentless communication of language. While this subjectivity is tortured, ironic, and fragmented, it is nonetheless always present, which is further evidence of the impossibility of proceeding, via poetry or any other means, to the *néant* in Baudelaire. Even if it is so, as Agamben contends, that poetry's goal is in fact to let language communicate itself, Baudelaire demonstrates the impossibility of fulfilling that goal, of completing the fall into silence, as opposed to remaining endlessly within that fall.

There is also divergence between Baudelaire and Agamben on the question of the redemptive value of the poem itself. Agamben suggests, based on an analysis of the sestina form that he extends to "every poem," that the poem is

> a soteriological device which, though the sophisticated *mēchanē* of the announcement and retrieval of rhyming end words (which correspond to typological relations between past and present), transforms chronological time into messianic time. Just as this time is not other to chronological time or eternity, but is the transformation that time undergoes when it is taken for a remnant, so too is the time of the sestina the metamorphosis that time undergoes insofar as it is the time of the end, the *time that the poem takes to come to an end.* (*Time* 82–3)

As I have argued, while the comparison of the transformation from chronological to messianic time to the temporal space of the poem holds in the case of Baudelaire, it does not necessarily follow that the poem operates as a soteriological device, since, in the case of Baudelaire's poetics as in his esthetics and his theology, the moment of redemption never comes. Not merely held in potentiality or virtuality, it is never even announced, suggested, or prefigured. The end of the poem is thus not redemptive in Baudelaire's case, despite the transformation of time that his poems, like those of others, perform.

To return to the question we posed above, what would it mean in Baudelaire to come to a cadence, to come to rest? And would that rest be an abyss or an escape from the abyss? Here, a difficulty arises analogous to our incapacity to view the world from beyond messianic time, from what Adorno labeled the standpoint of redemption. Messianic time, as Agamben describes it, is the time it takes for time to come to an end, not the actual end of time nor the time beyond time, which is necessarily inconceivable to us. In a similar way, if we were to perceive the poem's coming to rest, that in no way cancels the abyss as it is represented in Baudelaire's poetry, since to perceive the end means that there is still a consciousness present to perceive, and thus the problem of consciousness as the source of anguish remains unaltered. In order to find some consolation in the coming to cadence of the poem, we as readers would have to cease to exist along with the poem itself. So, to Agamben's tension between the semiotic and the semantic, we can add another tension between the poem which must come to an end and the eternity of the perceiving subjectivity for whom there can be no end that can be recognized as such. This, then, is the tragedy performed in *Les Fleurs du Mal*, the endlessly future-oriented subject in search of the *nouveau* at the conclusion of "Le voyage," in conflict with the subject condemned to eternity despite a desire to come to an end in a nothingness even more final than death. One could say, then, that given the theological conditions of the impossibility of redemption as Baudelaire traces them, it is impossible for him to come to an end. Fondane had already suggested as much when he made a distinction between unjust societies, which can be changed, and the fundamentally "unjust" conditions of human experience no matter what the particular historical conditions may be:

> Ah, qu'il serait bon de ne vivre qu'en une société *injuste*, afin de la pouvoir corriger dans le sens révolutionnaire, et non dans un *monde* injuste, que l'on ne peut corriger, et qui nous afflige de maladie, de secret, d'impuissance et de mort! Qu'il serait bon de vivre en un monde où l'on puisse conclure! Mais Kleist, Baudelaire, Rimbaud, *ne peuvent pas conclure*! C'est là leur tragédie, non une « voluptueuse tragédie », mais la tragédie pure et simple. (*Faux traité* 86)

> [Ah, it would be good to live in just an *unjust* society, in order to be able to correct it in the revolutionary sense, and not in an unjust *world*, that one cannot correct, and which afflicts us with sickness, secrets, impotence and death! It would be good to live in a world where one could conclude! But Kleist, Baudelaire, Rimbaud *cannot conclude*! That is their tragedy, not a "voluptuous tragedy," but tragedy pure and simple.]

While Fondane speaks of concluding in the sense of drawing conclusions in a rational argument with a gesture toward a systematic philosophy, there are important implications, as his list of literary figures rather than philosophers suggests, for the notion of concluding a literary work here as well. Fondane recognizes the tension between the impossibility of concluding that he has just asserted and the fact that poems do conclude. Poets, he concedes, "concluent, puisqu'ils écrivent des poèmes" ["conclude, since they write poems"] (*Faux traité* 87). Poetry since Baudelaire and Rimbaud is marked by the demystificatory aspect that gives the lie to a poetic conclusion that would also be a definitive conceptual conclusion, an acceptable solution to the problem of existence as Fondane has defined it through his analysis of Baudelaire. How, then, to conlude *within* poetry, even under the condition of the original sin of knowledge, as Baudelaire did, as opposed to *beyond* it, as Rimbaud chose to do (*Faux traité* 88)?

As Agamben has helped us to see, there are high, and highly intertwined, poetic and theological stakes in a consideration of how poems end, and all the more so in the work of a poet like Baudelaire, for whom the theological plays such an important role. What, then, can we say about the way poems end in Baudelaire? I will examine poems that offer several kinds of models of an ending, including the two that served as the ending of *Les Fleurs du Mal* as a whole. To begin, let us consider "L'irréparable," which takes up several of the thematic aspects we have been considering in Baudelaire, in a form that repeats the first line of each stanza at the stanza's conclusion. The first stanza poses a question that prepares the development of the nine remaining stanzas:

> Pouvons-nous étouffer le vieux, le long Remords,
> > Qui vit, s'agite et se tortilla
> Et se nourrit de nous comme le ver des morts,
> > Comme du chêne la chenille?
> Pouvons-nous étouffer l'implacable Remords? (1: 54)

> [Can we stifle the old, the lingering Remorse,
> > That lives, quivers and writhes,
> And feeds on us like the worm on the dead,
> > Like the grub on the oak?
> Can we stifle implacable Remorse? (189)]

This structure encourages us to see each stanza as a closed unity, while the question posed pushes the poem on toward an answer, thus replicating the tension that Agamben identifies between the poem's desire to come to an end and its tendency to defer that end. With each stanza, the return to the first line at the end gives the effect of an echo, a revisiting of familiar territory unaltered by the intervening development, which suggests a temporality that, paradoxically, remains still even in its movement.

Baudelaire uses a similar structure of a repeating line to close each stanza in other poems of *Les Fleurs du Mal* such as "Réversibilité" ["Reversibility"] and "Moesta et errabunda" ["Grieving and Wandering"]. In those two poems, the pattern of repeated lines is never altered. In "Le Balcon" ["The Balcony"] the pattern is broken only in the final stanza where the line "Ces serments, ces parfums, ces baisers infinis" is transformed into "—Ô serments! ô parfums! ô baisers infinis!" ["—O vows! O perfumes! O infinite kisses!" (125)]: a gesture which provides closure to the poem, paradoxically, by slightly altering, rather than confirming, the pattern of repetition that had been established in the preceding five stanzas. In "L'irréparable," by contrast, the pattern is broken earlier and in increasingly less subtle ways. In the second stanza, there is an alteration of the punctuation only:

> Dans quel philtre, dans quel vin, dans quelle tisane, […]
> Dans quel philtre?—dans quel vin?—dans quelle tisane? (OC1: 54)

[In what philtre, in what potion, what wine (189)][3]

The fourth stanza introduces the first semantic change:

> À cet agonisant que le loup déjà flaire
>   Et que surveille le corbeau,
> À ce soldat brisé! s'il faut qu'il désespère
>   D'avoir sa croix et son tombeau;
> Ce pauvre agonisant que déjà le loup flaire! (1: 55)

[To this dying man whom the wolf already scents
    And whom the crow watches,
To this broken soldier! if he must despair
    Of having his cross and his grave,
This poor, dying man whom the wolf already scents! (189)]

And the sixth stanza provides a more substantial alteration from the first to the last line:

> L'Espérance qui brille aux carreaux de l'Auberge
>   Est soufflé, est morte à jamais!
> Sans lune et sans rayons, trouver où l'on héberge
>   Les martyrs d'un chemin mauvaus!
> Le Diable a tout éteint aux carreaux de l'Auberge! (1: 55)

[Hope that shines in the windows of the Inn
    Is snuffed out, dead forever!
Without the moon, without light, to find where they lodge
    The martyrs of an evil road!
The Devil has put out all the lights at the Inn! (191)]

This change is significant, as the last line cancels the idea of hope presented in the first by introducing, in his only appearance in this poem, the Devil. We need to be cautious about an overly facile interpretation of this stanza. If what the Baudelairean subject aspires to is nothingness, then hope, which looks forward to a future, only prolongs existence rather than driving it toward its end, leaving the subject in a prolonged state of expectation for something which, as we shall see in "Le Rêve d'un curieux," is destined to disappoint. On this view, the Devil's action of extinguishing hope, and with it a form of desire that will necessarily remain unfulfilled, would represent a welcome step toward the desired *néant* if not for the fact that, in this case, the consciousness persists, thus blocking the move toward nothingness. This doubled sense of an end without a true end is echoed in the form of the poem itself, as this stanza, the sixth of ten, suggests the possibility of an ending by its significant break with the pattern of repetition established in the first five, while at the same time refusing actually to bring the poem to an end. The form thus enacts the "ending which is not an ending," the extinguishing of hope without the corresponding desirable *néant*, that is at stake in the content. And after this stanza, the poem does begin again in the following stanza with another question: "Adorable sorcière, aimes-tu les damnés?" ["Adorable sorceress, do you love the damned?" (191)] (1: 55), repeated verbatim at the close of the stanza.

The play between the verbatim repetitions and the altered final lines establishes a new set of expectations for a pattern, since we now notice a pattern, beginning at the start of the poem, of three stanzas with exact or nearly exact repetition, followed by one stanza of slight alteration ("A cet agonisant…" quoted above), then a stanza of exact repetition followed by a significant repetition ("L'Espérance…" quoted above). Once the poem begins again after the reference to the Devil having extinguished hope, we have what appears to be a reprise of the larger pattern of repetition and difference, since the next three stanzas feature, as the first three had, exact repetition of the first line in the last line. If that whole larger-scale pattern were to repeat itself, the result would be a twelve-stanza poem, since the first cycle developed over six stanzas. Baudelaire violates the expected pattern of repetition, however, by bringing the poem to an end earlier than the expected twelfth stanza. After the three stanzas that include identical repetition of the first line in the last, the final stanza features a near total transformation of the first line in what is the final line of the poem. Moreover, the last stanza is the only one that is syntactically inseparable from the preceding one, an enjambment between the two making it impossible for the last stanza to stand on its own as a unit of sense:

> —J'ai vu parfois, au fond d'un théâtre banal
>   Qu'enflammait l'orchestre sonore,
> Une fée allumer dans un ciel infernal
>   Une miraculeuse aurore;
> J'ai vu parfois au fond d'un théâtre banal
>
> Un être, qui n'était que lumière, or et gaze,
>   Terrasser l'énorme Satan;
> Mais mon coeur, que jamais ne visite l'extase,
>   Est un théâtre où l'on attend
> Toujours, toujours en vain, l'Etre aux ailes de gaze! (OC1: 55)

[—Sometimes I have seen at the back of a trite stage
    Enlivened by a deep-toned orchestra,
A fairy set ablaze a miraculous dawn
    In an infernal sky;
Sometimes I have been at the back of a trite stage

A being who was only light, gold and gauze,
    Throw down the enormous Satan;
But my heart, which rapture never visits,
    Is a playhouse where one awaits
Always, always in vain, the Being with gauze wings! (191)]

The theatrical allusion is a new element introduced in these final stanzas, but the circumstances in which the poem was composed indicate that the entire scenario was inspired by a theatrical *féerie* [fairy play] entitled *La Belle aux cheveux d'or* [*The Beauty with the Golden Hair*] in which Marie Daubrun played the title role.[4] The theatrical context accounts for some of the more mysterious references earlier in the poem, such as the "sorcière" ["sorceress"] evoked in the third and seventh stanzas. More importantly, however, the theatrical context provides a contrast between the melodramatic, conventional story of good triumphing over evil, which is the Christian narrative of redemption, and the more complex situation that Baudelaire describes here. The "miraculeuse aurore" ["miraculous dawn"] of the penultimate stanza is revealed to be a fabrication, an impossible *coup de théâtre*, and when Satan makes an appearance in the final stanza, it is not the actual Devil that had figured in the sixth stanza but rather a theatrical Satan. The plot of the *féerie* ends, then, before the poem describing it ends. The half stop of the semi-colon in the second line of the final stanza pushes the poem along to its conclusion, a conclusion confirmed by the near-total transformation between the first and last line of the final stanza. And yet, the finality implied by this break in the formal pattern is counteracted by the semantic content of the final three lines, which open onto an eternal waiting. The seemingly definitive ending, which came toward the middle of the poem as the Devil extinguished hope, is replaced at the end by an eternally deferred ending, an impossible ending that makes the semiotic end of the poem a mere indication of the impossibility of its actual ending. This opening at the end of the poem shares key features with several other of Baudelaire's most characteristic endings of poems, most notably "Le rêve d'un curieux," which also features a theatrical metaphor for a mental landscape, and "Le voyage," both of which I shall analyze further below.

The repeated "toujours" of the final line underscores the contrast between the formal poetic closure and the opening of the poem onto eternity, in this case an eternity of sameness. This kind of open ending is not infrequent in Baudelaire, the most famous case being the series of objects of the poet's thought in "Le cygne": "Je pense aux matelots oubliés dans une île,/Aux captifs, aux vaincus! … à bien d'autres encor!" ["I think of the sailors forgotten on some isle,—Of the captives, of the vanquished! ... of many others too!" (293)] (1: 87). We find a more metaphysically inflected end in "L'héautontimorouménos":

> Je suis la plaie et le couteau!
> Je suis le soufflet et la joue!
> Je suis les membres et la roue,
> Et la victime et le bourreau!
>
> Je suis de mon coeur le vampire,
> —Un de ces grands abandonnés
> Au rire éternel condamnés
> Et qui ne peuvent plus sourire! (1: 79)
>
> [I am the wound and the dagger!
> I am the blow and the cheek!
> I am the members and the wheel,
> Victim and executioner!
>
> I'm the vampire of my own heart
> —One of those utter derelicts
> Condemned to eternal laughter,
> But who can no longer smile! (265)]

Like "Le cygne," this poem risks falling into an endless series, as the poet enumerates a long sequence of opposites. The continuation of the penultimate stanza's series of enunciations in the first line of the final stanza at first seems to confirm the continuation of the series, albeit with a variation in syntactical structure. The dash inflicts a formal violence on the series, a forced removal of the poem from the eternal sets of opposites into which it has fallen. But as in "L'irréparable," the lines that enforce closure on the poem do so in ways that open it onto eternity. This closure is not really one after all, since one set of eternal repetitions (the enumeration of opposites) is replaced by another eternal, this time the laughter that Baudelaire in his essay "De l'essence du rire" associates with the satanic. The laughter here is that of fallen humanity, which, without redemption, remains trapped in an eternal fall, a persistence of sameness which is one form of the *gouffre* we explored in Chapter 2 and which only the *néant* could effectively cancel. And this despite Baudelaire's assertion in "De l'essence du rire" ["On the Essence of Laughter"] that there is some kind of redemption to be had in laughter: "C'est avec le rire que [l'homme] adoucit quelquefois son Coeur [...]; car les phénomènes engendrés par la chute deviendront les moyens du rachat" ["It is with laughter that [man] soothes his heart sometimes [...]; for the phenomena engendered by the fall will become the means of redemption"] (OC2: 528). This redemption can only be temporary though, a passing moment in the generally eternal fall, just as any notion of a unified self will be shown, in "L'héautontimorouménos," to be a temporary and false conception whereas the permanently enduring sense of self is the one that is eternally doubled. As Michele Hannoosh has pointed out, for Baudelaire "the movement that surpasses the comic is itself an essentially comic one, affirming unequivocally the comic nature of the abolsute, the fallenness and humanity of the ideal" (38), and thus we can say that the very logic of the comic mitigates any permanence in the "redemption" of laughter by laughter, which becomes a move that only implicates us further into the fall that is marked by the comic. The poetic assertion of the eternally doubled subject in "L'héautontimorouménos" finds its confirmation in "De l'essence du rire" as well. In the essay, Baudelaire claims that perception of the self as doubled is rare; in the essay he claims it is reserved not to the poet but to the philosopher: "Ce n'est point l'homme qui tombe qui rit de sa propre chute, à moins qu'il ne soit un philosophe, un homme qui ait acquis, par habitude, la force de se dédoubler rapidement et d'assister comme spectateur désintéressé aux phénomènes de son moi" ["It is not at all the man who falls who laughs at his own fall, unless he be a philosopher, a man who has acquired, by habit, the strength to double back rapidly on himself and witness, as a disinterested spectator, the phenomena of his self"] (OC2: 532).

To be at all is to be caught, conscious or not, in the "eternal laughter," and to cancel being would also cancel the doubled subjectivity that gives birth to this poem. This fact highlights the unusual status of poetry for Baudelaire. Agamben had indicated that the poem both strives for and seeks to resist its own ending; in this poem, however, the double consciousness, represented as a sado-masochistic self relation, implies a desire to end, whereas the end at which we arrive effectively cancels the possibility of the end of subjectivity by the indication of the condemnation of the subject to eternal laughter. Like the subject itself, then, the end of the poem is relentlessly double: it ends only by indicating the eternal impossibility of an end, thus resolving the tension between ending and resisting an ending by making both continuing and ending come to the same result, that is, an eternal continuation.[5] By ending, it continues, via an end that can never come to an end. This challenges the very definition of cadence as a resting point, or what Agamben calls a falling into prose at the end of a poem, since the fall enacted and represented by this poem is not a fall *into* anything but rather an eternal fall.

How, then, does Baudelaire address endings when it is a question not of an individual poem but of the collection *Les Fleurs du Mal*, a work whose final section, "La Mort" ["Death"] explicitly invites reflection on the connections among the end of the poem, the end of the collection, and the end of a life? The 1857 and 1861 editions of *Les Fleurs du Mal* end quite differently. The final section of the 1857 edition includes just three poems: "La mort des amants," "La mort des pauvres," and "La mort des artistes," ["The Death of Lovers," "The Death of the Poor," "The Death of Artists"], whereas the 1861 edition includes these three but adds "La fin de la journée," "Le rêve d'un curieux," and "Le voyage," ["The End of the Day," "The Dream of a Curious Man," and "The voyage"], thus significantly altering our perception of the end both of Baudelaire's poetic project in *Les Fleurs* and of the metaphysical implications of death for the subject awaiting it. I turn now to a comparison of the final poem of 1857, "La mort des artistes," and the last poem of the 1861 edition, "Le voyage," claiming that the latter complicates our sense of an ending of *Les Fleurs* on account of the portrayal of the end in the penultimate poem, "Le rêve d'un curieux."

The 1857 edition ends with the death not of a generalized subject, that "Hypocrite lecteur,—mon semblable,—mon frère!" ["—Hypocritish reader,—my fellow,—my brother!"] evoked from the very start of the collection, but of a certain subset of artists:

> Il en est qui jamais n'ont connu leur Idole,
> Et ces sculpteurs damnés et marqués d'un affront,
> Qui vont se martelant la poitrine et le front,
>
> N'ont qu'un espoir, étrange et sombre Capitole!
> C'est que la Mort, planant comme un soleil nouveau,
> Fera s'épanouir les fleurs de leur cerveau! (1: 127)
>
> [There are some who have never known their Idol
> And those sculptors, damned and branded with shame,
> Who are always hammering their brows and their breasts,
>
> Have but one hope, bizarre and somber Capitol!
> It is that Death, soaring like a new sun,
> Will bring to bloom the flowers of their brains! (445)]

Death is figured here as a source of comfort, as it had been in more explicit terms in the preceding sonnet, "La mort des pauvres," where death is viewed as consoler and as "le seul espoir" ["the only hope"] of the poor. That comfort, and the resulting hope, are presented in rather different terms in "La Mort des artistes," since it is far from assured that death will "bring to bloom the flowers of their brains," and thus we are left with what is probably a vain hope, a hope that is nothing like its theological counterpart, which aligns with trust but is rather more like wishing. Claude Pichois notes the parallel between this vision and the more explicitly violent one in the prose poem "Le *Confiteor* de l'artiste" ["The Artist's *Confiteor*"] whose conclusion asserts that "L'étude du beau est un duel où l'artiste crie de frayeur avant d'être vaincu" ["Studying the beautiful is a duel in which the arist shrieks with fright before being defeated" (4)] (1: 1090). The artists of "La Mort des artistes" are no longer active creators consciously manipulating their destiny in an act that parallels divine creation, but are rather reduced to a state similar to that of the helpless poor, without even the reassuring potential of the "portique ouvert sur les Cieux inconnus" ["the portal opening on unknown Skies!" (443)] (1: 127) with which "La Mort des pauvres" comes to its end. Death, for these artists, is merely an endpoint that defines the failure of their life's project.

The 1861 edition, by contrast, features a far more universalizing vision of the end, both of the poetry collection and of the human subject. The long poem "Le voyage," which closes the definitive edition of *Les Fleurs*, engages a collective "nous" ["we"] from the very start of the poem, an inclusive gesture that goes far beyond the particular populations of lovers, the poor, and artists represented in the original three poems that comprised the section "La Mort." With this poem, Baudelaire returns to the more expansive metaphysical vision with which he began the collection in "Au lecteur," a poem that seeks to reduce rather than reinforce the division between the author and the reader and among readers themselves. While the "nous" is sometimes, presumably, universal and sometimes restricted to the group of travelers who speak in the poem,[6] the final section puts the "nous" in a particular situation of expectant longing:

> Ô Mort, vieux capitaine, il est temps! levons l'ancre!
> Ce pays nous ennuie, ô Mort! Appareillons!
> Si le ciel et la mer sont noirs comme de l'encre,
> Nos coeurs que tu connais sont remplis de rayons!
>
> Verse-nous ton poison pour qu'il nous réconforte!
> Nous voulons, tant ce feu nous brûle le cerveau,
> Plonger au fond du gouffre, Enfer ou Ciel, qu'importe?
> Au fond de l'Inconnu pour trouver du *nouveau*! (1: 134)
>
> [O Death, old captain, it is time! let's weigh anchor!
> This country wearies us, O Death! Let us set sail!
> Though the sea and the sky are black as ink,
> Our hearts which you know well are filled with rays of light
>
> Pour out your poison that it may refresh us!
> This fire burns our brains so fiercely, we wish to plunge
> To the abyss' depths, Heaven or Hell, does it matter?
> To the depths of the Unknown to find something new! (463)]

At first glance, this final section of the poem represents quite a different look at death than the one we see in the other poems of the section. Rather than a mere consolation, Death here is the vehicle of adventure, the motor of a continuing existence that looks beyond the end of the poem toward an open set of possibilities, replacing the vain hope of "La Mort des artistes" with the thrill of the new and unknown. On this reading, even the notion of the *gouffre* would in a sense be redeemed because the abyss would now be the space where the new could be found and subject removed from the torturous stasis of *Ennui* and transported toward something currently undefined but presumably desirable.

Reading this poem in the context of another that Baudelaire added to the 1861 edition of this section of *Les Fleurs* throws a redemptive interpretation of the conclusion of "Le voyage" into question. The penultimate poem of the 1861 edition is "Le rêve d'un curieux":

Connais-tu, comme moi, la douleur savoureuse
Et de toi fais-tu dire: « Oh! l'homme singulier! »
—J'allais mourir. C'était dans mon âme amoureuse
Désir mêlé d'horreur, un mal particulier;

Angoisse et vif espoir, sans humeur factieuse.
Plus allait se vidant le fatal sablier,
Plus ma torture était âpre et délicieuse;
Tout mon coeur s'arrachait au monde familier.

J'étais comme l'enfant avide du spectacle,
Haïssant le rideau comme on hait un obstacle …
Enfin la vérité froide se révéla:

J'étais mort sans surprise, et la terrible aurore
M'enveloppait.—Eh quoi! n'est-ce donc que cela?
La toile était levée et j'attendais encore. (1: 128–9)

[Do you know as I do, delectable suffering?
And do you have them say of you: "O! the strange man!"
—I was going to die. In my soul, full of love,
A peculiar illness; desire mixed with horror,

Anguish and bright hopes; without internal strife.
The more the fatal hour-glass continued to flow,
The fiercer and more delightful grew my torture;
My heart was being torn from this familiar world.

I was like a child eager for the play,
Hating the curtain as one hates an obstacle …
Finally the cold truth revealed itself:

I had died and was not surprised; the awful dawn
Enveloped me.—What! is that all there is to it?
The curtain had risen and I was still waiting. (449)]

Under the apparently simple guise of an anecdote, this poem complicates the notion of subjectivity and the sense of an ending to a greater extent than we have seen in the conclusion of "Le voyage." The setting of the poem as dream, made explicit by the title but never referred to in the poem itself, allows the poet to speak as a kind of disembodied, detemporalized subjectivity, looking back on his own experience and narrating it from the point of view of the end. Yet the end is of course not definitive, since the subject is still present and able to double back on itself, thus putting us in something like the temporality of "L'héautontimorouménos," which drives toward an end and desires the end to come, all the while preventing its coming by the continuation of discourse. There is a further resemblance between the two poems in the opening out onto an eternal temporality (the "eternal laughter" of the former and the indefinite "I was still waiting" of this poem), which ends by not ending, coming to rest in a point of unrest that prolongs the messianic moment, in Agamben's sense of the time that time takes to come to an end, without providing the means for arriving at the end. In other words, the poem not only defers the arrival of redemption but renders it impossible precisely because of the infinite prolongation of this temporal moment which nonetheless does not allow us to cancel temporality.

The poem interrupts itself several times, with the dashes that announce those interruptions coming at moments that do not correspond to the sonnet's divisions into quatrains and tercets. The typical poetic structure of the sonnet is thus both posited and questioned here, as is the notion of the "end." The poem's first two lines stand alone as a direct address to the reader, without apparent relationship to the anecdote that follows. The "Rêve" in question thus only begins in earnest in line three of the poem, once the opening question has come to an end. The poem itself ends twice, the first time prematurely in the middle of line 13, following an enjambment which, we recall, is for Agamben the defining feature of a poem. Furthermore, the tone itself changes after the dash, highlighting the double ending of the poem by a lapse into highly prosaic language and syntax. It is unclear whether the question and comment that end the poem are a continuation of the dream or the poet's commentary about the dream after the fact. Either way, the poem resists coming to a definitive end, or rather the definitive end of the poem is simultaneously an infinitely extended waiting, as it was at the end of "L'irréparable" as well, where the poet writes that his heart is "un théâtre où l'on attend/Toujours, toujours en vain" ["Is a playhouse where one awaits/Always, always in vain" (191)] (1: 55). "Le rêve d'un curieux" introduces disappointment as the inevitable reaction to death, an indication that, so long as subjectivity persists, it will not be able to find consolation in death, which turns out in this poem to be, for the subject able to perceive it, just as ineffectual a solution to the problem of Ennui as satanic revolt had been.

As it is framed in "Le Rêve d'un curieux," the problem is one of knowledge, which is in play from the very first word of the poem, "Connais-tu, comme moi, la douleur savoureuse?" On one hand, this is another device to reduce the distance between the poet and the "hypocrite lecteur" and to indicate the potentially perverse desire for death. But what is unusual about desire in this poem is that it is fulfilled, and the knowledge about desire about which the poet inquires at the outset becomes knowledge about death and consequently about the inevitable disappointment of a phenomenon that does not live up to our expectations. The hopeful expectation, even if it is figured as "torture," is canceled by the disappointment that knowledge brings with it. If we agree with Benjamin Fondane that knowledge, rather than disobedience, is in fact the source of original sin and that we are unable to cancel its effects without canceling our very humanity, then this poem too brings us back to the primacy of the theological domain in Baudelaire. The greater the effort to extract himself from the "familiar world," the more unseverable his bond to it grows. The theme of knowledge also figures in the penultimate section of "Le voyage," which begins with the exclamation, "Amer savoir, celui qu'on tire du voyage!" ["Bitter is the knowledge one gains from voyaging!" (461)] (1: 133). The poet hardly provides a ringing endorsement of travel: "Si tu peux rester, reste;/Pars, s'il le faut" ["If you can stay, remain;/Leave, if you must" (461)] (1: 133). While there are indications that it is *Ennui* that makes us restless and converts every new discovery into a new source of anguish, the condition of knowledge is prior to the condition of *Ennui* and could said to be generative of it, constantly returning us to the disappointment that knowledge inevitably brings with it.

Given the irredeemable image of the poet/child eternally waiting before the already revealed spectacle, we need to question any interpretation of the last section of "Le voyage" (the last words of *Les Fleurs du Mal* themselves) that sees in it a hopeful tone. I would like to propose, in light of Agamben's remarks on the way poems both strive toward and resist their endings, and in light of the notion of the eternal fall that we have seen operating in several of Baudelaire's poems, that *Les Fleurs du Mal* ends twice, the first time in "Le rêve d'un curieux" and again in "Le voyage." This reading sees in the latter poem an enactment of the fall into fruitless expectation that the former poem had already dismantled as a possibility. The poetic subject cannot come to an end in "Le rêve d'un curieux," lost as he is in eternal waiting or, if we imagine the subject recounting his dream, suspended in the present moment of that narration of the dream. Either way, the subject does not, cannot die, and even if it were to die, it would not reap the benefits of that death in terms of the cancellation of the suffering brought about by knowledge, since the perceiving subject would then cease to exist and thus to perceive. We can only imagine what it would be like to be free of the torment of existence, but that imagination is made all the more disturbing by the knowledge of the impossibility of bringing about that freedom from torment. Thus the imagination of a better circumstance becomes a temptation, and once again we remain in the realm of the unredeemable. If "Le rêve d'un curieux" presents an accurate summation of Baudelaire's conception of knowledge and eternal irreparation, a view confirmed by the identification of the "amer savoir" in "Le voyage," then the final section of the latter poem, in its eager call for death to lead the subject on to its next adventure in novelty, needs to be read as another deluded cry from a subject unaware that death, as an experience, will not bring any redemptive experience of the new. The speaking subject here is akin to the one in the first part of "Le rêve d'un curieux," naïve in his anxious expectation, unaware that disappointment inevitably awaits.

The final lines of *Les Fleurs du Mal* leave us in breathless expectation of the new, with an implied hint of the possibility of redemption to be found there, but the infinite expansion of that ending has already been cancelled in advance by the ending of "Le rêve d'un curieux"; hence the double ending of *Les Fleurs du Mal*. "Le rêve d'un curieux" is a more definitive ending, by virtue of the way it shuts down the possibility of hope for escape by reinforcing the quasi-theological underpinning of the necessary suffering, because of knowledge, of the perceiving subject. Yet, by the openness of the ending as well as the fact that it is the penultimate and not the final poem of the collection, it is clearly not completely definitive as an ending. "Le voyage," on this reading, presents us in the final section with yet another example of a desiring subject oblivious to the fact that death, like satanic revolt, intoxication, or any number of potential solutions, will not bring about the desired relief from suffering. In that sense, it is an ending that both closes the collection and sends us back to "Le rêve d'un curieux" and its refusal of the kind of open launch into the *nouveau* that "Le voyage" offers. Thus the last poem of the collection is not definitive as an ending; futhermore, it also forces a forgetting of the penultimate poem in order to seem viable as an approach both to death and to the conclusion of the collection.

The poetic effect of the juxtaposition of the endings of the final two poems of *Les Fleurs du Mal* is thus quite striking: the collection itself both strives for and resists its own end by setting up a structure whereby the final two poems turn back in on themselves, as the end of the penultimate poem leads us on to "Le voyage," only to have the end of that poem lead us inevitably back to the frustrated sense of an ending implied by the disappointed spectator awaiting something beyond the end. The conclusion of *Les Fleurs du Mal* thus performs the link between poetic closure and the problem of ironic subjectivity as constructed in poems such as "L'héautontimorouménos," which can conclude only by spiraling into the eternity of satanic laughter.[7] The definitive end, here as in the concluding poems of the collection, could only come with the extinguishing of subjectivity in the *néant*, a definitive closure that is refused at the same time as definitive poetic closure. The refusal of the possibility of redemption has implications not only for the (impossible) death of the subject but also for the structure of poetry itself, which is denied the definitive ending toward which it strives. The prototheological considerations we have seen operating throughout Baudelaire's thought and poetry thus turn out to be inseparable from formal considerations of poetic structure, in ways consonant with Agamben's theorizing of the end of the poem and its relation to the end of time and the end of poetry more largely. The ending of the 1861 edition is thus far more faithful to the non-messianic vision of Baudelaire's poetry articulated even in the 1857 edition, whose ending, it turns out, is also a penultimate end when we see it in the light of the 1861 revision. The poetry thus itself mirrors or prefigures its own reception, in that it has proven especially resistant to attempts to identify definitive meaning; that resistance to immediate or transparent meaning is often evoked as one of the aspects of Baudelaire's "modernity." But here the fragility of terms such as modernity and antimodernity comes to the fore, since it is precisely the poetry's refusal of linear progression, its infinite doubling back, that subtracts it from the linear logic of the modern while making the problem of endings central to its esthetic and metaphysical concerns.

The Order of Impossible Salvation:
From Baudelaire to Cioran

Baudelaire's working through of the consequences of his asoteriology has resonance far beyond his own time period. A host of thinkers have revisited the kinds of metaphysical and esthetic questions we have been raising in light of the ever more explicit declaration of God's death in the nineteenth century, and in the attempt to grapple further with the implications of the impossibility of redemption. For, as in the case of the concept of the death of God itself, it is not and cannot be simply a question of abandoning soteriological logic altogether, as if we could leave behind that pattern of thought once and for all, with no remainder, and adopt another one. An important inheritor of Baudelaire's asoteriological thinking and writing, one who, like him, retains elements of a Christian framework but abandons both the crucial matter of belief and the central doctrine of redemption, is Emil Cioran. Like Baudelaire, Cioran's writings take up both the philosophical and esthetic implications of what turns out, in Cioran's case, to be a most difficult struggle to abandon what he knows to be an impossible logic of redemption. In Cioran we see Baudelaire's project reconceived in light of the cultural, intellectual, and esthetic developments of the early and mid twentieth century.

By virtue of his intertwining of these philosophical and esthetic concerns around the transformed discourse of Christianity, Cioran can be considered Baudelaire's heir, although he does not explicitly position himself that way. Like the nineteenth-century poet, the twentieth-century aphorist renders explicit the struggle to resolve the question of the full implications of the impossibility of redemption rather than just attempting to pass over the difficulty inherent in overcoming that mode of thinking. At stake, of course, is the set of concerns that is sometimes referred to as nihilism, the complex issue of revaluing values, of attempting to salvage strands of a redemptive logic where one no longer exists. The history of philosophical engagement with that question is inextricably bound up with esthetic engagement, and the mid to late twentieth century, that is, the moment that is foundational for thinkers of Cioran's generation, saw an intensification of the discourse that one might label "nihilism" and a renewed skepticism about the ability of art to cancel its effects or to redeem meaningless or catastrophic experience. Simon Critchley traces back to Kant the attributing of such powers to the esthetic: "The category of the esthetic is the place where the problem of nihilism—the dilemma as to what might count as a meaningful life without the founding certainties of religion—is broached" (*Very Little* 90). He goes on to inquire, following Kierkegaard, "as to whether the esthetic can perform the lofty function" formerly undertaken by religion (90). A central preoccupation of Cioran's is lucidity, and thus in his reflections on art and writing, he will seek to articulate a vision of esthetics that resists illusion. Key among these illusions is the implicit or explicit assumption that art carries, in the wake of the eclipse of the Christian soteriological vision, some redemptive value, and so Cioran will throughout his writings attempt to articulate the place of art in a world that he wishes to see freed from the illusion of a falsely comforting or redemptive vision.

Cioran's implicit interlocutor in this articulation of the role of the esthetic is Friedrich Nietzsche, and so a brief consideration of the question of art and redemption in Nietzsche is in order, all the more so since the German philosopher, by his vehement critique of Christianity and his desire to draw the sometimes disturbing consequences of the death of God that he announces, could be seen as the prototypical representative of the view that seeks to place art in the salvific role once held by the Christian religion. Shane Weller takes up the question of art and transfiguration in Nietzsche:

> If Christianity as the moral interpretation of the world is a "craving for the nothing" or a "*No* to life," then the aesthetic interpretation must be an affirmation of that same life. The life (Leben) that is to be affirmed, however, is itself nothing other than art, as is made clear when Nietzsche asserts that "all of life is based on semblance [Schein], art, deception, points of view, and the necessity of perspectives and error" (BoT 23). Thus, if art is a "supplement" to natural reality, as an affirmation of life it is in fact an affirmation of itself. It is not simply that *life* overcomes itself as art, then, but rather that *art* overcomes itself *as art*. What art transfigures is nothing other than itself. (Weller 30)

Already it is possible to see the logic of redemption in the idea of affirming life as art. The notion of transfiguration places us within the realm where the theological and esthetic meet, and the self-overcoming carries more than an echo of resurrection recast in esthetic terms. To affirm life as art is to redeem what is not affirmable (presumably, illusion) by the transvaluation of illusion now recast entirely in the domain of art. By an act that looks something like redemptive grace, the unaffirmable aspect of life is canceled in its rebirth as art. If what Nietzsche affirms and redeems as life is in fact art, we return here to Agamben's notion of redemption that is ultimately empty because it saves only itself, thus becoming a content-less redemption in light of the fact that, *pace* Nietzsche, creation must fade away: redemption's "exigency is […] lost in the unsavable. Born from a creation that is left pending, it ends up as an inscrutable salvation that no longer has an objective" (*Nudities* 9).

Weller's analysis goes on to show that "it would seem […] that nihilism as Nietzsche determines it is ultimately impossible, given that the arch-nihilist is in fact already a 'yes-creating' force" (34), but still the transfiguration that is the self-overcoming of art "cannot be a purely affirmative act [...] since the artist is characterized by negation, and more precisely by a negation in the form of a self-transfiguration, which is always also a mode of veiling" (34). Several key concepts that Cioran takes up in his cumulative writings on esthetics, lucidity, and redemption are present in this reading of Nietzsche. Of particular importance is the notion of veiling, which stands opposed to the disclosive function of art and places the artist (as well as the human subject more generally, given the way that art encroaches on and becomes synonymous in a sense with life) back into the realm of illusion. This view works against an affirmation of art's ability to provide lucid insight. If art, through its self-transfiguration, returns to the realm of illusion, it cannot really have any redemptive value because it, ironically, affirms itself as illusory in a way that blocks our ability to transcend that illusion. Coming to rest in itself, art can thus save only itself, and is reduced to the same impotence as redemption, forced to turn in on itself in a salvific gesture that we must label meaningless. We shall see, in this chapter and the next, that Cioran may sometimes affirm the redemptive characteristics of art but only as a temporary redemption, one that is subject to its own self-negation and, in that sense, there is nothing more redemptive in art than there would be in, say Baudelaire's state of intoxication, which, while it provides temporary and illusory respite from a lucid vision of the world, we would be tempted to label redemptive.

As for Nietzsche, his version of redemption through art is not so much temporary as constant. He writes in *The Birth of Tragedy*:

> The more aware I become of those omnipotent art impulses in nature, and find in them an ardent longing for illusion and for redemption by illusion, the more I feel compelled to make the metaphysical assumption that the truly existent, the primal Oneness, eternally suffering and contradictory, also needs the delightful vision, the pleasurable illusion for its constant redemption: an illusion that we, utterly caught up in it and consisting of it [...] are required to see as empirical reality. If we look away from our own "reality," then, for a moment, if we see our empirical existence, like that of the world in general, as an idea of the primal Oneness created in a moment, then we must see the dream as the *illusion of illusion*, and hence as an even higher satisfaction of the original desire for illusion. (*Birth* 25)

It is not surprising that Nietzsche goes on to engage a painting of a Christian scene, Raphael's *Transfiguration*, as an allegorical illustration of the kind of transformation he describes here, for it is clear that Nietzsche's description of the redemptive function of art depends heavily on Christian notions of redemption, which Nietzsche applies to esthetic experience without fundamentally altering the logic of redemption on which both Christian and Nietzschean transfiguration depend. While Nietzsche arguably offers a "secularized" esthetic redemption, the certainty that underlies his claims about access to a higher reality, the "illusion of illusion," gives the lie to its purported removal from Christian patterns of thought. The unity effected by esthetic vision here is even a comforting vision, one that satisfies "desire" in a way that brings the tension of unsatisfied desire to rest in the supposedly eternal presence of the desire, illusion. The world thus imagined is caught in a structure of mutual interdependence that cancels the content of the illusion in favor of the structure or form of the illusion, and thus creates a self-perpetuating world, eternal and complete unto itself, that parallels messianic time by its removal from dynamic movement. The celestial vision is precisely what is revealed in the transfiguration, and so once again, Nietzsche's secular esthetics remains uncomfortably but necessarily tied to the logic of redemption from which, presumably, he would like to escape:

> From this illusion there now arises, like an ambrosial vapour, a new and visionary world of illusion of which those caught up in the first illusion see nothing—a radiant gloating in the purest bliss and painless contemplation beaming from wide-open eyes. Here, in the highest artistic symbolism, we behold that Apolline world of beauty and its substratum, the terrible wisdom of Silenus, and we intuitively understand their reciprocal necessity. […] With sublime gestures [Apollo] reveals to us how the whole world of torment is necessary so that the individual can create the redeeming vision, and then, immersed in contemplation of it, sit peacefully in his tossing boat amid the waves. (*Birth* 25–6)

Such a rendering of art's transfiguration of empirical reality satisfyingly accounts for the simultaneity of the visions but not for their "reciprocal necessity"; Nietzsche's vision here reads more like an esthetic theodicy attempting to account for evil but claiming that it is necessary for it to exist in order for us to be free of it, which seems to beg the question. We have already seen that early twentieth-century engagement with similar questions will come to rather different conclusions, hearkening back to Baudelaire in order to alter the function of contemplation. For Nietzsche, contemplation equals serenity and is a by-product of the reciprocal mutual dependence of reality and its esthetically transfigured other face.

But as we have seen in the network of ideas that circulate among Benjamin, Fondane, and Baudelaire, contemplation aligns itself with an unredeemable vision inspired by evil, stemming from a view of knowledge that sees it as knowledge of evil only. If there is no transfigured reality, there can be no redemption, and so the theologically inflected vocabulary of Baudelaire and his later interpreters gets us, paradoxically, further from the logic of redemption than Nietzsche's brand of estheticism, which, for all its adoption of pagan deities, clings strongly to the logic of redemption in ways that Baudelairean atheology is compelled to refuse. While the subject under Baudelairean original sin may be *incurvatus in se*, turned in on itself, the Nietzschean vision makes no room for such an individual subject, creating instead an entire esthetic world that is closed in upon itself in its mutually self-completing and redemptive movement from illusion to the illusion of illusion. This subject-less world is what leads toward what Agamben has identified as the redemption that becomes pure subject for itself. We have seen Agamben's atheological analysis of this structural move; he writes analogously in *The Man without Content* about art's own similar move, akin to Nietzsche's self-enclosed esthetic world, toward an art of pure form that results, ultimately, not in Nietzschean harmony but in nihilism:

> Art is the annihilating entity that traverses all its contents without ever being able to attain a positive work, because it cannot identify with any content. And since art has become the pure potentiality of negation, nihilism reigns in its essence. […] The essence of nihilism coincides with the essence of art as the extreme point of its destiny insofar as, in both, being destines itself to man in the form of Nothingness. (*Man* 57–8)[1]

The esthetic nothingness of pure form is, however, even if it were achievable, incompatible with the nothingness that plays such a crucial role, as we have seen, in Baudelaire's esthetics and metaphysics of non-redemption. In this instance, it is Baudelaire rather than Nietzsche who inaugurates an esthetic and critical heritage that seeks to come to terms with the elimination of redemption as a mode of thought rather than simple reversing or secularizing the way in which redemption is achieved. Subjectivity persists in Baudelaire's poetry, which opposes itself on these grounds to the Nietzschean view as he articulates it here.

As an inheritor of both traditions in the twentieth century, Emil Cioran enters into dialogue with both but ultimately must be seen to side with Baudelaire when it comes to the impossibility of an extended redemptive esthetic vision. Sylvain David is right to note that Cioran follows Nietzsche in the latter's attempt at "pillaging" (the word is Cioran's)

> poetry's material in order to give back a little vigor to philosophy. It is a question of opposing the semantic freedom of verse to the logical rigor of the sentence […]. By breathing a dose of lyricism into the exercise of thought, the essayist attempts a redemptive transmutation that seeks to replace the frozen concept with the vivacity of the image, to triumph over the spirit of the system and the false objectivity that it implies, by a return to the vigor of the passions. (David 90)

Cioran's philosophical project borrows its style and something of its form, then, from Nietzsche. Paradoxically though, the return to the poetic turns him away from Nietzschean esthetic redemption and toward Baudelaire; the latter's poetry, by its relentless insistence on the poetic subject unable to engage in self-cancellation, opposes itself in terms of content to Nietzsche's vision. Nietzsche's view must be dismissed on the same grounds as traditional Christianity is dismissed, as an overly and unjustifiably optimistic vision of a redemption that is in fact impossible. Cioran himself says as much:

> A un étudiant qui voulait savoir où j'en étais par rapport à [Nietzsche], je répondis que j'avais cessé de le pratiquer depuis longtemps. Pourquoi? me demanda-t-il. – Parce que je le trouve trop *naïf*…

Je lui reproche ses emballements et jusqu'à ses ferveurs. Il n'a démoli des idoles que pour les remplacer par d'autres. […] Il n'a observé les hommes que de loin. Les aurait-il regardés de près, jamais il n'eût pu concevoir ni prôner sur le surhomme, vision farfelue, risible, sinon grotesque. (Pl 799)

[To a student who wanted to know where I stood regarding [Nietzsche], I replied that I had stopped engaging with him a long time ago. Why, he asked. Because I find him too *naïve*.

I reproach him for his flights of enthusiasm and even his fervors. He demolished idols only to replace them with other ones. […] He observed men only from afar. If he had looked at them from up close, he could never have conceived or extol the overman, far-fetched vision, laughable, if not grotesque.]

This is not to say that, by rejecting Nietzsche as overly optimistic, Cioran's writings provoke a gloomy despair. Rather, as Michel Jarrety has argued, for Cioran "only the happiness of negating allows us to tolerate the real as it actually is" (Jarrety 130). He thus substitutes a model of tolerance for Nietzsche's notion of transfiguration, resulting in what Jarrety labels "a double negation; the one that contests—the world, God, progress in history, etc.—by the refusal to recognize in them a full reality, and at the same time the one that triumphs over itself by this second thrust that constitutes the joy of denouncing the absence or precariousness of it: to hold the world in derision is to put it at a distance" (Jarrety 130). What emerges is something like a therapeutic model, which places Cioran closer to the Stoics than to any more modern precursors.

From the start of his appearance on the French literary scene, it became apparent that Cioran was not easily classifiable in terms of literary or esthetic precedents, and that, like Baudelaire, he undoubtedly announced something new while retaining a forceful vocabulary from several traditions that had gone before. Cioran's literary début in French was the 1949 publication of *Précis de décomposition* [*A Short History of Decay*], famously hailed by Max Nadeau in terms that point to the distinctness of Cioran's literary voice while at the same time claiming that voice as somehow representative of a post-World War II culture seeking an expression appropriate to the radical historical and culture rupture of that event. In his article "Un penseur crépusculaire" ["A Twilight Thinker"], Nadeau writes: "The one we were waiting for has come, the prophet of concentrational era and of collective suicide, the one whose arrival was prepared by the philosophers of nothingness and the absurd, the bringer of bad news *par excellence*" (Nadeau 211). The choice of the term *prophet* is revealing here, since it situates Cioran's vision, like those of the prophets, as both idiosyncratic and prescient of the kind of vision that will become common rather than unusual in the future. Nadeau also complicates the reference to prophecy by placing Cioran at the end as well as at the beginning of an intellectual geneaological line, since he situates the existentialists as precursors of Cioran. The logic of the contradiction, or of the both/and, dominates all of Cioran's thought and writing, and so it is fitting that his arrival on the French literary scene is noted under the complex sign of the prophet in his ability both to typify contemporary experience and to render it in a form we find disturbingly or unsettlingly new. Nadeau goes on perceptively to identify another productive tension, one that will animate all of Cioran's work, between the embodied, particular voice of a suffering subject and a more abstract, generalized, disembodied voice: "It is not a monster, nor a phenomenon, barely an agitator […] but it is surely a being submerged in shame and disgust and who suffers. On the shore of the triumphal way that leads to atomic destruction he puts down his sack and sits down, exhausted, refusing all consolations and all pity" (211). And, significantly, Nadeau raises the question of belief: "He still believes in something since he writes, confesses, and sings his distress" (212). Already, it is clear that Cioran's nihilism is not a simple or simplistic one, but Nadeau's observation opens up several difficult questions lurking beneath the seemingly straightforward assertion that he makes. If Cioran does not simply negate everything, what is in fact left? Nadeau links belief here to the act of writing: Cioran believes *since* he writes. What kind of belief would be indicated by the act of writing, exactly? A belief in writing itself? In its worth? In its potential not just to record but to transform experience? And what exactly does it mean to believe, in this context?

As with Baudelaire, it can be difficult to write about Cioran because of his dedication to contradiction and to doubleness. His aphorisms lend themselves easily to quotation, but getting a grasp on his work as a whole is a more challenging enterprise.[2] While he actively resists a systematic approach, there are several themes that recur regularly throughout his work. Positing a global rather than a local interpretation of them, however, risks mischaracterizing his work as a whole, as Patrice Bollon has noted:

> One would have to cite all of Cioran in order to account for this unclassifiable and properly untenable position that affirms in the same move—when it is not *within a single sentence*—the demand for the most illuminating lucidity *and the* necessity of the most obscurantist illusion, the search for wisdom *and* acquiescence to the most vile drives, a mystical drawing toward saintliness *and* attachment to the most atheistic materialism, incredulousness concerning change and *a fortiori* progress *and* the romantic ineluctability of revolt! As if in him coexisted permanently and about all subjects the affirmer and the negator, the ideologue and one who contests him, the pleader and the judge, in an eternal contradictory soliloquy, an infinite dialogue with self, between the divided parts of his personality. (Bollon 150)

The philosophical, the theological, and the esthetic are already complexly intertwined in Nadeau's simple observation about Cioran, and as his own writing develops over the ten books that will follow the *Précis*, Cioran returns constantly to the kinds of questions we have already been raising. One of his several obsessional themes is redemption. At the most basic level, we could simply assert that Cioran finds salvation impossible and untenable, and indeed I will show below how this follows from several of his most important postulations.[3] But, as with Baudelaire, such a simple observation raises more issues than it resolves because, as was also the case with Baudelaire and the other authors we have examined, enumerating the consequences of the impossibility of redemption is anything but straightforward and draws us right back to the philosophico-esthetic web of questions we have just begun to pursue. Beyond that, we also need to contend with the fact that, much more so than in Baudelaire, the notion of redemption constantly reappears throughout Cioran's works, despite its impossibility as a working hypothesis, which demonstrates the incredible difficulty of the task of thinking beyond redemption even if we were to want (or indeed, need) to. Redemption reappears in several guises and as a result of a variety of kinds of experience (none of which relate back to a Christian redemptive sacrifice), but none of these appearances cancels the impossibility of redemption which governs Cioran's thought, thus making it necessary for Cioran's reader to account for redemption's simultaneous presence in the writing and impossibility as an active and viable concept.

From the outset, we should be clear that Cioran does not operate within a paradigm of belief in God, a fact easily obscured by the constant reference to God, the devil, and other borrowings from the lexicon of Christianity. Even more so than Baudelaire had done, Cioran separates the use of the Christian framework from the question of belief, and is more explicit about the refusal of that belief than Baudelaire had been. In interviews, for instance, he affirms directly, "Je ne crois ni en Dieu, ni en rien" ["I believe neither in God nor in anything"] (*E* 130) and calls himself a "théologien athée" ["atheist theologian"] (*E* 164). This is not to say, however, that Cioran's writings may be justifiably or helpfully labeled "atheistic." Even though he indicates that his "attitude est celle d'un théologien non croyant" ["attitude is that of a non-believing theologian"] (*E* 164), it would be overly simplistic, and ultimately misleading, to call Cioran a partisan of an atheistic theology. (It is in fact significant that even in the phrase just quoted, he claims that his attitude is that *of* such a theologian, not that he is one himself. In other words, there is an attitude that informs his writing, but the writing itself is not, and could not be, the work of a theologian, since that would invest more force in the unbelief than Cioran is ever willing to concede.) As in Baudelaire, Christian concepts, devoid of their central tenet of redemption, have a force much greater than a metaphor; they are retained and refuted simultaneously in ways that no convenient label can capture. Thus, one of the greatest understatements from Cioran, not usually known for reducing the force of his assertions, lurks in this claim: "Je ne suis pas croyant mais la religion m'intéresse" ["I am not a believer but religion interests me"] (*E* 106).[4] The precise nature and extent of that interest in religion can emerge only through a prolonged engagement with the multifaceted ways Cioran uses these terms and concepts throughout his writings, as concentrating on any one particular use at any given moment gives a misleading picture of the whole. As was the case with Baudelaire, this is not to say that a coherent whole eventually emerges. The theological for both of them functions as something more like a fiction, but to assert that, it is necessary to understand the full force, and uncommon meaning, that they give to the notion of fiction as well.

It would be premature, however, to propose such an answer even as a tentative hypothesis; this is so because, by explicitly rejecting systematic philosophy, Cioran forces us to read him in a way different than searching for the identification of a problem and its subsequent solution. The serious attention paid to style, noted by every commentator on Cioran, and the frequent choice of aphorism or very short essay as a form suggest that there is insight into Cioran's process of thinking to be gained from approaches that pursue alternatives to linearity and systematicity. Of all of the antinomies operating in Cioran's process and works, Sylvain David identifies one that is primary in that it forms the fundamental pair of moves between which Cioran vacillates:

> In a general way, the aporias at the heart of Cioran's work can be reduced to a dichotomy between an attraction for the venomous charm of "negative exercises" and a paradoxical but nevertheless present "temptation to exist." Beyond doubt a will, or even a need, to believe remains. From this irreducible interior quartering, Cioran draws his great watchword: that of "thinking against oneself." This exercise of dangerous intellectuality seems to correspond to certain esthetic practices of modernity, as the references to those three masters who remain with the author, Nietzsche, Dostoyevski, and Baudelaire, testify: "'I am the wound and the knife,' there is our absolute, our eternity" (*TE* 826). (David 104)

Thinking against oneself, the subtitle of a section of the *Précis de décomposition* but also a more than adequate brief charaterization of all of Cioran's enterprise, is, like all of the terms we have considered so far, plural in its meanings, but all of the possible meanings of the term return to the self-torture of the divided subject, which David rightly links to Baudelaire. Not simply a romantic subject attracted at some level to intellectual masochism, Cioran's writing subject emerges in part out of the intellectual history it often stubbornly refuses to evoke explicitly but with which it engages by its impression of coming "after everything" and attempting to think from the ruins of a long tradition or rather to return to a tradition seen in a new light to ask what might still be either available or adaptable. But lest that description imply confidence on the part of Cioran's speaking subject, we need to remember that thinking against oneself also implies constant doubt, another key leitmotif in Cioran's work. Doubt in turn contains its own division against itself, since to think against doubt would mean temporarily to affirm certainty. Such emphasis on aporia and paradiox may seem like the stuff of intellectual games, but the stakes are always high in Cioran, and tragedy is a much more apt comparison than the ludic enterprise, even if an ironic sense of humor often shines through Cioran's vituperation.

Cioran provides the most sustained discussion of redemption in two of his three works that consist of extended essays rather than shorter fragments, *La chute dans le temps* and *Le mauvais démiurge*, both from his middle period, but before turning to those works, it is important to spend some time with the *Précis* since it announces so much of the thematic materials that Cioran would develop over the next forty years and also allows us to get a fuller grasp on how he appropriates and transforms

Christian concepts. At times in the *Précis*, he adapts a specifically monastic Christianity, generalizing the medieval concept of *acedia* far beyond the cloister:

> *Acedia.* Cette stagnation des organes, cette hébétude des facultés, ce sourire pétrifié, ne te rappellent-ils pas souvent l'ennui des cloîtres, les cœurs déserts de Dieu, la sécheresse et l'idiotie des moines s'exécrant dans l'emportement extatique de la masturbation? [...]
>
> La terre, le ciel, sont les parois de ta cellule, et, dans l'air qu'aucun souffle n'agite, seule règne l'absence d'oraison. Promis aux heures creuses de l'éternité, à la périphérie des frissons et aux désirs moisis qui pourrissent à l'approche du salut, tu t'ébranles vers un jugement sans faste et sans trompettes, cependant que tes pensées, pour toute solennité, n'ont imaginé que la procession irréelle des espérances.
>
> Et tu retombes dans le monde comme une Trappe sans foi, traînant sur le boulevard, Ordre des filles perdues—et de ta perdition. (Pl 70)

> [*Acedia.* That stagnation of the organs, that stupor of the faculties, that petrified smile, do they not remind you often of the ennui of cloisters, hearts that God has deserted, dryness and idiocy of the monks hating themselves in the ecstatic transport of masturbation? [...]
>
> The earth and the sky are the walls of your cell, and, in the air that no breath agitates, only the absence of prayer reigns. Promised to the empty hours of eternity, to the periphery of shudders and the moldy desires that rot at the approach of salvation, you set off toward a judgment without splendor and without trumpets, whereas your thoughts, for all solemnity, imagine only the unreal procession of hopes.
>
> And you fall back into the world like a Trappist without faith, dragging along the boulevard, the Order of Lost Girls—and of your perdition.]

The passage makes clear that Cioran forces a new, antilinear approach to time, much in line with his rethinking of time in the later works we will explore below, when we wish to trace the intellectual or cultural genealogy of the concepts he evokes. While undoubtedly "contemporary" in the refusal of religious faith, and indeed in the approach consisting of piecing together fragments of earlier cultural attitudes in order to form a new one from the ghosts or traces of the old, this excerpt establishes just as much continuity as rupture with the Middle Ages, expanding the purview of *acedia* and thereby making contemporary society resemble its medieval counterpart if we are able to subtract the question of religious faith and salvation from the equation.

Cioran returns to a monastic framework later in the *Précis*:

> A nous autres il nous faudrait des cloîtres aussi dépossédés, aussi vides que nos âmes, pour nous y perdre sans l'assistance des cieux, et dans une pureté d'idéal absent, des cloîtres à la mesure d'anges détrompés qui, dans leur chute, à force d'illusions vaincues, demeureraient encore immaculés. Et d'espérer une vogue

de retraites dans une éternité sans foi, une prise d'habit dans le néant, un Ordre affranchi des mystères, et dont nul « frère » ne se réclamerait de rien, dédaignant son salut comme celui des autres, un *Ordre de l'impossible salut...* (Pl 150)

[We others would need cloisters as dispossessed, as empty as our souls, to lose ourselves there without the assistance of the heavens, and in the purity of an absent ideal, cloisters on the scale of demystified angels who, in their fall, by dint of vanquished illusions, still remained immaculate. And to hope for a vogue of retreats in an eternity without faith, a taking of the monastic habit in nothingness, an Order empancipated from mysteries, and of which no "brother" would ask anything, disdaining his salvation and that of others, an *Order of Impossible Salvation...*]

Here the focus is sharper than in the earlier reference to an imaginary "Order of Lost Girls"; in this reformulation of the monastic framework, Cioran lays out the terrain on which he will operate over the course of the next several decades. The new monks are now explicitly linked to a fall, but not one that would simply result in a valorization of Satanism. Rather, the fall purifies in some sense and is the condition of possibility of the emergence of the new monasticism. This new order, which one could only half-appropriately call "post-Christian," represents the end product of the process by which what is salvageable from older redemptive models of thought is retained while the soteriology itself is removed. Neither the original monasticism, nor a parody of it, nor its elimination, the Order of Impossible Salvation is the new conceptual model, necessarily imaginary but powerful as a base from which an asoteriological thinking might emerge. Such thinking, the passage implies, would involve fidelity to practice but not on account of an act of faith; it would be based on lucidity but not a lucidity that cancels all action. And above all, the monastic model implies fidelity to its founding notion, a commitment to live out the consequences of the Impossible Salvation which it adopts as its founding principle. Here, Cioran appears to subtract redemption effortlessly from the model of faithful commitment to an intellectual ideal, but as we shall see, soteriological logic is not often easily surpassed, and least so by any simple attempt to negate it without remainder.

Beyond linking the medieval and the contemporary, however, Cioran here establishes an important connection to Baudelaire as well via the notion of *acedia*, easily transposed, as Cioran here describes it, into the register of Baudelairean *ennui*, which owes a debt to romantic despondency but far surpasses it in the troubling generalizing of the sentiment as opposed to its reservation for a select few. Thus there are at least three temporalities, often opposed to one another by those with an eye to periodization (pre-modern, high modern, postmodern), superimposed in Cioran's fragment and shown to reveal points of commonality or dialogue that invite us to move beyond a linear temporality when it comes to tracing the history of the ideas at play here. The point of my analysis of Cioran is not simply to establish a comparison to Baudelaire, but given I argue that they are two crucial figures in the story of the fall out of the logic of redemption and that there are indeed patterns of similarity in their approach to reappropriating de-Christianized Christian themes for other purposes, it is worth pausing, before forging ahead, over the links between the two. While Cioran does not often make explicit reference to other authors in his own works, he pays brief but significant homage to Baudelaire in *De l'inconvénient d'être né* [*The Trouble with Being Born*]: "Un écrivain ne nous a pas marqués parce que nous l'avons beaucoup lu mais parce que nous avons pensé à lui plus que de raison. Je n'ai pratiqué spécialement ni Baudelaire ni Pascal mais je n'ai cessé de songer à leurs misères, lesquelles m'ont accompagné partout aussi fidèlement que les miennes" ["A writer has not made an impression on us because we have read him extensively but because we have thought of him more than is reasonable. I have not spent particularly large amounts of time reading Baudelaire or Pascal but I have not ceased dreaming of their miseries, which have accompanied me everywhere as faithfully as my own"] (Pl 873–4).[5] Other critics have noted points of affinity between Baudelaire and Cioran in certain thematic areas. Mariana Sora, for instance, identifies a "Baudelairean trait" in Cioran's interest in women saints which features a "mix of estheticism and morbid pleasure" (Sora 226), and also, more significantly, in the link between religion and knowledge of evil. Sora rightly identifies a distinction between the two regarding the particulars of the relation: for Baudelaire it is a question of "consciousness of sin," whereas for Cioran it is "the becoming conscious of an ontic evil" (226), about which we shall have more to say below.

I have already suggested another important point of continuity between the two writers stemming from the central role of the "héautontimorouménos," the self-torturer, the product of a fragmented subjectivity caught in a suspension of time that produces torment for the divided self who perceives himself as divided. Baudelaire's figure of the self-torturer in the poem of that name finds its echo in the constant skepticism and doubt of Cioran's writing voice, unable to root himself in any particular position (save for the paradoxical and impossible certainty about the appropriateness of doubt as an unquestionable position) and thus condemned to think against himself. This self-tormenting position is one that Sylvain David has labeled Cioran's "negative heroism" (David 15).[6] Both Baudelaire and Cioran make this figure foundational to their ontology and metaphysics. While neither of them dwells at disproportionately great length on the idea, it necessarily colors virtually all of their other inquiries, and leads both of them to prefer the void of non-existence to the torture of existence. Like Baudelaire, Cioran publishes a prayer to a God he hardly believes in; whereas Baudelaire had asked God to grant that he may not be inferior to those he despises,[7] Cioran uses prayer as a means toward being free of prayer itself:

(Seigneur, donnez-moi la faculté de ne jamais prier, épargnez-moi l'insanité de toute adoration, éloignez de moi cette tentation d'amour qui me livrerait pour toujours à Vous. Que le vide s'étende entre mon cœur et le ciel! Je ne souhaite point mes déserts peuplés de votre présence, mes nuits tyrannisées par votre lumière, mes Sibéries fondues sous votre soleil. Plus seul que vous, je veux mes mains pures, au rebours des vôtres qui se souillèrent à jamais en pétrissant la terre et en se mêlant des affaires du monde. Je ne demande à votre stupide omnipotence que le respect de ma solitude et de mes tourments. Je n'ai que faire de vos paroles; et je crains la folie qui me les ferait entendre. Dispensez-moi […] la paix que vous ne pûtes tolérer et qui vous incita à ménager une brèche dans le néant pour y ouvrir cette foire des temps, et pour me condamner ainsi à l'univers,—à l'humiliation et à la honte d'être.) (Pl 86)

[(Lord, give me the faculty of never praying, spare me the insanity of all adoration, remove from me this temptation of love that would deliver me over forever to You. May the void spread itself out between my heart and heaven! I do not wish for my deserts to be peopled with your presence, my nights tyrannized by your light, my Siberias melted under your sun. More alone than you, I want my hands to be pure, the opposite of yours that sullied themselves for good by forming the earth and getting involved in the affairs of the world. I only ask from your stupid omnipotence the respect of my solitude and my torments. I have no use for your words, and I fear the madness that would make me hear them. Exempt me from the peace that you could not tolerate and that led you to contrive a breach in the nothingness to open there this fair of time, and to condemn me thus to the universe—to the humiliation and the shame of being.)]

Although Cioran offers this prayer in parentheses, it contains an essential aspect of his vision and an important source of distinction from Baudelaire. We saw that the latter blasphemes, in the satanic poems of "Révolte," in a way that simply reverses good and evil by singing the praises of Satan. In Baudelaire, this was an intermediary step, a fruitless negation en route to the ultimate (and impossible) solution of non-existence. While Cioran would agree that non-existence is ultimately preferable to existence, his form of blasphemy in the prayer quoted here has nothing to do with the simplistic Satanism through which Baudelaire's speaking subject passes. Rather, God himself becomes the temptation here. By asking to be free from prayer and to have the void interposed between his heart and the heavens, Cioran implies that conventional prayer is a temptation to be resisted, not because, in a quasi-Nietzschean sense, it would be a sign of weakness or slave mentality but because it would anchor the subject even more firmly in an existence from which he knows it is best to flee. In this sense, the temptation to interact with God is related to what Cioran calls in the title of one of his books the "temptation to exist"; both of those temptations stem from the difficulty we have not only in admitting that non-existence is preferable (at least until suffering convinces us) but also in having the courage to follow through and draw all the consequences of that realization.[8]

It should be clear by now that the stakes are high in Cioran in terms of elaborating the full complexity of the asoteriology he proposes in sometimes terrifyingly brief aphoristic form. The remnants of the theological emerge in his writings in forms comparable to those of thinkers such as Agamben, Žižek, and others who have turned toward similarly-minded investigations of the theological in the early twenty-first century. It would thus be wrong to see Cioran simply as a nihilist, as he has sometimes been interpreted. Nicolas Cavaillès indicates at the outset of his book-length study of

Cioran that "despite himself, no doubt, Cioran sees his work divided up among three exclusive types of readers: the adolescent, the philosopher, and the poet" (Cavaillès 17), and it is true that certain passages of Cioran, taken on their own, do seem to suggest a sort of post-romantic adolescent revolt against the world by a tormented soul: "*Tout est rien; rien n'est. L'une et l'autre formule apportent une égale sérénité. L'anxieux, pour son malheur, reste entre les deux, tremblant et perplexe, toujours à la merci d'une nuance, incapable de s'établir dans la sécurité de l'être ou de l'absence d'être*" ["*Everything is nothing; nothing is. Both formulas bring an equal serenity. The anxious man, to his misery, remains between the two, trembling and perplexed, always at the mercy of a nuance, incapable of establishing himself in the security of being or of the absence of being*"] (Pl 736). But the theological and philosophical stakes implied by the attempt to think beyond idealism, existentialism, and every other systematic philosophy, and to pursue a revisionary path that differs significantly from that of Nietzsche even as it shares some of the same impulses to negate but not simply destroy what came before, make it impossible to reduce Cioran to a form of adolescent nihilism that would be content to proclaim the meaninglessness of human endeavor. He does, to be sure, repeatedly assert such meaninglessness, but those assertions need to be taken as a local moment within his larger project of working through the implications of a refusal of the soteriological vision, since his question of "à quoi bon?" ["what's the use?"] repeatedly yields to an impulse to keep writing and to refuse to come to rest in a simple and simplistic negative vision. This perpetuation of writing is a source of both satisfaction and torment, and as I have implied, the torment is a necessary product of existence, which is set up to preclude the possibility of resolution in anything other than non-existence, at which point there would be no subject available to perceive the end of the torment. Cioran is no more able to come to an end than Baudelaire, despite the necessity of the literary text coming to an end. That is perhaps the most "poetic" character of Cioran's writing, far more so than his moments of lyricism. He participates in the problematics of the end that we analyzed in Baudelaire through Agamben's esthetico-theological meditations on the notion of closure.

Cioran goes further than refusing closure, however; he also suggests that new *beginnings* are impossible: "Chercher la souffrance pour éviter le rachat, suivre à rebours le chemin de la délivrance, tel est notre apport en matière de religion: des illuminés bilieux, des Bouddhas et des Christs hostiles au salut, prêchant aux misérables le charme de leur détresse" ["To seek suffering to avoid redemption, to follow the way of deliverance backwards, that is what we bring when it comes to religion: irritable enlightened ones, Buddhas and Christs hostile to salvation, preaching to the wretched the charm of their distress"] (Pl 276). He goes on to claim in this passage that a step beyond the Judeo-Christian worldview (corrupt since Adam but not for the reasons typically given) would be to "débaptiser l'univers, par ôter l'étiquette qui, apposée sur chaque apparence, la relève et lui prête un simulacre de sens" ["unbaptize the universe, to remove the label which, appended on each appearance, raises it and lends it a simulacrum of sense"] (Pl 276). There is an echo of the Rimbaud of *Une saison en enfer* [*A Season in Hell*] here, who claims to be "esclave de [s]on baptême" ["the slave of [his] baptism"] (Rimbaud 274), meaning that the effects of baptism are permanent in that even if one were to renounce one's faith, baptism itself cannot be canceled or reversed. Cioran implies here that with the act of naming comes a conferring of meaning that is, like the baptismal act itself, impossible to cancel even though it may be shown to be false or, more likely in Cioran's case, even though one sees the assigning of meaning as a step in the wrong direction, a fall into the human world of meaning, progression, linearity, and all the rest of the fundamentally human experience that Cioran wishes to cancel. Aurélien Demers identifies three potential solutions to the problem of irredeemable human experience as Cioran defines it, namely, via the child, the primitive, or the insane, but goes on to demonstrate why all of these are not ultimately tenable as potential solutions: "the child possesses an enviable but ephemeral and unrecoverable destiny, the primitive enjoys a relatively preferable but impossible condition, the crazy man has received a touch of the providential hand of chance on his existence, but his luck is inaccessible. […] One thus never escapes the fatality of the fall. What *makes* the fall is thus consciousness" (Demers 167).

Once meaning is established with the naming of the universe and the things in it, the drama of humanity's perdition and then its potential redemption is put in motion, and this is precisely the narrative that Cioran wishes to invalidate by invalidating all sense of linear temporal progression. His own writings, often taking the form of isolated fragments, perform the kind of change he advocates by refusing to follow a narrative scheme or a systematic progression of argument. This refusal of narrative echoes the refusal of the idea of redemption, which is, at least before Agamben theorizes them as simultaneous, fundamentally temporal and linear in nature: a fall, followed by the cancellation of the fall. If one accepts even this basic minimum of redemptive structure, the Christian narrative appears to contain at least a "simulacrum of sense," which is precisely what we should refuse to pretend to give to lived reality. Instead, we should recognize the permanence of human corruption: "Aucunement accidentelle, notre corruption est permanente, elle est de toujours. De même l'iniquité: abusivement taxée de « mystère », elle est une évidence, elle est même ce qu'il y a de plus *visible* ici-bas, où remettre les choses en place exigerait un sauveur pour chaque génération, pour chaque individu plutôt" ["Not at all accidental, our corruption is permanent and from all time. The same goes for iniquity: abusively labeled a 'mystery,' it is something obvious, it is even what is most *visible* here below, where to put things back in place would require a savior for each generation, or rather for each individual"] (Pl 684). Recognizing what is immediately visible to us is what allows us successfully to surpass the logic of redemption and the linear temporality on which it depends.

But once again, this is no easy feat, despite the fact that it simply involves taking account of what is already visible to us in the world. This is so because salvation appears to us as a temptation, and like all temptations, its results are ultimately nefarious and lead us into error.

Le salut finit tout; et il nous finit. Qui, une fois *sauvé*, ose se dire encore vivant? On ne vit réellement que par le refus de se délivrer de la souffrance et comme par une tentation religieuse de l'irréligiosité. Le salut ne hante que les assassins et les saints, ceux qui ont tué ou dépassé la créature; les autres se vautrent—ivres morts—dans l'imperfection ... (Pl 27)

[Salvation finishes everything; and it finishes us. Who, once *saved*, dares to call himself still living? One only really lives by the refusal to deliver oneself from suffering and as if by a religious temptation of irreligiosity. Salvation haunts only assassins and saints, those who have killed or gone beyond the creature; others wallow—dead drunk—in imperfection ...]

Salvation joins God and existence in a network of temptations to which we succumb by the act of living daily life. Cioran extends this analysis by calling hope a sickness, a position that would be difficult to defend without these preliminary observations about the related notion of salvation as a temptation:

Qui n'est pas imbu de la conviction que tout est vain? Mais qui ose en affronter les suites? L'homme à vocation métaphysique est plus rare qu'un monstre— et pourtant chaque homme contient virtuellement les éléments de cette vocation. [...] Nous ne pouvons renoncer à quoi que ce soit; cependant les évidences de la vanité sont à notre portée. Malades d'espoir, nous attendons toujours; et la vie n'est que l'attente devenue hypostase. Nous attendons tout— même le Rien plutôt que d'être réduits à une suspension éternelle, à une condition de divinité neutre ou de cadavre. Ainsi, le cœur qui s'est fait un axiome de l'Irréparable, en espère encore des surprises. L'humanité vit amoureusement dans les événements qui la nient .... (Pl 45)

[Who is not steeped in the conviction that all is vanity? But who dares to confront the consequences of that? The man with a metaphysical vocation is rarer than a monster—and yet each man contains virtually the elements of this vocation. [...] We cannot renounce anything; yet the proofs of vanity are within our reach. Sick with hope, we wait forever; and life is only a wait that has become hypostasis. We await everything—even the Nothing, rather than be reduced to an eternal suspension, to a condition of neutral divinity or cadaver. Thus, the heart that has made for itself an axiom of the Irreparable, still hopes for surprises from it. Humanity lives lovingly in events that negate it.]

The advantage of the sickness metaphor is that it removes the question of agency potentially inherent in the notion of temptation. In its place, sickness provides the context of our minds and bodies against or beyond our will in order to accomplish an action which is detrimental or destructive to us. Cioran's emphasis on our incapability to renounce, not only hope but anything else we might want, brings us back to the difficulty of thinking beyond redemption and suggests that it acts in a somewhat parasitic way on our thought, imposing its logic even on the most valiant attempts to think beyond it. The problem, then, is not so much that we cannot renounce hope but that we cannot even imagine what it would be like to do so. The same will be true of redemption, despite Cioran's many attempts to surpass it and fulfill the dictates of lucid knowledge. But as we shall see in the next chapter, an intermittent or temporary redemption is ultimately the furthest his own thought can take him.

Cioran overturns traditional thinking about redemption but not by a simple reversal. Again, a we have already seen with Baudelaire, simple negation, while it may be a stop on the way toward mature thinking, is not part of what I have been calling asoteriological thinking because such negation depends on the structure of redemption itself, in the same way that Satanism depends on the existence of Christianity in order to have any sense whatsoever. Rather, Cioran is seeking to think beyond the category of redemption itself precisely because of the killing effect it has on the human subject. But as we see yet again here, thinking beyond redemption also implies thinking beyond *endings*, not only in the eschatological sense but also in the expanded sense that we need to read in the assertion that "salvation finishes everything." The reason that no simple negation is possible in the case of salvation is that, since salvation brings a definitive and final answer, thinking beyond salvation necessarily implies a refusal of those kinds of answer.[9] Cioran's constant return to paradox is co-committant with his obsessive focus on salvation. Simona Modreanu identifies a link between paradox and the fall:

> Cioran sees paradox as the figure *par excellence* of the Fall, as a materialization of *difference*, irony of the human condition and verbal irony at the same time. Adam fell with an imperfect viaticum: a language inept at naming precisely and a thought insufficient for apprehending or circumscribing the Absolute; from whence comes the permanent discomfort that Cioran acknowledges in his existence and that paradox translates best, because it "expresses the incapacity to be *naturally* in the world" (499). (*Dieu* 47–8)

Moreover, the attempt to think beyond redemption necessarily results in paradox because any sort of definitive answer, even one that resembled damnation, would be dependent on the logic of redemption precisely because it is the logic of the definitive end.

Intriguingly, Cioran goes on in this same passage to link poetry to the refusal of redemption:

> Le tort de toute doctrine de la délivrance est de supprimer la poésie, climat de l'inachevé. Le poète se trahirait s'il aspirait à se sauver: le salut est la mort du chant, la négation de l'art et de l'esprit. Comment se sentir solidaire d'un aboutissement? Nous pouvons raffiner, jardiner nos douleurs, mais par quel moyen nous en émanciper sans nous suspendre? (Pl 27)

> [What every doctrine of deliverance does wrong is to suppress poetry, climate of the unfinished. The poet would betray himself if he aspired to save himself: salvation is the death of song, the negation of art and spirit. How to feel solidarity

with an end? We can refine, cultivate our sorrows, but by what means can we emancipate ourselves from them without suspending ourselves?]

We should avoid the temptation to read "poetry" here in the generalized and superficial sense of emotional excess in a romantic vein. Such a reading might be encouraged by the reference to suffering. But in light of the deeper and more complex connections we have been working out between philosophical and esthetic concerns or more specifically between metaphysics and poetry, Cioran explores territory here that we have traced in a complex intratemporal web between Baudelaire and Agamben. Those two writers have helped us see what is at stake in Cioran's remarks here, which is something far beyond the idea of redemption putting an end to physical or emotional pain. The poet betrays himself if he strives for redemption not because it is the poet's function to give voice to raw emotion but because redemption is linked to endings, and as we have seen, the poem both strives toward and actively resists its own ending, which would be the end of the poem itself. Thus the poet must always reach a compromise solution between, on the one hand, abandoning poetry itself by accepting the logic of redemption and, on the other, remaining incapable of ending a poem and thus fulfilling the creative act.

But if it is impossible definitively to abandon hope, poetry's status becomes problematic, since Cioran describes poetry as a corrective to hope:

Entre la poésie et l'espérance, l'incompatibilité est complète; aussi le poète est-il victime d'une ardente décomposition. Qui oserait se demander comment il a ressenti la vie quand c'est par la mort qu'il a été vivant? Lorsqu'il succombe à la tentation du bonheur,—il appartient à la comédie…Mais si, par contre, des flammes émanent de ses plaies, et qu'il chante la félicité—cette incandescence voluptueuse du malheur—il se soustrait à la nuance de vulgarité inhérente à tout accent positif…. (Pl 95)

[Between poetry and hope, the incompatibility is complete; therefore the poet is the victim of an ardent decomposition. Who would dare wonder how he felt life when it is by death that he was living? When he succumbs to the temptation of happiness,—he belongs to the comedy…. But if, on the other hand, flames emanate from his wounds, and he sings his felicity—that voluptuous incandenscence of unhappiness—he subtracts himself from the hint of vulgarity inherent in all positive accent….]

Cioran leads us to two competing versions of the way to go on with life, since both poetry and hope fulfill the function of allowing life to continue, yet they are at odds with each other, which suggests that one of the two should be incompatible with life's continuation. The end of either poetry or hope would be the end of existence, but in the case of Cioran it is not possible to affirm definitively that existence is preferable to non-existence. In fact, just the opposite may be true, but again, in the absence of our ability to experience nothingness, a definitive position is impossible, and at any rate a definitive position-taking would constitute the kind of definitive end that all of Cioran's thought and style refuse. The temporal space of his writing is, rather, messianic in Agamben's sense; his writing represents the time it takes for time to come to an end rather than itself coming to rest, conceptually or esthetically, in an end itself.[10]

All of this might seem to lead to a clear and definitive, if at first counterintuitive, conclusion. If God and existence are temptations, if nothingness is at least hypothetically better than existence, and if redemption is not a helpful but an illusory category, it would seem that redemption would lie in getting beyond redemption. Cioran in fact states this in *De l'inconvénient d'être né*: "La certitude qu'il n'y a pas de salut est une forme de salut, elle est même *le* salut. À partir de là on peut aussi bien organiser sa propre vie que construire une philosophie de l'histoire. L'insoluble comme solution, comme seule issue ... " ["The certainty that there is no salvation is a form of salvation, it is even salvation itself. From there one can organize one's own life as well as construct a philosophy of history. The insoluble as solution, as the only way out ... "] (Pl 886). So abandoning salvation is itself a salvation: while the formulation is paradoxical, it is consistent with virtually all of Cioran's reflections on related topics. We seem to have arrived at a satisfying conclusion: salvation is illusory and dangerous, and while it may seem undesirable to try to get beyond it, it is in our best interests to do so, and liberation from an illusion about our own good lies in the balance.

Such a simple and categorical answer is not, however, possible, and not just because humans hold their illusions dear. First of all, certitude is itself a problematic category in Cioran. Bringing thought and writing to a definitive end in certitude is not the same as bringing existence to an end in nothingness, and while we continue to exist, it is impossible to assert certitude, according to Cioran's most powerful assertions. Other aspects of Cioran's thought mitigate the definitive abandoning of redemption as a category. Even the statement I have just quoted and provisionally labeled definitive does not withstand scrutiny; in fact it demonstrates its own impossibility. If knowing that there is no salvation is salvation, we are effectively locked in the logic of salvation, and not just because it is a comforting illusion. Removing the comforting illusion does nothing to remove the redemptive logic at work in affirming no redemption as a kind of redemption; the more we attempt to think beyond that category, the further we become mired in it. Moreover, Cioran's statement could in fact be read as a critique, and not an assertion, of the position that getting beyond salvation is itself redemptive: salvation is illusory, and certitude about the lack of salvation is salvation and is thus illusory. Seeing the statement as a critique is in line with what Cioran would often imply about such activities as "organizing one's life" and "constructing a philosophy of history," both of which seem like impossible tasks according to much of Cioran's writing. So while the statement about certitude of no salvation seems definitive, it itself escapes condemnation as a dead end by being legible simultaneously in two contradictory senses. At the moment when Cioran seems closest to certainty and to definitive assertion, he is in fact most fully mired in duality. This, then, is our first suggestion of an answer to the question of why it cannot be so easy as to assert the end of salvation, and our attempt to explain why this is the case leads us to the heart of Cioran's thought, the notion of the fall, which links the lack of redemption to an irrepressible duality. Thus we need to take a closer look at his writing on original sin and the fall in order to gain deeper insight into his infinite struggle with redemptive logic. We shall see in the next chapter that, as was the case with all the theological terrain we have examined so far, Cioran both depends on and subverts it, removing theological discourse from the category of belief and assigning it greater heuristic value than myth but stopping short of elevating it to a systematic philosophy.

The Eternal Fall: Cioran

Cioran's conception of the fall is multifaceted and articulated throughout his work, sometimes in brief references and sometimes in more elaborated development. The idea of the fall for which he is best known is the double conception of it as a fall both into and out of time. We shall consider this idea further below, but it would be far too simple to frame Cioran's notion of the fall around a single idea, given the weight it has as a foundational concept it has in all of his thought. As an originally theological concept, it holds primacy over all other explanatory conceptualizations, even though it is important to emphasize, once again, the separation we should maintain here from traditional questions of belief. Cioran comments on this distinction in the *Cahiers* [*Notebooks*]: "Je ne crois pas au Péché dans le sens chrétien. Mais je crois que l'homme est un animal *marqué*, qu'il est réellement affecté d'une tare initiale, et c'est grâce à elle qu'il a glissé de la condition animale à la condition humaine" ["I do not believe in Sin in the Christian sense. But I believe man is a *marked* animal, that he is really affected by an initial stain, and that it is thanks to that that he slid from the animal condition to the human condition"] (C 639). Best, then, to see the theological as a competing discourse with philosophy, psychology, and so on, and as the winner in that competition precisely because the way Cioran appropriates theological discourse gives it tremendous heuristic power and allows us to see competing approaches as an outgrowth of theology rather than its competitor. Thus, for instance, this comment from the *Cahiers*: "La fameuse « agressivité » que Freud a présentée comme une grande découverte est une des composantes essentielles du Péché originel. La psychanalyse est pour l'essentiel tributaire de la théologie. Chez l'une et l'autre, la même vision impitoyable de l'homme" ["The famous 'aggressivity' that Freud presented as a great discovery is one of the essential components of Original Sin. Psychoanalysis is essentially a tributary of theology. In both, the same merciless vision of man"] (C 630). Given the overarching importance of the fall, it is thus necessary to establish a web of related concepts which Cioran addresses near and through his considerations of it. First of all, Cioran continues Baudelaire's use of the fall as a critique of, or corrective to, the notion of progress. The fall's cancellation of linear time precludes a notion of development by condemning humans to an eternal return to the conditions of the fall:

Tout pas en avant, toute forme de dynamisme comporte quelque chose de satanique: le « progrès » est l'équivalent moderne de la Chute, la version profane de la damnation. Et ceux qui y croient et en sont les promoteurs, nous tous en définitive, que sommes-nous sinon des réprouvés en marche, prédestinés à l'immonde, à ces machines, à ces villes, dont seul un désastre exhaustif pourrait nous débarrasser. Ce serait là pour nos inventions l'occasion ou jamais de prouver leur utilité et de se réhabiliter à nos yeux. (Pl 541)

[Every step forward, every form of dynamism includes something satanic: "progress" is the modern equivalent of the Fall, the profane version of damnation. And those who believe in it and are its promoters, all of us no doubt, what are we if not condemned ones on the move, predestined to the vile, to these machines, these cities, of which one exhaustive disaster could rid us. That would be the now-or-never chance for our inventions to prove their utility and rehabilitate themselves in our eyes.]

There are echoes here of Baudelaire's satanic revolt as an effort to break through *ennui* toward potential action, even if it is the negative action of the disaster. But, like Baudelaire, Cioran is unable to confirm the desirability or even the possibility of the catastrophic "solution" to the problem of the fall, since it is hard to see how the catastrophe could do anything but reinforce the conditions of the fall that it purportedly cancels. Cioran extends this critique of progress by identifying the way each attempt to surpass our humanity only leads us further away from our ability to transcend ourselves: "On peut attribuer à une tare cette force centrifuge, cette force funeste qui l'éloigne [l'homme] de lui-même; plus il cherche sa vraie nature, plus il s'en écarte et la fuit, et quand il sera arrivé à l'extrême de cette fuite, il éclatera ou sombrera" ["One can attribute to a stain this centrifugal force, this diastrous force that moves [man] away from himself; the more he seeks his true nature, the more he distances himself from it and flees it, and when he arrives at the end of this flight, he will explode or sink"] (C 639).

A key passage of the *Précis* extends Cioran's interpretation of the fall while identifying the breach with traditional theology's linkage of the fall and redemption:

Qu'est-ce que la Chute sinon la poursuite d'une vérité et l'assurance de l'avoir trouvée, la passion pour un dogme, l'établissement dans un dogme [...]. Un être possédé par une croyance et qui ne chercherait pas à la communiquer aux autres, –est un phénomène étranger à la terre, où l'obsession du salut rend la vie irrespirable ... regardez autour de vous: partout des larves qui prêchent [...]. L'envie de devenir source d'*événements* agit sur chacun comme un désordre mental ou comme une malédiction voulue. La société, –un enfer de sauveurs! Ce qu'y cherchait Diogène avec sa lanterne, c'était un *indifférent*. (Pl 4)

[What is the fall if not the pursuit of a truth and the assurance of having found it, the passion for a dogma, establishment in a dogma [...]. A being possessed by a belief and who would not seek to communicate it to others, — is a phenomenon foreign to the earth, where the obssession of salvation render life unbreathable … look around you: everywhere larvae who preach […]. The desire to become a source of *events* acts on each person like a mental disorder or a welcome curse. Society—a hell of saviors! What Diogenes was looking for with his lantern was an *indifferent* person.]

Paradoxically at first glance, remaining faithful to the logic of the fall would thus require forgetting the traditional ways in which the consequences of the fall are lived. The movement that Cioran traces here is a fundamentally negative one that attempts to rebuild the notion of the fall on a different basis and with significantly different consequences for a philosophy of lived experience. Not surprisingly, a reconsideration of salvation appears at the heart of this challenge to traditional thinking about the fall. But the first move here is to establish distance between the fall and certitude, no easy feat for a thinker who expresses such certainty each time he addresses the question of humanity's tainted fallen nature. The solution at which he arrives involves not so much the existence of certainty but the kinds of consequences for action that one draws from that certainty. Cioran establishes a break between certitude and action by refusing to proclaim, as opposed to simply living out, the certainty of the fall. Already the fall is double here: Cioran the theorist of the fall, who is, by virtue of that role, committed to the notion of the fall, separates himself from the proselytizers of the fall, who only proclaim it because of their remaining within the logic of salvation. For them, salvation originates from proclaiming the fall, presumably with an eye toward its cancelation. To be caught in the logic of redemption is, however, another sign of the fall, given that redemption is impossible; those who cannot get beyond redemption are enmeshed even further in the consequences of the fall. So for both Cioran's speaking subject and for the proclaimers of the fall from whom he distances himself, the fall is operational. Lucidity about its irreparability does nothing to cancel its effects while proclaiming it only buries us deeper in its consequences. Such a totalizing phenomenon will not allow a loosening of its effects; it is for this reason that, as we have already seen, knowledge that there can be no salvation cannot itself be a form of salvation. If Cioran's speaking voice here takes on something of the prophet, it is only to condemn and refuse even a trace of soteriological logic; that logic is, as Cioran indicates, what makes life "unbreatheable," and therefore we need to see any salvific promise to make life more bearable as a contributor to that unbreatheable atmosphere.

Rather than casting an eye at a future-oriented redemption, the best we can do is to engage in fictions in order to be able to continue to live, since lucidity about the possibility of redemption, release, or progress renders other options impossible.[1] The Cioranian subject still engaging with the world must do so in the domain of the as-if; this is the realm of fictions not as dangerous illusion but rather as a hypothesis whose validity must be declared impossible but which allows us to function in the world in the absence of a perceivable passage into non-existence. There is more to say about the role of fiction for Cioran, but for now, it suffices to note its potential as an alternative to the discourse of redemption, a positively valued kind of lucid illusion that Cioran opposes to history, which the French Cioran consistently dismisses as not only illusory but dangerous, the worst kind of delusion on account of its horrific consequences. Cioran's post-World War II engagement with the idea of history is a wholesale dismissal of his early political engagement which sought the transformation of his native Romania through a misguided alliance with fascism, a view on which he comments in 1970 in his *Cahiers*: "C'est la pire folie de ma jeunesse [...]. Si je suis guéri d'une maladie, c'est bien celle-là" ["It is the worst folly of my youth [...]. If I am cured of one sickness, it is surely that one"] (C 832).[2] His later view of history condemns the pursuit of historical progress or transformation by both the right and the left, both of which fall prey too easily to the myth of the betterment of humanity, with the disastrous and bloody consequences we see lived out in the twentieth century as in any other period that dedicated itself to such misguided ends as human improvement:

> L'Histoire: manufacture d'idéaux ... , mythologie lunatique, frénésie des hordes et des solitaires ... , refus d'envisager la réalité telle quelle, soif mortelle de fictions [...]. Mais vivre, c'est s'aveugler sur ses propres dimensions ... [...]. Qui, avec la vision exacte de sa nullité, tenterait d'être efficace et de s'ériger en sauveur? (Pl 6)

> [History: factory of ideals ... , lunatic mythology, frenzy of hordes and solitaries ... , refusal to envisage reality as is, deadly thirst for fictions [...]. But to live is to blind oneself about one's own dimensions ... [...]. Who, with a precise vision of his nullity, would attempt to be effective and to set himself up as a savior?]

Several categories of Cioran's thought come together here, with history aligned with redemption and refused outright while the proper pursuit becomes the appropriate attitude toward fiction as lucid tool for living rather than vehicle of the "lunatic mythology" of history and its worst kind of realization of illusory thought through bloody action.[3] As Sylvain David indicates, Cioran "does not directly evoke his error and aberrations [...] but he transposes the problematic of adhesion to common values to an ontological, absolute level. [...] By doing this, Cioran finds himself projecting on all of humanity what, at its origin, constitutes a personal mistake" (David 31), an important move in what David calls Cioran's "negative heroism" (31).

The question is thus not one of illusion versus truth but rather of distinguishing between nourishing and poisoning fictions in the realm of quasi-lucidity which is the only conceptual zone in which any kind of living activity is possible for Cioran. It is crucial not to try to overcome belief but rather to come to consciousness of belief as belief, in order to remain within the realm of nourishing fiction. In a passage whose opening ideas echo the famous opening of *Les Fleurs du Mal* in their evocation of "la sottise, l'erreur, le péché, la lésine" ["folly, error, sin, avarice"] which "occupent nos esprits et travaillent nos corps" ["occupy our minds and labor our bodies" (3)] (OC1: 5), Cioran declares:

> Nous croyons tous à bien plus de choses que nous ne pensons, [...] et, défendant nos idées avec des moyens extrêmes, nous parcourons le monde comme des

forteresses ambulantes et irréfragables. Chacun est pour soi-même un dogme suprême; nulle théologie ne protège son dieu comme nous protégeons notre moi; et ce moi, si nous l'assiégeons de doutes, et le mettons en question, ce n'est que par une fausse élégance de notre orgueil: la cause est gagnée d'avance. (Pl 58)

We all believe in many more things than we think, […] and, defending ideas with extreme measures, we travel the world like walking uncontradictable fortresses. Each one is for himself a supreme dogma; no theology protects its god the way we protect our self; and this self, if we besiege it with doubts and put it in question, it is only by a false elegance of our pride: the cause is won in advance.]

This passage suggests that there can be a tyranny of thought as well as action; certainty in one's convictions leads to poisonous cognitive as well as historical results. What masquerades as positive or creative energy in defending ideas becomes a destructive force precisely because a basis of certainty can never be established, thus making the coercive power of thought inherent in the thought itself rather than in any externally verified source. In light of the possibility of fictions becoming a danger rather a vehicle for living, we need to inquire whether redemption can be a fiction of the non-totalizing, healthy variety, given that Cioran has linked it to history by virtue of their common teleological orientation. Can the notion of salvation itself be saved by considering it a fiction in a positive sense? As long as we are lucid about the fictional nature of salvation, can we admit it as an appropriate conceptual framework?

The answer, based on the passage just quoted, has to be no, because of salvational logic's totalizing nature. The very fact that it is difficult, if not impossible, to think beyond redemption clearly indicates that by Cioran's criteria, soteriology is a totalizing discourse that manifests itself tyrannically, not necessarily by always presenting itself as dogmatic but rather by not allowing a space by which we might think beyond it. Salvational logic in this sense "colonizes" all other thought and pushes us in the direction of certainty rather than doubt, making it difficult to maintain salvational logic at the level of fiction in the positive sense, and reinforcing the link that Cioran establishes between redemption and history. What certainty of historical vision does to the historical actor, salvational logic does to the thinker even if the thinker attempts to deny the certainty of that logic, and thus salvational logic becomes even more insidious than historical logic, since the latter does allow conceptual space for thinking beyond it.

Once again, poetry comes to play an important role in articulating some of the relationships we have been tracing here among history, redemption, and lucid illusion. While Cioran's comments on poetry are fewer in number than his references to these other topics, a careful reading of those remarks can provide helpful insight into the way Cioran attempts to think through and beyond soteriological discourse.

Mais un Shelley, mais un Baudelaire, mais un Rilke interviennent au plus profond de notre organisme qui se les annexe ainsi qu'il le ferait d'un vice. Dans leur voisinage, un corps se fortifie, puis s'amollit et se désagrège. Car le poète est un agent de destruction, un virus, une maladie déguisée et le danger le plus grave, encore que merveilleusement imprécis, pour nos globules rouges. Vivre dans ses parages, c'est sentir le sang s'amincir, c'est rêver un paradis de l'anémie, et entendre, dans les veines, des larmes ruisseler .... (Pl 967)

[But a Shelley, a Baudelaire, a Rilke intervenes in the deepest part of our organism which annexes them as it would a vice. In their vicinity, a body fortifies itself, then softens and disintegrates. For the poet is an agent of destruction, a virus, a disguised illness and the most serious danger, even though marvelously imprecise, for our red corpuscles. To live in his vicinity is to feel one's blood thin and to dream of a paradise of anemia and to hear, in one's veins, tears streaming ....]

Like many of Cioran's comments on poetry, this one at first seems to reveal a straightforward and not terribly interesting or original point, that is, that poets are decadent or degenerate and thus, as has been repeated since Plato, have a nefarious effect on their audience. In the larger context of Cioran's thought, however, a more complex reading emerges from the concept of the poet as "agent of destruction." Given the positive role that destruction has in terms of bringing us out of the dogmatic slumber that Cioran identifies with the dangerous fictions and mythologies that generate the catastrophes of history and its action, poets play an important role here. If they turn us away from our taste for acting in the world, that can only be to our advantage under the conditions of Cioranian lucidity. The "danger" is only operative for our selves as we normally construct them in the haze of the illusions that allow us to continue normal functioning in the world.

In that sense, the poets are agents not only of destruction but of the kind of lucidity that would generate the positive kinds of fiction that allow us to live without falling prey to the dangerous kind of illusions. In that sense, poets become a kind of model for how to mitigate between the lucidity that leads to total inaction and agency in the world that leads to illusion. As artistic creators, poets already navigate the terrain of lucid illusion, a point to which we shall have occasion to return. Cioran confirms the reading of the advantages of the supposedly "dangerous" poets by rendering more explicit the way in which poets can perform the work of philosophers better than the philosophers themselves, still in a corrective or destructive mode:

Bien plutôt qu'à l'école des philosophes, c'est à celle des poètes qu'on apprend le courage de l'intelligence et l'audace d'être soi-même. Leurs « affirmations » font pâlir les propos les plus étrangement impertinents des sophistes anciens. Personne ne les adopte: y eut-il jamais un seul penseur qui fût allé aussi loin que Baudelaire [...]? (Pl 96)

[Rather than at the school of philosophers, it is at that of the poets that one learns the courage of intelligence and the audacity of being oneself. Their "affirmations" make the most strangely impertinent propositions of the ancient sophists pale in comparison. No one adopts them: was there ever a single thinker who went as far as Baudelaire [...]?]

If, as we have seen, Cioran posits his own writing voice as a kind of prophet, the poet as he is figured here becomes a kind of model. Rather than seeing maxims or prescriptions in the poems, we are asked to admire and imitate the mode of thought that generates the poetry, a participation in esthetic creation that involves the courage to situate oneself within doubt in a way that no systematic philosopher can allow himself to do without contradicting the very nature of a proposition.

At many points, then, Cioran tends toward a philosophy of practice, one rooted in a thought that would take lucid account of futility and the ideal of nothingness but that would nonetheless allow some kind of functioning, and some kind of thought *as* functioning, in the world. This linking of the esthetic and the ethical returns us to the terrain of redemption and allows us further insight into the way it functions for Cioran. We have already seen that it would be liberating to be rid of the idea of redemption, but this kind of liberation is impossible, so that the elimination of redemption becomes a kind of regulatory ideal, something to which we should aspire in full knowledge of the impossibility of fulfilling the goal. In that sense, asoteriology performs the kind of endlessness that it theorizes: if a refusal to come to an end is a hallmark of the attempt to think beyond redemption, since getting beyond redemption also means surpassing teleology and thus eschatology, then the endless and fruitless pursuit of the impossibility of redemption is the appropriate path to take. This puts us in a better position to understand Cioran's notion of an "Order of Impossible Salvation." The monastic reference enforces the notion of practice along with the idea of fidelity in thought and action to a guiding principle, in this case the easily demonstrable impossibility of salvation. The context is one of a religious practice without the trappings of belief in the traditional sense, one in which the creative work of the poets could be seen as a practice that enacts and reacts to the consequences of impossible salvation, a kind of creative destruction.

In all of this, there is an ambiguous relation to the concept of "mystery." The "Order of Impossible Salvation" itself will be, we recall, "un Ordre affranchi des mystères, et dont nul « frère » ne se réclamerait de rien, dédaignant son salut comme celui des autres" ["empancipated from mysteries, and of which no 'brother' would ask anything, disdaining his salvation and that of others"] (Pl 150). But as in the case of salvation itself, mystery is not so easy to refuse, and in some sense the practice of the hypothetical Order of Impossible Salvation would also involve conceiving and living out the consequences of this declared liberation from mystery. Elsewhere, Cioran writes:

> A l'aide de quels artifices trouverions-nous la force de l'illusion pour aller en quête d'une autre vie, d'une vie nouvelle? […] Je n'ai connu aucune vie « nouvelle » qui ne fût illusoire et compromise en ses racines. J'ai vu chaque homme avancer dans le temps pour s'isoler dans une rumination angoissée et retomber en lui-même, avec, en guise de renouvellement, la grimace imprévue de ses propres espoirs. (Pl 67–8)

> [With the aid of what artifice would we find the strength of illusion to go on a quest for another life, a new life? […] I have known no "new" life that was not illusory

and compromised at its roots. I have seen each man advance in time in order to isolate himself in an anguished rumination and to fall back in himself with, in the guise of renewal, the unexpected grimace of his own hopes.]

The question is far from merely rhetorical; the status of illusion, in its manifestation through thought, action, artistic creation, and so on, and in its link with or opposition to lucidity, is what is most at stake for Cioran when he is working through the consequences of asoteriology as a faithful practitioner in the Order of Impossible Salvation. The complexity of these questions, as it reveals itself in the web of contexts throughout Cioran's entire corpus, is what takes Cioran's thought and writing far from the world of adolescent pleasures of vituperation against the world. The resurging up from mystery into lucidity is always followed by a complication of the conceptual scenario that plunges us back into the arena of thought as praxis in the impossible yet crucial task of articulating, and then living, or articulating *while* living, the consequences of impossible salvation.

Poets are in a unique position for Cioran, for not only do they perform the destructive work that allows us to break through to lucidity, but they also, as we saw through Agamben and Baudelaire, struggle with what it means to live in the time of coming-to-an-end without actually achieving the end, via the nature of the poem as that which both pushes on toward its end and actively resists it. Moreover, their working in the medium of language also further implicates them in the consequences of Cioranian lucidity:

> Si par chaque mot nous remportons une victoire sur le néant, ce n'est que pour mieux en subir l'empire. Nous mourons en proportion des mots que nous jetons tout autour de nous. […] La vie n'est que cette impatience de déchoir, de prostituer les solitudes virginales de l'âme par le dialogue, négation immémoriale du Paradis. (Pl 17)

> [If by each word we score a victory over nothingness, it is only the better to fall under the influence of its empire. We die in proportion to the words that we throw around us. […] Life is only this impatience to demean oneself, to prostitute the virginal solitude of the soul by dialogue, immemorial negation of Paradise.]

Cioran's comment reminds us that that while esthetic creation might be a kind of temporary overcoming of nothingness, it cannot be itself a kind of redemption, as Nietzsche conceived it. The multifaceted conception of nihilism is evident here in that esthetic creation both cancels and participates in the nothingness. Neither simple negation nor construction, nothingness takes on a dynamic character that is evident in the proliferation of words by which and in which we live and die. Each word preferred is a robbery from the virtual into the actual. This is not to say, however, that silence has any salvific effect, since our silence is only the imitation of a genuine silence: "Point de salut, sinon dans l'*imitation* du silence. Mais notre loquacité est prénatale. Race de phraseurs, de spermatozoides verbeux, nous sommes *chimiquement* liés au

Mot" ["No salvation at all, unless in the *imitation* of silence. But our loquacity is prenatal. Race of sentence-makers, verbose spermatozoids, we are *chemically* linked to the Word"] (Pl 176).

In *La Tentation d'Exister* [*The Temptation to Exist*], Cioran continues to associate poets and a creative form of nihilism linked to the poet's destructive work on the ordinary use of language, itself a kind of refusal of everyday reality and its alliance with illusion:

> Le poète, lui, […] prend le langage au sérieux. Il s'en crée un à sa façon. Toutes ses singularités procèdent de son intolérance aux mots tels quels. Inapte à en supporter la banalité et l'usure, il est prédestiné à souffrir à cause d'eux et pour eux; et cependant c'est par eux qu'il essaie de se sauver, c'est de leur régénération qu'il attend son salut. Quelque grinçante que soit sa vision des choses, il n'est jamais un vrai négateur. (Pl 400)

> [The poet […] takes language seriously. He creates himself one in his own manner. All his singularities proceed from his intolerance of words as they are. Incapable of tolerating the banality and wear of them, he is predestined to suffer because of them and for them; and yet it is by them that he attempts to save himself, it is from their regeneration that he awaits his salvation. No matter how grating his vision of things may be, he is never a true negator.]

We can ask the same question about poets as we can about Cioran's speaking subject himself: is it in fact ever possible to be "a true negator?" Does absolute negation act as a kind of regulatory ideal, or is there in fact a way to be a "true" nihilist? The passage reveals more about the complex status of nihilism for Cioran than it does about the task of the poet, who in this instance seems, again like Cioran's speaking subject, an intensified version of the human subject generally, given as he is to nihilism while unable to sustain an actual affirmation of nothingness, and accomplishing creative work that both destroys and affirms. Cioran makes an exception for the poets not because they have access to "truth" (in fact, they operate fully within illusion), but because of their particular kind of illusion:

> Puisque le poète est un monstre qui tente son salut par le mot, et qu'il supplée au vide de l'univers par le symbole même du vide (car le mot est-il autre chose?), pourquoi ne le suivrions-nous pas dans son exceptionnelle illusion? Il devient notre recours toutes les fois que nous désertons les fictions du langage courant pour nous en chercher d'autres, insolites, sinon rigoureuses. Ne semble-t-il pas alors que toute autre irréalité est préférable à la nôtre, et qu'il y a plus de substance dans un vers que dans tous ces mots trivialisés par nos conversations ou nos prières? Que la poésie doive être accessible ou hermétique, efficace ou gratuite, c'est là un problème secondaire. Exercice ou révélation, qu'importe. Nous lui demandons, nous autres, qu'elle nous délivre de l'oppression, des affres du discours. Si elle y réussit, elle fait *pour un instant*, notre salut. (Pl 400–1)

[Since the poet is a monster who attempts his salvation by the words, and since he replaces the void of the universe with the very symbol of the void (for is the word anything else than that?), why would we not follow him in his exceptional illusion? He becomes our recourse every time that we desert our fictions of ordinary language in order to seek others, unusual, if not rigorous. Does it not seem then that all other unreality is preferable to ours, and that there is more substance in a line of poetry than in all those words trivialized by our conversations or our prayers? That our poetry must be accessible or hermetic, effective or gratuitous is a secondary problem. Exercise or revelation, what does it matter? We ask of it, we others, that it deliver us from oppression, from the torments of discourse. If it succeeds, it makes, *for an instant*, our salvation.]

It is significant that it is in the context of poetry that Cioran presents this crucial observation about redemption, one to which we shall return in greater detail, namely, that if any redemption is available to us at all, it is as a temporary phenomenon. By this conception of redemption, Cioran distinguishes himself from the other writers we have been considering, for whom presumably redemption is either permanent or non-existent. For now, it is important to note that this redemption is not simply synonymous with illusion, as, for instance, altered states of consciousness might be for others who hint at temporary redemption. Rather, this temporary redemption is linked specifically and exclusively to language: poets save us from "the torments of discourse," in ways that Cioran does not enumerate more specifically here.

If we take into consideration the link between language and fiction, we can begin to make the link between linguistic redemption and other modes. Fictions, we recall, are a kind of lucid illusion, entirely constructed in and through language, so the work of the poets, though not in narrative form, allows us to free existing words from their long-established contexts in order not so much to remove ourselves from illusion as to reshape those illusions consciously. Cioran goes so far as to equate our existence and our fictions:

Nous durons tant que durent nos fictions. [...] Exister équivaut à un acte de foi, à une protestation contre la vérité, à une prière interminable ... Dès lors qu'ils consentent à vivre, l'incrédule et le dévot se ressemblent en profondeur, puisque l'un et l'autre ont pris la seule décision qui marque un être. (Pl 427)

[We last as long as our fictions last. [...] Existing equals an act of faith, a protest against the truth, an interminable prayer .... As soon as they consent to live, the faithless person and the devout one resemble each other deeply, since both have made the only decision that marks a being.]

This passage, while affirming what Cioran claims about the impossibility of perceiving the desired state of nothingness, further highlights the impossibility of surpassing religious structures of thought even as we reject belief in a God. The challenge then becomes escaping the logic of redemption while being forced to remain inside the proto-Christian structures of thought or action, that is, the gesture of living in the first place. The production of illusion that we call living can be seen as either a heroic protest or a taking refuge in illusion. But once again artistic creation and lived experience as creation are brought together as similar acts, both stripped of their redemptive aspect, at least in any permanent sense.

One specific literary mode of living the consequences of the unavailability of redemption is that of tragedy, which allows us to see new meaning in a version of the story of Jesus stripped of the resurrection: "Si Jésus avait fini sa carrière sur la croix, et qu'il ne se fût pas engagé à ressusciter, –quel beau héros de la tragédie! Son côté divin a fait perdre à la littérature un admirable sujet. […] Rien de plus étranger à la tragédie que l'idée de rédemption, de salut et d'immortalité!" ["If Jesus had finished his career on the cross and had not been engaged in rising from the dead,—what a beautiful tragic hero! His divine side made literature lose an admirable subject. […] Nothing more foreign to tragedy than the idea of redemption, salvation and immortality!"] (Pl 82). Far from shutting down literary creation, then, the removal of salvation enables it, while preserving the notion of salvation inhibits it. To understand why, it is helpful to turn to Paul Audi's notion of paradise in his theory of esthetics. For Audi, paradise is the (conceptual) space where everything is possible. While this sounds inviting, if everything is possible, then everything is also virtual, and nothing is actual:

> qu'au paradis tout soit possible, cela signifie qu'aucun possible n'y est *à soi*. Rien de cette virtualité pure (de cette virtualité inentamée par une quelconque actualisation des possibles), rien qui relève de ce champ de possibilités ouvert au maximum « n'appartient » à qui que ce soit. C'est ce qui explique que le « péché »–l'acte qui cause la « chute », ce terme désignant *l'assignation de soi à la finitude, c'est-à-dire l'assignation à soi d'un ensemble réduit de possibles*— resulte de la « possession », c'est-à-dire d'une décision consistant à *s'appoprier un possible*. (Audi 242)

> [That everything be possible in paradise signifies that no possible belongs to itself there. Nothing of this pure virtuality (of this virtuality unaccomplished by whatever actualization of possibilities), nothing from that field of possibilities open to maximum "belongs" to anybody at all. That is what explains that "sin"— the act that causes the "fall," that term designating *the assignation of the self to finitude, that is the assignation to oneself of a reduced totality of possibles*—results from "possession," that is, from a decision consisting of *appropriating a possible for oneself*.]

The conceptual space of paradise, which is the locus of redemption, inhibits esthetic production on account of the inability to move from the virtual to the real or actual: "Au paradis, non seulement tout est possible, mais *la possibilité est tout ce qu'il y a*" ["In paradise, not only is everything possible, but *possibility is all that there is*"].[4] This move is a crucial one for beginning to understand the role of sin in Cioran and its relationship to creation, both of the world and of art. Audi's conception of sin is helpful because he removes it from its traditional Christian connotations as disobedience to divine law and puts it squarely within a human context while still retaining the force of the original theological concept.

We are always already fallen, and always already unable to be redeemed, and this space of the real and unalterable is the world in which we operate. And as we have seen, operating is the next best thing to the impossible scenario of perceiving ourselves ceasing to exist altogether. This constant commitment to action is what distinguishes us, to our detriment, from animals according to Cioran:

> Loin de fuir la monotonie, les animaux la recherchent, et ce qu'ils redoutent le plus c'est de la voir cesser, car elle ne cesse que pour être remplacée par la peur, cause de tout affairement.
>
> L'inaction est divine. C'est pourtant contre elle que l'homme s'est insurgé. Lui seul, dans la nature, est incapable de supporter la monotonie, lui seul veut à tout prix que quelque chose arrive, n'importe quoi. Par là, il se montre indigne de son ancêtre: le besoin de nouveauté est le fait d'un gorille fourvoyé. (Pl 884)

> [Far from fleeing monotony, animals seek it out, and what they fear the most is to see it end, for it ceases only to be replaced by fear, cause of all bustling activity.
>
> Inaction is divine. It is, however, against it that man has revolted. Only he, in nature, is incapable of tolerating monotony, only he wants at all cost for something, anything, to happen. By that, he proves himself unworthy of his ancestor: the need for newness is the fact of a misled gorilla.]

Inoperativity is what the animals and the divinity have in common, and it is precisely the zone that is impossible for humans to occupy, in our position of opposition to both animals and divinities. If we follow Audi's lead in associating the fall, and thus what has traditionally been labeled "sin," with our necessary relegation to the realm of the actual as opposed to the potential or virtual, we have an atheistic yet theological account of the relation of sin to creation, and of artistic creation to other kinds of lived praxis. In order to be saved, on this account, we would need to be something other than human, and a saved humanity would be a fundamentally altered humanity precisely on account of its entry into inoperativity. Cioran lays out the basic foundation of his asoteriology already in the *Précis de décomposition*, but he goes on to develop the idea of the fall more extensively in his middle period, in *La chute dans le temps* [*The Fall into Time*] (1964) in particular. Now that we have sketched the reason why the theological is of utmost importance to Cioran even though he separates it from any quetson of actual traditional belief in God, we can enter further into Cioran's recasting of original sin and the way it operates independently of any notion of Satan, disobedience, or potential cancellation through redemptive sacrifice.

Cioran's opening move in *La chute dans le temps* draws upon the fundamental duality of the human person that had theorized earlier:

Nous ne sommes réellement nous-mêmes que lorsque, dressés en face de soi, nous ne coïncidons avec rien, pas même avec notre singularité. La malédiction qui nous accable pesait déjà sur notre premier ancêtre, bien avant qu'il se tournât vers l'arbre de la connaissance. Insatisfait de lui-même, il l'était encore plus de Dieu qu'il enviait sans en être conscient; il allait le devenir grâce aux bons offices du tentateur, auxiliaire plutôt qu'auteur de sa ruine. (Pl 523)

[We are only truly ourselves when, standing in front of ourselves, we do not coincide with anything, not even with our singularity. The curse that weighs us down already weighed on our first ancestor, well before he turned toward the tree of knowledge. Unsatisfied with himself, he was even more so with God whom he envied without being conscious of it; he was going to become conscious thanks to the good services of the tempter, auxiliary rather than author of his ruin.]

From the start it is evident that Cioran retains only the general conceptual outlines of the story of the fall and posits an extremely unorthodox interpretation. The first major departure from traditional interpretation is also a departure from Baudelaire's own take on the fall, equally central to his thought and writing but derived from different initial assumptions. Of particular note is that original sin predates the encounter at the Tree of Knowledge, and is thus not the result of any temptation. In this Cioran distinguished himself from Joseph de Maistre, whom he identifies as an admirable thinker but from whom he, like Baudelaire, he takes his distance, especially around questions of original sin and redemption. Cioran writes that de Maistre

se trompe lorsqu'il ramène le Péché à une trangression primitive, à une faute immémoriale et concertée, au lieu d'y voir une tare, un vice de nature; il se trompe également quand, après avoir parlé à juste titre d'une « maladie originelle », il l'attribue à nos iniquités, alors qu'elle était, ainsi que le Péché, inscrite dans notre essence même: dérèglement primordial, calamité affectant indifféremment le bon et le méchant, le vertueux et le vicieux. (Pl 1143)

[is mistaken when he traces Sin back to a primitive transgression, to an immemorial and concerted fault rather than seeing in it a stain, a vice of nature; he is mistaken equally when, after having spoken rightly of an "original malady," he attributes it to our iniquities, whereas it was, as Sin was, inscribed in our very essence: primordial undoing, calamity indifferently affecting the good and the bad, the virtuous and the vicious.]

Human duality is, for Cioran unlike for de Maistre, irredeemable. Just as inoperativity is central to our definition as human beings, so too is the inherent duality of the human person, not so much in the sense of a tension between good and evil (those terms are conspicuously absent here) but in a distance from self that is constitutive of the human. Knowledge of this duality is, as it was also for Fondane, the main consequence of this primal scene, rather than disobedience to a divine command or even a rupture with an original wholeness. It follows naturally from this interpretation that the devil is reduced to the role of accomplice, an almost unnecessary figure rather than a central character in the drama. In that sense, Cioran's theology corresponds to Jean-Luc Nancy's notion of the auto-deconstruction of Christianity. The resulting atheistic theology leaves the place of God open and empty and retains the force of a theological vision without an all-powerful God driving it. According to Nancy, God must necessarily disappear into the world at the moment of creation (otherwise there would then be two worlds), "and with this disappearance a decisive episode of the entire movemement that I have sometimes named the 'deconstruction of Christianity' occurs" which would be "the integral absenting of God in the unity that reduces it in and where it dissolves" (*Creation* 68).[5]

Also crucial here is the emphasis on knowledge rather than eternal life, as humanity's aspiration:

L'homme […] ne demandait qu'à mourir; voulant égaler son Créateur par le savoir, non par l'immortalité, il n'avait nul désir d'approcher de l'arbre de vie, n'y portait aucun intérêt; c'est ce dont Yahweh parut s'aviser, puisqu'il ne lui en interdit même pas l'accès; pourquoi craindre l'immortalité d'un *ignorant*? (Pl 524)

[Man […] asked only to die; wanting to equal his Creator by knowledge, not by immortality, he had no desire to approach the tree of life, was not at all interested in it; that is what Yahweh seemed to realize, since he did not even forbid him access to it; why fear the immortality of *one who does not know*?]

Cioran retains the notion of humanity's having been created in God's image, but once again, he reinterprets the meaning of that idea based on a non-traditional identification of the attributes of God: for Cioran, what we share with God is his inability to be happy: "En lui se manifestait déjà cette inaptitude au bonheur, cette incapacité de le supporter dont nous avons tous hérité. […] Qu'attendre d'autre d'une carrière commencée par une infraction à la sagesse, par une infidelité au *don d'ignorance* que le Créateur nous avait dispensé?" ["In him manifested itself already that inaptitude for happiness, that incapacity to tolerate it that we have all inherited. […] What else to expect from a career begun by an infraction to wisdom, by an infidelity to the *gift of ignorance* that the Creator had dispensed to us?"] (Pl 524). If humans are defined by their distance from themselves, there is continuity with the notion of God here, who, in order to create, needed to make something that would be differentiated from himself; thus one could see the act of creation itself as a distancing of God from himself, from a unity to a multiplicity of being. Moreover, we inherit our inability to be happy not from Adam but from God himself, and thus by our very misery participate in the divine. For God to save us from this condition would mean the ability of God to save himself as well, a capacity clearly not in his power. What God could not have done for himself, he attempts to do for a humanity which then refuses the gift, and by doing so defines itself as human.

Cioran's idiosyncratic take on the fall sees it as double. Traditionally, the fall inaugurates historical time, putting into motion the series of events that will culminate, at the end of chronological time, in the messianic event which cancels the fall into history. Cioran acknowledges that fall but, speaking in his quasi-prophetic first-person singular in a way that de-individualizes that speaking subject, he asserts:

> Les autres tombent dans le temps; je suis, moi, tombé du temps. A l'éternité qui s'érigeait au-dessus de lui succède cette autre qui se place au-dessous, zone stérile où l'on n'éprouve qu'un seul désir: réintégrer le temps, s'y élever coûte que coûte, s'en approprier une parcelle pour s'y installer, pour se donner l'illusion d'un chez-soi. Mais le temps est clos, mais le temps est hors d'atteinte: et c'est de l'impossibilité d'y pénétrer qu'est faite cette éternité négative, cette *mauvaise* éternité. (Pl 612–13)

> [Others fall into time; as for me, I have fallen from time. Following on that eternity that built itself up above him is that other history that places itself beneath, in a sterile zone where one only feels one desire: to reintegrate time, to raise oneself in it whatever the costs, to appropriate a parcel of it in order to install oneself there, to give oneself the illusion of a home. But time is closed off, but time is beyond our grasp: and it is from the impossibility of entering it that is made this negative eternity, this *bad* eternity.]

The second fall, the fall *from* time, rather than correcting the effects of the first, repeats them, as Sylvie Jaudeau has remarked, "at another level since [the second fall] reproduces, with regard to time, the absolutist illusion of historical man with regard to the origin: fallen man places paradise, that he had formerly assimilated to eternity, in the temporal universe" (Jaudeau 39). At the end of *La chute dans le temps*, Cioran turns to the question of will in order to suggest that, if lack of it is a sickness, "la volonté elle-même en est une autre, pire encore" ["will itself is another, still worse one"] (Pl 618). If man were to attain the status of Nietzsche's overman, "il éclaterait sans doute et s'écroulerait sur lui-même. Et c'est par un détour grandiose qu'il serait amené alors à tomber du temps pour entrer dans l'éternité d'en bas, terme inéluctable où peu importe, en fin de compte, qu'il arrive par dépérissement ou par désastre" ["he would doubtless explode and would crumble on himself. And it is by a grandiose detour that he would thus be brought to fall from time to enter eternity from below, ineluctable endpoint where it matters little, finally, whether he enters by wasting away or by disaster"] (Pl 618). In place of the logic of slavation, Cioran sets up a no-win situation whereby humanity is forced to choose between two kinds of annihilation, the active one of history being the worse of the two options. In this key passage, Cioran definitively dismisses not only the Christian notion of redemption but also the modern philosophical echoes of it, as well as the political incarnations inherent in any notion of progress.

Like Fondane, Cioran places the desire to know at the heart of what he will characterize as original sin, a view incompatible with the notion that happiness could derive from acting on that desire:

> Le désir de connaître, empreint de perversité et de corruption, plus il nous tient, plus il nous rend incapables de demeurer *à l'intérieur* de quelque réalité que ce soit. […] Si l'homme avait eu la moindre vocation pour l'éternité, au lieu de courir vers l'inconnu, vers le nouveau, vers les ravages qu'entraine l'appétit d'analyse, il se fût contenté de Dieu, dans la familiarité duquel il prospérait. Il aspira à s'en émanciper, à s'en arracher, et y a réussi au-delà de ses espérances. (Pl 525)

> [The desire to know, imprinted with perversity and corruption, the more it holds us, the more it renders us incapable of remaining *on the inside* of any reality at all. […] If man had had the least vocation for eternity, instead of running toward the unknown, toward the new, toward the ravages that the appetite for analysis brings, he would have contented himself with God, in whose familiarity he was prospering. He aspired to emancipate himself, to tear himself away, and succeeded beyond his hopes.]

The sign that humanity was not cut out for eternity is *ennui*, the emotional manifestation of the metaphysical fact of incompatibility of human restlessness and divine changelessness. We recall that, for Baudelaire, satanic revolt is conceived as a potential point of exit from *ennui*, albeit one that eventually proves false. For Cioran, history itself plays an analogous role to Baudelaire's Satanism, a fruitless temptation as a potential remedy to *ennui*: "L'ennui au milieu du paradis fit naitre chez notre premier ancêtre un appétit d'abîme qui nous a valu ce défilé de siècles dont nous entrevoyons maintenant le terme. Cet appétit, véritable nostalgie de l'enfer, ne manquerait pas de ravager la race qui nous succéderait et d'en faire la digne héritière de nos travers" ["Ennui in the middle of paradise gave birth, in our first ancestor, to an appetite for the abyss which has gained us this parade of centuries of which we see the endpoint now. This appetite, a veritable nostalgia for hell, would not fail to ravage the race that would follow us and make it the worthy inheritor of our shortcomings"] (Pl 939). Despite the shift in emphasis to history, a pattern emerges in Cioran that is familiar from Baudelaire: given that divine redemption is impossible, we seek it in other channels, but remain blind to the fact that our incontrovertible doubleness renders any potential redemption impossible. Our being human has the consequence of revealing an aspiration to us while that aspiration must necessarily go unfulfilled.

On account of this, we have the right to be envious even of an insect, who easily attains what a human being cannot: "Ayant perdu le secret de la vie et emprunté un trop grand détour pour pouvoir le retrouver et réapprendre, [l'être humain] s'éloigne chaque jour un peu plus de son ancienne innocence, il déchoit sans arrêt de l'éternité" ["Having lost the secret of life and taken an overly large detour in order to find it and learn it again, [the human being] distances himself a little more each day from his former innocence, he falls away from eternity without stopping"] (Pl 526). Similarly, rats are also superior to us: "Comment ne pas reconnaître les avantages qu'a sur nous un rat, justement parce qu'il est rat et rien d'autre? Toujours différents, nous ne sommes nous-mêmes que dans la mesure où nous nous écartons de notre définition" ["How can we not recognize the advantages that a rat has over us, precisely because he is a rat and nothing else? Aways different, we are only ourselves to the extent that we separate ourselves from our definition"] (Pl 530). If we are defined by duality, that is, if our singularity is itself doubled, then we are condemned always to be at a distance from ourselves, always looking to bridge a gap to arrive at a coherent view of self that is, however, permanently inaccessible to us precisely because closing the gap would eliminate our self as we have known it: "Etre conscient, c'est être divisé d'avec soi, c'est se haïr" ["To be conscious is to be divided against oneself; it is to hate oneself"] (Pl 402). Cioran links this doubleness to our insatiable appetite for illusion; the illusion that we have a unified self to which we could somehow have access feeds other illusions, such as the improvement of ourselves, which itself stems from the illusion of superiority that we feel toward other animals. "Obnubilés par la métamorphose, par le possible, par la grimace imminente de nous-mêmes, nous accumulons de l'irréel et nous nous dilatons dans le faux, car dès qu'on se sait et qu'on se sent homme, on vise au gigantisme, on veut paraître plus grand que nature" ["Obsessed by metamorphosis, by the possible, by the imminent grimace of ourselves, we accumulate the unreal and we dilate ourselves in the false, for as soon as one knows and feels oneself to be a man, one aims at gigantism, one wants to seem bigger than nature"] (Pl 530). We should also note that Cioran here identifies the possible as the source of our perdition; this is precisely the defining characteristic of paradise as Audi defined it. When translated to the world, however, which is necessarily the realm of the actual as opposed to the virtual, precisely because we cannot cease all movement and operativity, the possible becomes a source of torment because we fall under the illusion that the possible is realizable, when in fact there is a radical incompatibility between the possible and the actual. The stakes are high if we fail to attain lucidity about the illusion of the possible.

Cioran is almost always concerned with describing things as they are, rather than as they could or should be. He does occasionally engage the level of the virtual, and these moments help solidify the distinction between the possible and the actual, or, as we have just framed it, the world of what we mught call paradise and the lived reality that opposes itself to it. In yet another condemnation of humanity's engagement in history, Cioran writes: "Au lieu de s'évertuer à se retrouver, à se rencontrer avec soi, […] il a tourné ses facultés vers l'extérieur, vers l'histoire. Les eût-il interiorisées, en eût-il modifié l'exercice et la direction, qu'il eût réussi à assurer son salut" ["Rather than striving to find himself again, to meet up with himself, […] he turned his faculties toward the exterior, toward history. Had he interiorized them, had he modified their exercise and direction, he would have succeeded in assuring his salvation"] (Pl 531). At first glance, this seems like an odd affirmation for a thinker like Cioran, in that it seems to advocate a rich interior life as leading to a satisfying human experience, as if we could be happier by being more reflective. But in light of the tortures of the mind that result from any kind of contemplative activity, Cioran could hardly affirm such a position, all the less so in that it seems so easy to accomplish this turn from exteriority to interiority here. Moreover, the fact that Cioran situates knowledge at the heart of what he labels original sin suggests that acts of contemplation, which would sink us even further into the heart of knowing, indicates that Cioran would need to suggest that Cioran reject interiority as a route to salvation. After all, the self only tortures itself by contemplating itself, because that contemplation only reveals the self's irreparable doubleness as a constitutive property, thus revealing that we get further from any desired unity of self the more we meditate on that condition, which can only divide us further from ourselves. The key here is in the hypothetical past of the last sentence that I've quoted. Given that Cioran simply cannot affirm that redemption was available to a humanity that refused it, we need to read this hypothetical beyond the surface level. Cioran cannot be suggesting that things could have been otherwise for humanity, given the duality that constitutes humanity as distinct from the animals. What he describes here, then, is pure virtuality, the existence of a conceptual space where redemption would have been possible. This space is what we can call "paradise," a place where everything is possible and, therefore, nothing is actual. Would this, then, be redemption? Yes and no, since there would have been no condition from which we would have needed to be saved, thus rendering the conceptual category of "redemption" inoperative. If rendering salvation inoperative is indeed a kind of salvation, it can only be in Agamben's sense of a virtuality, a "pure" salvation that saves nothing because it is without object. What is happening in this quoted passage, then, is that Cioran's writing becomes performative, illustrating the consequences of the fall as he characterizes it. For the fact that the speaking subject here can imagine a virtual world where there would have been some kind of salvation suggests the irrepareable divide between what we can imagine and what we know to be reality in terms not only of our condemnation to irreparable duality but, more importantly, of our consciousness of that duality. What the hypothetical mood indicates is the deep consequences of human knowledge as constitutive of the always already occurring fall.[6]

This idiosyncratic view of the fall is accompanied by an equally idiosyncratic treatment of God, and this is a key component of what separates Cioran's view of the fall from the traditional Christian reading of human sin as the refusal of God's offer of happiness. Creation is, for Cioran, the work of an imperfect creator, the *mauvais démiurge* [evil demiurge]; it is more like a disaster resulting from the effort of an incompetent artisan. It is not only humanity who falls, in his view, but also God himself. Thus Cioran shares the traditional view that we aspire to be like God, but deforms it to suggest that we are in God's image not in our tendency toward good or perfection but rather in the disasters that result from our own imperfection:

> En compétition avec Dieu, nous singeons ses côtés douteux, son côté démiurge, cette partie de lui qui l'entraîna à créer, à concevoir une œuvre qui devait l'appauvrir, le diminuer, le précipiter dans une *chute*, préfiguration de la nôtre. L'entreprise amorcée, il nous laissa le soin de la parachever, puis rentra en soi, dans son éternelle apathie, d'où il eût été preferable qu'il ne sortît jamais. […] Où nous

réfugier, sinon auprès de celui qui, l'épisode de la creation mis à part, fut toujours coupé de tout? [...] Nous aurions connu alors une autre face de la divinité et peut-être, aujourd'hui, enveloppés d'une lumière pure, non entachée de ténèbres ni d'aucun élément diabolique, serions-nous aussi incurieux et aussi exempts de la mort que le sots et les anges. (Pl 534)

[In competition with God, we ape his dubious aspects, his demiurgic aspect, that part of him that brought him to create, to conceive a work that had to impoverish him, to diminish him, to throw him into a *fall*, prefiguration of ours. Once the operation was begun, he left us the responsibility to finish it, then retreated into himself, in his eternal apathy, from which it would have been preferable that he never leave in the first place. [...] Where can we take refuge? If not near him who, with the exception of the episode of creation, was always cut off from everything? [...] We would have known then another face of the divinity and maybe, today, wrapped in a pure light, not sullied by darkness or any other diabolical element, we would have been as uncurious and as exempt from death as idiots and angels.]

Humans thus complete God's work on earth by continuing the disaster and catastrophe inaugurated by the creation in the first place, and which we now call "history." Our inability to remain within inaction is not the result of a decision but rather, like our duality, something inherent in our nature, without which we would be something other than human, but on account of which we share in the divine image, since God also could apparently not refrain from action. Given that this push into the action of creation is a departure from God's nature, traditionally defined as eternal and inoperative and therefore changeless, we see that God himself falls when he creates the world, yielding just as humans do to the temptation to act and thus reinforcing another link between humanity and divinity, to the detriment of both. Cioran's appeal to the gnostic concept of the demiurge helps him avoid some of the conceptual ambiguity that Baudelaire faced when attempting to uphold the duality of God and the devil. While Cioran often adapts gnostic concepts rather than adopting them strictly as presented in the gnostic tradition itself, the idea of a not necessarily benevolent and certainly not omnipotent demiurge allows Cioran to develop his notion of an imperfect and irredeemable universe.[7]

Cioran is not so much attempting to provide a perverse reading as to draw all of the consequences from the givens of the Christian myth of the origins of creation and humanity. He himself evokes the notion of considering all the consequences of one's foundations: "Si l'homme n'est pas près d'abdiquer ou de reconsidérer son cas, c'est qu'il n'a pas encore tiré les dernières consequences du savoir et du pouvoir" ["If man is not ready to abdicate or reconsider his case, it is that he has not yet drawn the last consequences from knowing and power"] (Pl 535). While Cioran puts aside questions of belief, his project in books such as *La chute dans le temps* and *Le mauvais démiurge* is not to reject the fundamental tenets of Christianity but to try to draw the proper conclusions from them, working from within Christian theological logic to arrive at conclusions that differ widely (and, Cioran would claim, necessarily) from those that

Christian theology draws, and most notably around the ideas of God's goodness and perfection and the possibility of redemption.

In his middle period books, as in his earlier ones, Cioran maintains the impossibility of salvation but does not cease returning to the idea, in a haunting that suggests that one cannot be rid of the notion of salvation merely by affirming and arguing for its impossibility. In *La chute dans le temps*, he makes a distinction between salvation and deliverance:

> Détaché de ses entreprises [...], [le sceptique] est arrivé à la délivrance, mais à une délivrance *sans salut*, prélude à l'expérience intégrale de la vacuité, dont il approche tout à fait lorsque, après avoir douté de ses doutes, il finit par douter de soi, par se déprécier et se haïr, par ne plus croire à sa mission de destructeur. Une fois rompu le dernier lien, celui qui le rattachit à soi, et faute duquel l'autodestruction même est impossible, il cherchera refuge dans la vacance primordiale, [...]. Son incuriosité atteint à une telle ampleur qu'elle confine au dépouillement total, à un néant plus dénudé que celui dont les mystiques s'enorgueillissent ou se plaignent après leurs pérégrinations à travers le « désert » de la divinité. (Pl 557)

> [Detatched from his undertakings [...], [the skeptic] has arrived at deliverance, but at a deliverance *without salvation*, prelude to the full experience of vacuousness, which he approaches entirely when, after having doubted his doubts, he ends up doubting himself, deprecating and hating himself, no longer believing in his mission of being a destroyer. Once the last link is broken, the one that attached him to himself, and without which even self-destruction is impossible, he will seek refuge in the primordial vacancy [...]. His uncurosity attains such large size that it confines to total deprivation, to a more naked nothingness than the one which the mystics were so proud of or complained about after their peregrinations through the "desert" of the divinity.]

This is at first glance an unexpected line of thought from Cioran in that it speaks of deliverance not as an unfulfillable hypothetical but as an accomplished reality, as well as referring to self hatred not as a sense of torture resulting from the inevitable doubling of the self but rather as a positive move in the direction of breaking the ties that block us from deliverance. There is a creative destruction of the self here. We seem to witness the transformation of the human being into what Cioran often considers impossible, namely, a creature that can experience the "vacance primordiale" that would be a form of deliverance. Baudelaire's impossible *néant* appears accessible in this passage, but we must recall that ultimately, for Cioran, this can only be a temporary condition, for reasons that have to do with the act of knowing, which is tellingly absent from this passage. Maintaining the state of the *néant* here would involve a permanent refusal of consciousness, and once again we return to the problem of knowledge as it presents itself for Cioran, namely, that deliverance would involve surpassing knowledge, but that such a condition would render us something other than human. What Cioran describes is something aligned with mystical experience (and even superior to it, as he suggests at the end of the passage), but like mystical experience, it is rare and certainly not able to be prolonged. Moreover, any awareness of this state of deliverance would already be a step away from it, since knowledge is a characteristic of the divided self that the *néant* was intended to conquer. The deliverance-without-salvation that Cioran describes here is similar to other moments, connected especially with writing, where Cioran affirms something like redemption but only in the mode of the temporary, thus negating one of redemption's essential features, its eternity and its removal of the saved subject from the changes of temporality.

Cioran makes a similar move when considering what kind of relief might be available to us from the torturous thoughts that he pursues throughout most of his works:

> S'il nous est interdit de recouvrer l'innocence primordiale, en revanche nous pouvons en imaginer une autre et essayer d'y accéder grâce à un savoir dépourvu de perversité, purifié de ses tares, changé en profondeur, « repenti ». Une telle métamorphose équivaudrait à la conquête d'une seconde innocence, laquelle, survenue après des millénaires de doute et de lucidité, aurait sur la première l'avantage de ne plus se laisser prendre aux prestiges, maintenant usés, du Serpent. La disjonction entre science et chute une fois opérée, l'acte de connaître ne flattant plus la vanité de personne, aucun plaisir démoniaque n'accompagnerait encore l'indiscrétion forcément agressive de l'esprit. [...] Il s'agirait ni plus ni moins que de *recommencer la Connaissance*, c'est-à-dire d'édifier une autre histoire, une histoire dégrevée de l'ancienne malédiction, et où il nous fût donné de retrouver cette marque divine que nous portons avant la rupture avec le reste de la création. Nous ne pouvons vivre avec le sentiment d'une faute totale [...]. Comme c'est notre corruption qui nous fait sortir de nous-mêmes, [...] l'empressement à produire nous dénonce, nous accuse. Si nos oeuvres témoignent contre nous, n'est-ce point parce qu'elles émanent du besoin de camoufler notre déchéance, de tromper autrui, et, plus encore, de nous tromper nous-mêmes? Le *faire* est entaché d'un vice original dont l'*être* semble exempt. Et pusique tout ce que nous accomplissons procède de la perte de l'innocence, ce n'est que par le désaveu de nos actes et le dégoût de nous-mêmes que nous pouvons nous racheter. (Pl 579)

[If we are forbidden from recovering primordial innocence, in return we can imagine another one and try to access it thanks to a knowledge deprived of perversity, purified of its stains, deeply changed, "repented." Such a metamorphosis would be equivalent to the conquest of a second innocence, which, arrived after thousands of years of doubt and lucidity, would have the advantage over the first one of no longer letting itself fall victim to the glamour, now faded, of the Serpent. Once the disjunction between science and the fall is accomplished, the act of knowing no longer flattering the vanity of anyone, no demonic pleasure would still accompany the inevitably aggressive indiscretion of the mind. [...] It would be a question, no more and no less, of *recommencing Knowledge*, that is, to build another history, a history disencumbered of the former curse, and where it would be given to us to find again that divine sign that we wore before the rupture with the rest of creation. We cannot live with the feeling of a total fault […]. Since it is our corruption that made us go out of ourselves, […] the rush to produce denounces us and accuses us. If our works testify against us, is it not because they emanate from the need to camouflage our decay, to fool others, and, moreover, to fool ourselves? *Doing* is sullied with an original vice of which *being* seems exempt. And since everything we accomplish proceeds from the loss of innocence, it is only by disavowing our acts and our disgust at ourselves that we can redeem ourselves.]

Once again, as the passage continues, it reveals the impossibility of what it seems to affirm at the outset. The key to gaining access to the "second innocence" to which Cioran initially refers is the overcoming of production, which would need to be dissociated from knowledge in order to make the latter palatable. While Cioran does not say so directly, however, such a reduction of production and its "original vice" is impossible, since the refusal of all doing or making would place us in the domain of inoperativity. In other words, what at first seems to be a major alteration in Cioran's position on the possibility of redemption turns out to be yet another instance of the thought of redemption haunting the thinker without an actual possibility of it emerging from the thought. It is as if, by writing this passage, Cioran were enacting the impossibility of redemption; the sheer fact of producing the passage reveals a reversion to the state of making, which is precisely the logic one would need to transcend in order to begin to think about a new state of innocence. And once again, Cioran flirts with traditional theological concepts while radically altering them: if, for traditional theology, humans participate in God's nature and action through their own creativity, for Cioran our creative acts do indeed align us with God but only to demonstrate God's participation in the fall as well.

For Cioran, the medium is never separate from the message. He never claims to be making systematic philosophical arguments; in fact he actively resists such an approach. His writings also betray a keen interest in stylistic perfection, which suggests that he crafts his thoughts with an eye to their esthetic status. Although his work often resists classification, it is possible to analyze the first-person speaking voice as well as the progression (or lack thereof) from aphorism to aphorism as they exist in dialogue or contradiction. This suggests that we should consider Cioran's writings within the domain of the broadly literary, that is, in a genre that, while not opposed to exploring non-fictional "truths," would not have truth in a conventional philosophical sense as a main goal. Rather, the truth produced by literary works is situational, provisional, and dynamic. In this sense, Cioran is strongly invested in what we could call "fiction," as long as we understand that term not as the opposite of truth or the synonym of fakery or falsehood, but rather as a creative (in the strong sense) use of language that bears a complex relationship to illusion, truth and lucidity. The confident way in which Cioran presents his ideas about the fall and its consequences clashes with his frequent affirmation of skepticism and doubt as the only appropriate reactions to any solidly formed and confidently expressed ideas.

There is, of course, an element of paradox necessarily built into any consistently skeptical position, since eventually one would have to be skeptical of one's own skepticism, but here the concept of fiction as a context-bound, situational, and provisional kind of truth can be helpful. Two excerpts from Cioran's *Cahiers*, written five years apart, reveal the way he comes to nuance his confidence-laden propositions. In 1965 Cioran pens this short aphorism defining himself by his superior level of lucidity: "Qui êtes-vous? Je suis le Détrompé" ["Who are you? I am the one without illusions"] (C 283).[8] In 1970, the statement is both elaborated and nuanced:

> Chacun sa démence: la mienne est de me croire l'homme le plus détrompé qui fut jamais. L'excès de cette prétention en prouve l'irréalité. N'empêche que parfois j'ai la sensation que personne n'est ni ne pourra être moins dupe que je ne l'ai été à certains moments, à certains moments seulement. Car tout est chez moi occurrence, date, instant, *sensation* précisément. (C 878)[9]

> [To each his madness: mine is to believe myself the man most devoid of illusions that ever was. The excess of this pretention proves its irreality. Nevertheless sometimes I have the sensation that no one is and no one could be less duped than I was at certain moments, and only at certain moments. For everything in my case is occurrence, date, instant, *sensation* precisely.]

The expanded and altered version is instructive both about what Cioran means by lucidity and about the nature of his aphorisms more generally. In it, he recognizes the potentially fictional quality of his assertion about his own lucidity, thus keeping open the possibility that his conviction about lucidity may in fact be an illusion and suggesting that we should read that assertion of lucidity as a kind of productive illusion. The statement is "fictional" in that it allows him to speak as a character from within the perspective of supposed lucidity, to bracket doubt for long enough to be able to craft an enunciation from within that point of view. In this way he temporarily suspends, but never fully transcends, the skepticism that lies at the base of all of his positions. Furthermore, he alters the enunciation in a quasi-Kantian way by claiming that he appears to himself as free of illusion, and that this is as far as we can go on the way to ultimate knowledge. His assertion is open-ended not in the sense of allowing for a near-infinite number of potential interpretations but rather in the sense of being provisional and thus allowing him to assert a contradictory claim at a different "instant." This revealing glance into the workshop of the aphorist sheds light on the way in which we should read the kinds of categorical statements that frequently appear in his collections of aphorisms, in forms similar to the one he provides in the shorter version of the aphorism we are considering. The expanded version does not cancel or falsify the shorter one so much as providing a key to its interpretation, one which emphasizes the situational aspect of a character speaking in a given way at a given time, even though that time and situation are never, of course, explicitly specified. The impression that the speaker is speaking from a vantage point of nowhere and at no particular moment is, of course, an important part of the fiction.

A crucial aspect of fiction as Cioran writes it is that it is a fertile kind of illusion; the certainty of absolute lucidity would shut down creative production since there would be nothing to add to the articulation of a fully lucid and definitive position. Such a writer would be caught in the trap of an eternal repetition of the same idea in exactly the same words; thus our fall into language—in its multiplicity and imperfection as a mode of transparent communicability—is also that which engenders literary production. Even if we affirm, with Cioran, that plant or animal existence, or (especially) nonexistence would be preferable to human existence as we are condemned to experience it, creative production has a role to play in making that experience more livable. Suspending lucidity long enough to enter a kind of illusion that allows for creative fertility does not exactly mire us deeper in the evil of existing, since barely anything could mire us more deeply than we already are. We might be tempted at this point to see writing, conceived along these lines, as a kind of redemptive act, but we must guard against that temptation or at least significantly qualify it.

Living requires the kinds of illusions that block our ability truly to conceive that nothing really exists. By definition for Cioran, what we call "life" depends on illusion: "Et comme [l'homme] avance en vertu de l'illusion acquise, pour s'arrêter il faudrait que l'illusion s'effritât et disparût; mais elle est indestructible tant qu'il demeure complice du temps" ["And as [man] avances according to the amount of illusion acquired, to stop it would be necessary for illusion to evaporate and disappear; but it is indestructible as long as man is complicit with time"] (Pl 536). All of this comes round once again to the notion of the fall, specifically the fall into time, from which there can be no release. And so we continue to fall both into time and into religious conceptions even though we know them to be illusions, thus guaranteeing that we can never be saved by refusing to maintain the importance of being saved in the first place. The vestiges of religious thinking in Cioran's writing are some of the illusions beyond which we find it hard to think and live for a sustained period of time; the atheist is no less delusional than the believer, since both require fictions to sustain life. And so, if living means believing in fiction, then making the affirmation that we are saved when we understand that nothing is, would involve renouncing the very skepticism that led us here, since, as Cioran writes in *De l'inconvénient d'être né* in a passage quoted above: "La certitude qu'il n'y a pas de salut est une forme de salut, elle est même *le* salut. À partir de là on peut aussi bien organiser sa propre vie que construire une philosophie de l'histoire" ["The certainty that there is no salvation is a form of salvation, it is even salvation itself. From there one can organize one's own life as well as construct a philosophy of history"] (Pl 886). To be able to follow these lines of thinking simultaneously, we would need to adopt both absolute skepticism and absolute certainty. This would be salvation, but here, once again, its conditions of existence are shown to be logically impossible.

Given that an acknowledgment of the nullity of existence, along with a concurrent reduction in all of the faculties typically associated with human nature, are what would bring us closest to something like salvation, it is not surprising that Cioran affirms the value of sleep as a potential relief from the suffering that characterizes existence:

N'importe qui se sauve par le sommeil, n'importe qui a du génie *en dormant*: point de différence entre les rêves d'un boucher et ceux d'un poète. Mais notre clairvoyance ne saurait tolérer qu'une telle merveille dure, ni que l'inspiration soit mise à la portée de tous: le jour nous retire les dons que la nuit nous dispense. Le fou seul possède le privilège de passer sans heurt de l'existence nocturne l'existence diurne: aucune distinction entre ses rêves et ses veilles. Il a renoncé à notre raison, comme le clochard à nos biens. Tous deux ont trouvé la voie qui mène hors de la souffrance et résolu tous nos problèmes; aussi demeurent-ils des modèles que nous ne pouvons suivre des sauveurs sans adeptes. (Pl 271)

[Anyone saves himself [or escapes] by sleep, anyone is a genius *while sleeping*: no difference between the dreams of a butcher and of a poet. But our clairvoyance would not tolerate that such a miracle would last, nor that inspiration be put at the disposal of all: the day takes away from us the gifts that the night gives us. Only the crazy man possesses the privilege of passing without a bump from nocturnal to diurnal existence: no distinction between his dreams and his waking state. He has renounced our reason, as the bum has renounced our goods. Both have found the way that leads beyond suffering and resolved all our problems; thus they remain models that we can follow of saviors without followers.]

From this it emerges that salvation is absolutely individual, since a person cannot follow someone else into insanity, as well as involuntary, and thus impossible by sheer act of will alone, not to mention undesirable for us as long as we cling to such inherently human tendencies as to believe that being sane is preferable to being insane. Still, sleep provides at least temporary or provisional salvation, since in sleep we have a taste of what the unconscious void is like. Sleep is the state that most resembles vegetal existence: "Plantes et bêtes portent sur elles les marques du salut, comme l'homme celles de la perdition" ["Plants and animals bear on themselves the marks of salvation, as man bears those of perdition"] (Pl 934). Once again, the fall into time is related to our permanent damnation on account of the fact that we are perpetually changing, not just in the sense of growing older, which we share with the animals, but in our ability to imagine the future and thus imagine humanity differently.

But what, then, of the act of creation itself? If sleep brings us a step closer to animal consciousness, then our active building and creating brings us nearer to God's work. Predictably, movement closer to God is not positively valued in Cioran: "De quoi sommes-nous coupables, sinon d'avoir suivi, plus ou moins servilement, l'exemple du créateur?" ["Of what are we guilty, if not of having followed, more or less slavishly, the example of the creator?"] (Pl 623). Cioran condemns parenthood by the same logic: "Cette incapacité de demeurer en soi-même, dont le créateur devait faire une si fâcheuse démonstration, nous en avons tous hérité: *engendrer* c'est continuer d'une autre façon et à une autre échelle l'entreprise qui porte son nom, c'est, par une déplorable singerie, ajouter à sa « création »" ["This incapacity to remain in oneself, of which the creator had to make such a regrettable demonstration, we have all inherited it: to *have offspring* is to continue by other means and on another scale the enterprise that bears his name; it is, by a deplorable imitation, to add to his 'creation'" (Pl 626–7). But we are in far more complex territory once we discuss not human creation in general but artistic creation specifically, and more precisely still, the act of writing. In a sense, Cioran's comments on the subject follow the same general trajectory that we saw operating in the case of redemption itself, namely, he at times provides the blanket condemnation of the idea that one would expect, yet that condemnation is nuanced and even called completely into question by many of his other writings.

An eminently human activity, writing is by its nature associated with the fall and with original sin according to Cioran:

> Ecrire des livres n'est pas sans avoir quelque rapport avec le péché originel. Car qu'est-ce qu'un livre sinon une perte d'innocence, un acte d'agression, une répétition de notre chute? Publier ses tares pour amuser ou exaspérer! Une barbarie à l'égard de notre intimité, une profanation, une souillure. Et une tentation. Je vous en parle en connaissance de cause. (Pl 332)

> [Writing books is not without some relationship to original sin. For what is a book if not a loss of innocence, an act of aggression, a repetition of our fall? Publishing one's defects in order to amuse or exasperate! An act of barbarism toward our intimacy, a profanation, a sullying. And a temptation. I speak from personal experience.]

Writing, on this account, draws us ever deeper into original sin rather than providing a way out of it, which is consistent with Cioran's appraisal of all human pursuits. Like living itself, writing requires a large dose of illusion in order to sustain itself:

> Produire, « créer », c'est s'interdire la clairvoyance, c'est avoir le courage ou le bonheur de ne pas percevoir le mensonge de la diversité, le caractère trompeur du multiple. Une œuvre n'est réalisable que si nous nous aveuglons sur les apparences; dès que nous cessons de leur attribuer une dimension métaphysique, nous perdons tous nos moyens. (Pl 600)

> [To produce, to "create," is to forbid oneself clearsightedness, it is to have the courage or the happiness to not notice the lie of diversity, the deceiving character of the multiple. A work is only achievable is we blind ourselves to appearances; as soon as we cease to attribute a metaphysical dimension to them, we lose all our means.]

But here a very different note emerges in the words "courage" and "bonheur." Unlike other proposed sources of redemption, which ultimately draw us ever deeper into perdition, writing seems to hold out hope for something more. If it requires just as much delusion about our condition as the other solutions, the difference seems to be the lucidity with which the writer undertakes the delusion that leads to the possibility of writing.[10] The delusion is controlled by the writer rather than encroaching upon him or her unwittingly. Writing thereby becomes a means of confronting, even if not vanquishing, the illusions inherent in human life, and therefore requires courage temporarily to enter those illusions so as better to illuminate and give voice to them. This is, perhaps, the appropriate degree of involvement in the human condition, this act of giving voice to it without drawing the full consequences of that condition: "Ne tirent les dernières conséquences que ceux qui vivent hors de l'art. Le suicide, la sainteté, le vice—autant de formes du manque de talent. […] C'est une diminution salutaire qui fait de tout acte de création un facteur de fuite" ["Only those who live outside of art draw the last consequences. Suicide, holiness, vice—so many forms of lack of talent. […] It's a saving diminution that makes of each act of creation a factor of evasion" (Pl 50). Passing into action to any greater extent than writing would be to fall into the same trap we explored above, that of not canceling but merely adding to the fall of humanity by seeking to overcome it through an action like suicide, which, by permanently suspending existence, permanently cancels lucidity without having changed the fallen human condition at all. The creative act, when applied to words, escapes the condemnation of action that Cioran applies almost universally elsewhere. Writing situates itself halfway between the continuation of illusion and the working through of lucidity; it is neither one in any complete sense and participates simultaneously in both. It is the kind of paradoxical act that can respond to the series of paradoxes that Cioran's tortured thinking about redemption has generated at every turn.[11]

Is this not, however, too easy a solution to a problem the complexity which Cioran has underscored throughout all the writings we have quoted? One would be tempted to think so, but the key aspect of this solution, which does not allow for redemption by a simple substitution of one kind of illusion for another, is in Cioran's indication, with his own italics, that poetry "fait, *pour un instant*, notre salut" ["makes, *for an instant*, our salvation"] (Pl 401). By abandoning the notion of permanence, we are able to achieve a temporary form of salvation which is in constant need of renewal. Since we are condemned to exist in time, and since changeless eternity is impossible, humanity's constant falling can only be lessened by constant renewal of redemption, the time of voluntary suspension of illusion through writing. From this constantly renewed redemption stems the cyclic nature of Cioran's own writings, which, often refusing linear development, turn around the same sets of ideas from aphorism to aphorism and from book to book. Cioran himself links his obsessional rewriting of key ideas to a notion of writing as therapy: "Si je n'ai fait qu'écrire le même livre, en marge des mêmes obsessions, c'est pour avoir constaté que cela me libérait, en quelque sorte. J'ai vraiment écrit par nécessité. La littérature, la philosophie, que sais-je encore, ne furent pour moi qu'un prétexte. L'acte d'écrire comme thérapeutique, c'était cela l'essentiel" ["If I have only written the same book [over and over again], in the margins of the same obsessions, it is because I noticed that it liberated me in some way. I truly wrote by necessity. Literature, philosophy, or whatever, were only a pretext for me. The act of writing as therapeutic, that was the essential thing"] (Liiceanu 85). Here, Cioran's theology aligns itself perfectly with his attitude on writing: he explicitly affirms both a provisional *theological* salvation and the momentary *personal* salvation available to us through poetry that he affirmed in the passage quoted above:

> Il en est de la délivrance comme du salut chrétien: tel théologien, dans sa scandaleuse naïveté, croit à la rédemption tout en niant le péché originel; mais si le péché n'est pas consubstantiel à l'humanité, quel sens attribuer à l'avènement du rédempteur, qu'est-ce qu'il [est] venu rédimer? Aucunement accidentelle, notre corruption est permanente, elle est de toujours. De même l'iniquité: [...] elle est même ce qu'il a de plus *visible* ici-bas, où remettre les choses en place exigerait un sauveur pour chaque génération, pour chaque individu plutôt. (Pl 684)

> [It is in the case of deliverance as in the case of Christian salvation: one theologian, in his scandalous naïveté, believes in redemption while denying original sin; but if sin is not consubstantial with humanity, what meaning can we attribute to the coming of the redeemer; what did he come to redeem? In no way accidental, our corruption is permanent, it has always been. The same with iniquity: [...] it is even what is most *visible* here below, where to put things back in their place would demand a savior for each generation, or rather for each individual.]

This individual savior, which is in fact each person for him or herself, is also a provisional savior. Cioran remarks a few pages further on:

> Dans la décision de renoncer au salut, il n'entre aucun élément diabolique, car, s'il en était ainsi, d'où viendrait la sérénité qui accompagne cette décision? Rien de diabolique ne rend serein. Dans les parages du Démon, on est au contraire morose. C'est mon cas ... Aussi ma sérénité est-elle de courte durée: juste le temps de me décider à en finir avec le salut. Par bonheur je m'y décide souvent, et, chaque fois, quelle paix! (Pl 717)

> [No diabolical element enters into the decision to renounce salvation, for, if it were thus, from whence would come the serenity that accompanies this decision? Nothing diabolical renders one serene. In the vicinity of the Demon, one is, on the contrary, morose. That's my case .... Therefore my serenity is short-lasting: just the time to make up my mind to be done with salvation. Happily I decide that often, and, each time, what peace!]

And so both the need for salvation and the constantly renewable decision to renounce salvation are provisional. Serenity is not impossible for Cioran; it comes both through writing and the conscious decision to renounce salvation, and perhaps the two acts function interdependently. [12] But the essential point is that serenity comes only with the realization that there can be no permanent salvation, and that, while it is in constant need of renewal, it is, all the same, perpetually renewable by a further act of writing or a renewed commitment to renounce the need for salvation in the first place.

A number of commentators on Cioran have focused on the role of writing. Rachel Mutin has emphasized the palliative aspect that, as we have seen above, Cioran himself sometimes evokes. Mutin writes:

> A cathartic gesture which permits him to channel his anguishes, his rages, his hauntings and obsessions, the fact of writing was thus for Cioran a means of delivering himself, of "expurging" himself from a nearly intolerable interior overflowing. […] Thus, it is very probably in writing that Cioran found a palliative resolution […], that of a nostalgic retreat imagined at the end of his life: to come back to a sort of cynical world, to arrive at a sumptuous decadence. (Mutin 240)

Even in this emphasis on the therapeutic value of writing, Mutin appeals to the vocabulary of redemption to describe the effect of writing, which leads us to suspect that there is more to the role of writing in Cioran, despite what he himself occasionally affirms, than a simple pharmaceutical aspect, a pure descent into illusion. Other critics have emphasized the theological dimension of writing, its characterization as a fall and thus as concomitant with our fall into time and into the degraded state which is the only possible human existence:

> Cioran does not forgive himself for continuing to write. Only silence is grand. He is of the race of those who, well aware of that, cannot for all that renounce the word, and the written word especially. Cioran the hopeless is a man of letters, a contradiction that to which he was sensitive. A new occasion to mock himself with a snicker that is not without indulgence. (Mauriac 215)

Claude Mauriac's descriptive vocabulary accurately reflects the relation between writing and the fall. If, as we have seen, Cioran refuses to assign a diabolical motive to the decision to renounce redemption, there *is* something that relates writing to our fallen condition. Condemned to language just as we are condemned to exist in time, unable thus to perpetuate silence, the palliative measure which is writing is also a sign of our further falling. As Mauriac emphasizes, however, Cioran is himself conscious of the fall, which to some extent mitigates its effects, allowing a kind of lucidity-in-illusion through ironic detachment.[13] Cioran in fact claims that condensing language into aphorisms is a way of taming language's inevitable expansion:

> Il est plus aisé de renoncer au pain qu'au verbe. Malheureusement le verbe glisse au verbiage, à la littérature. Même la pensée y tend, toujours prête à se répandre, à s'enfler; l'arrêter par la pointe, la contracter en aphorisme ou en boutade, c'est s'opposer à son expansion, à son mouvement naturel, à son élan vers le délayage, ver l'inflation […] Vous dirai-je le fond de ma pensée? Tout mot est un mot de trop. Il s'agit pourtant d'écrire: écrivons … , dupons-nous les uns les autres. (Pl 333)

> [It is easier to renounce bread than the word. Unfortunately the word slides into verbiage, into literature. Even thought tends toward that, always ready to spread

itself out, to puff itself out; to stop it at the stinging point, to contract it into an aphorism or a witty saying, is to oppose its expansion, its natural movement, its movement toward padding out and inflation […]. Shall I tell you the depth of my thought? Every word is one word too many. The thing is to write though: let us write … , let us dupe each other.]

Even though we are forever condemned, this does not cancel all interest in life, as Mauriac's phrase "a parcel of attachment" aptly conveys. We get the sense that it is not simply, as Cioran sometimes postulates, that an inability permanently to renounce life is a mark of our complicity with the fall but rather an affirmation, however provisional, temporary, and always open to skeptical interrogation, that writing can and does form a real attachment to life and allows us to take some degree of momentary but deep pleasure from it.

Here it is important to make a distinction between pessimism and nihilism, for while Cioran may sometimes be considered a nihilist, and while many of the assertions we have quoted would give partial credence to this view in that he repeatedly affirms that nothing would be better than something, nonexistence better than existence, the role that writing plays for Cioran would suggest that pessimism is a more helpful perspective through which to consider his writings. In his study of pessimism, which argues, in sympathy with Cioran, that it arises as a reaction to modern linear notions of time and its implications about progress, Joshua Foa Dienstag characterizes the difference this way: "Pessimism expects nothing. But this is not nihilism. Nihilism would be not *wanting* anything. Extreme nihilism? *Wanting nothing*" (Dienstag 256). In other words, pessimism provides a potential art of living, fully lucid about the "dissonance and disorder" of the world (Dienstag xii) and therefore able to find joy by tempering expectations.[14] It is not prohibited for the pessimist, as it would be for the nihilist, to believe that something may, at least temporarily, make life worth living. Cioran's earliest readers in French already saw this attitude emerging through his brutally pessimistic prose. Maurice Nadeau's review of *Précis de décomposition*, originally published in *Combat* in 1949, notes that Cioran's act of writing removes him from nihilism:

> On the side of the triumphal way that leads to atomic destruction he puts down his bag and sits, exhausted, refusing all consolations and all pity.
>
> He still believes in something since he writes, confesses, and sings his distress. Because he modulates it in a language that is all the more admirable since it is a borrowed one, because he distributes it artistically in lyrical phrasings, some easily oratorical, others of a concision like that of Nietzsche or Pascal, will we have the effrontery to say that this distress is feigned? (Nadeau 212)

While it cannot redeem us eternally, and while it may not even hold up to skeptical inquiry, writing remains for Cioran as necessary as living; he called it, in his last published book, a "defendable illusion."[15] Writing is never innocent, nor are the subjects of its pronouncements fixed or permanent; they are, rather, always subject to revision or even to perpetual restatement of the same. But lucidity about what writing can or cannot do as therapy, theology, or art of living, while it is not a definitive mode of redemption, is at least the beginning of the way to talk about it in terms that respect and reflect the full complexity of the idea. If we are unable, even in a post-theological age, to get beyond our attachment to the concept of redemption, writing lucidly about that failed attempt might just be the next best thing.

Asoteriological Ethics: Baudelaire and Nancy

In *La chute dans le temps*, Cioran writes: "Qui a fait une expérience analogue à celle de l'Ecclésiaste s'en souviendra toujours; les sévérités qu'il y aura puisées sont irréfutables autant qu'impracticables: des banalités, des évidences destructrices d'équilibre, des lieux communs *qui rendent fou*" ["The one who has had an experience analogous to the one of the author of Ecclesiastes will remember forever the severities that he will have drawn from it are as irrefutable as they are impracticable: banalties, obvious observations that destroy balance, commonplaces that *make you crazy*"] (Pl 594). In a way, this observation informs all of his writing, which poses questions of how to continue living, and how most appropriately to live, in the world, given the Cioranian subject's lucidity about the vanity of existence. Despair and insanity are two risks associated with this point of view; temporary escape via literature is, as we have already seen, another. Disregard for others, in recognition of the ethical relation as yet another form of absurdity and banality, is also a potential temptation, and yet Cioran's writings do not advocate such disregard or the abolition of ethical obligations. How, then, does Cioran's thought, and that of Baudelaire and others who could potentially carry the label "nihilist," move from the low point of despair suggested by the experience Cioran describes above, which permeates all aspects of existence and is irreversible, to the possibility of carrying on living? It is at this point that the temptation to revert to a logic of redemption is greatest, since the role of the messiah, or social utopias, or transfiguration via art, has typically been to cancel despair when nothing else can. This reversion is what Leo Bersani has criticized in what he calls the "culture of redemption," a crucial assumption of which is that "a certain type of repetition of experience in art repairs inherently damaged or valueless experience. Experience may be overhwleming, practically impossible to absorb, but it is assumed […] that the work of art has the authority to master the presumed raw material of experience in a manner that uniquely gives value to, perhaps even redeems, that material" (1). Far from falling into the tempting comforts of salvational logic, however, Baudelaire and Cioran point the way toward remaining within the experience Cioran describes here and becoming able to dwell there.[1]

All of the writers I have considered in this study pose the question of how to move from an esthetics to an ethics, or rather, how the two coexist. Nicole Parfait claims that what Cioran presents is "an esthetics under the guise of a moral philosophy" (119), whereas Patrice Bollon calls Cioran's thought an "evolutionary *art of living* without dogmas, a way of accustoming oneself to the world and to oneself, of filling what

Pavese called the 'profession of living': an ethics" (164). For Baudelaire and Cioran, both esthetics and ethics ultimately stem from the notion of original sin, but this is not to say that the idea provides a facile solution. Cioran himself comments:

> Comme toutes les grandes idées, celle de la Chute rend compte de tout et de rien, et il est tout aussi difficile de s'en servir que de s'en passer. Mais, enfin, qu'elle soit imputable à une faute ou à une fatalité, à un acte d'ordre moral ou à un principe métaphysique, il demeure qu'elle explique, tout au moins en partie, nos errements, notre inaboutissement, nos infructueuses recherches, la terrible singularité des êtres, le rôle du perturbateur, d'animal détraqué et inventif qui fut départi à chacun de nous. (Pl 1144)

> [Like all grand ideas, the Fall accounts for everything and nothing, and it is as difficult to use it as it is to do without it. But, finally, whether it is imputable to a fault or a fatality, to an act from the moral order or to a metaphysical principle, it remains that it explains, at least in part, our wanderings, our not arriving, our unfruitful searches, the terrible singularity of beings, the role of the troublemaker, the insane and inventive animal that was accorded to each of us.]

When he suggests that original sin is so total an explanation as to not really account for anything at all, Cioran makes clear the distance between his view and orthodox theological approaches to sin. The explicative value of the fall lies not in its actual truth but rather in its ability to serve as a generating principle for both esthetic creation and ethical relations.

Like Baudelaire, Cioran recognizes the power, and one could even say the seduction, of the fall as an explicative tale but guards against seeing esthetic creation as redeeming that fall. If anything, esthetic creation comes to depend on the fall as its condition of possibility rather than canceling it. Paul Audi develops what he calls an *esth/étique*, a convergence of ethics and esthetics that lays particular emphasis on the kind of despair Cioran evokes in the passage quoted above.[2] Audi writes:

> Pour ne plus désespérer de son propre désespoir il faut précisément désespérer *de* lui! Tel est le paradoxe sur lequel repose ce que j'appelle *la condition éthique*. Ce paradoxe veut que ce soit du tréfonds du désespoir, et pas du tout en s'efforçant de se dérober à son emprise fatale, que ce soit de la désespérance même que *l'esprit* vienne à émerger pour le meilleur comme pour le pire; et cela tant et si bien que cet esprit apparaît inévitablement comme quelque chose sinon de désespérant, du moins de désespéré—ce qui explique d'ailleurs qu'au fond de toute « pensée », si jubilante soit-elle, pour ne pas dire au fond de tout acte, fût-il un acte de création, il y a toujours une voix qui murmure sourdement, comme elle fit aux oreilles de Tolstoï: A quoi bon? ou Et puis après? ... (104)

> [In order not to despair over one's own despair one must, precisely, despair *of* it! Such is the paradox on which rests what I call *the ethical condition*. This paradox

desires that it be from the depths of despair, and not at all in trying to shy away from its fatal hold, that it be from despairing itself that *the mind* comes to emerge for better and for the worse and all the more so since this spirit appears inevitably as something, if not despairing, at least despaired—which explains, besides, that at the bottom of all "thought," as jubilant as it may be, not to mention at the bottom of every act, even if it be an act of creation, there is always a voice that murmurs quietly, as it did in Tolstoy's ears: what's the use? or, and then after that? ...]

Here, then, is the beginning of an ethics that emerges from nihilism but remains within that nihilism rather than transcending it, finding within it the basis for an *art de vivre*. I will argue that, if the main theoretical basis of asoteriology is established in Baudelaire's verse poems and Cioran's essays, it is primarily in Baudelaire's prose poems that we see emerge a sketch of what an ethics based on asoteriology might look like.

We have already considered how the aphorism places itself outside the usual sequence of diachronic time; Jacques Derrida sees in the unique temporality of the aphorism not a generalized removal from time but rather an affirmation of an immediate present that inevitably produces an ethical relation: "No aphorism without the promise of a now in common, without the pledge, the vow of synchrony, the desired sharing of a living present. In order that the sharing may be desired, must it not first be given, glimpsed, apprehended? But this sharing is just another name for aphorism" (*Acts* 421). Here, Derrida navigates complex territory in terms of what is desired as opposed to what is actualized through the aphorism; his language is not without echoes of the notion of the messianic that would place us back within soteriological thinking: promises, pledges, and vows suggest what is to come, perhaps forever deferred.[3] But the notion of givenness here suggests that the relation is already posited by the writing itself, in the immediate present as opposed to the future. Derrida goes on to say: "Because it traces, aphorism *lives on*, it lives much longer than its present and it lives longer than life. Death sentence [arrêt de mort]. It gives and carries death, but in order to make a decision thus on a sentence [arrêt] of death, it suspends death, it stops it once more [il l'arrête encore]" (421). This is not, then, a passage to eternal life but rather a suspension of time not in order to cancel death but in order to live with it, to account for it even though we can never actually experience death. We can read this suspension of death not as wishful thinking, for it is certainly not, for Derrida or Cioran, but rather as an attempt to think "as if not," a category of biblical origin that plays an important role for Agamben. As William Watkin explains, for Agamben there is an opposition between living "as if" and "as not." The former is associated with estheticization and carries dangers with it:

Living "as if," while seemingly creative and thus an act of poiesis, turns out to be self-defeating both for thought and for art. For not only does the spell over spells cast a false veil over thinking, it also misrepresents the poetic as well. In contrast to this, to live the "as not" is far from being nihilistic. If "as if" is a belated and blinded decadence, [...] the "as not" depicts an alternate futural moment of authentic being. If "as not" involves negation, as indeed it does, it is itself the negation of modern negativity in the form of a messianic moment to come which is the true state of modern now-time. The great question for modern thought, therefore, is "How does one travel from "as if" to "as not?" (Watkin 91)

Watkin is right to say that this preference for the "as not" in Agamben moves him toward a messianic mode of thinking (the phrase "as not" is Saint Paul's, a description of living in the end times that involves living in the world as if one were not really living in it)[4] that places him back within the logic of redemption.

As we have seen, it is literary writers such as Baudelaire and Cioran, rather than the critical theorists we have been examining, who remain most faithful to the refusal of the logic of redemption. The question arises in these writers, as the quotation from Cioran above already suggests, of how to live in a world that has shown to be devoid of redemptive possibility. Baudelaire often portrays the poetic subject awaiting death, frozen in contemplation, despite the fact that our fallen state requires us to continue to live, and with the added irony that while death may be thought to be a remedy, it cannot actually be so because it obliterates the subject altogether. If revolt is fruitless, what allows us to become "unfrozen" (to speak in the terms of "Le goût du néant" and its poetic subject awaiting an avalanche to carry him away)? It is helpful to return here to the notion of the artist's task of drawing out the eternal from the transitory, as Baudelaire states in "Le Peintre de la vie moderne" ["The Painter of Modern Life"]. It is, paradoxically, by an act of esthetic violence that Baudelaire clears the way for the possibility of shared experience with others, a basis of some kind for an ethical relation. The first step must be to reconsider the eternal and the transitory, since the former is the condition in which, by definition, nothing happens, since eternity implies a state of changelessness. For there to be artistic creation at all, there needs to be a violent rupture with this eternal, one that, for Baudelaire, takes its cue from the action of the fall which, by being unredeemable, is therefore also eternal. The fall thus combines movement and changelessness in a way that paradise cannot, and thereby becomes the basis of both esthetics and ethical relations in Baudelaire. Such an interpretation finds support in the traces of theological discourse in "Le Peintre de la vie moderne," an essay that at first seems far removed from metaphysical or theological concerns, with its famous discussions of transitory experience, the dandy, and the pleasures of makeup.

Baudelaire's principal contention in section one of the essay is well known: "le beau est toujours, inévitablement, d'une composition double, bien que l'impression qu'il produit soit une" ["the beautiful is always, inevitably, of a double composition, even though the impression it produces be unified"] (OC2: 791). This duality consists in an eternal and a relative element, the latter being "comme l'enveloppe amusante, titillante, apéritive, du divin gâteau" ["like the amusing, titillating, stimulating exterior of the divine cake"]. Immediately after this initial description, Baudelaire explains the origin of art's duality in these terms: "La dualité de l'art est une conséquence fatale de la dualité de l'homme" ["the duality of art is a fatal consequence of the duality of man"] and offers another comparison in order to explain the point: "Considérez, si cela vous plaît, la partie éternellement subsistante comme l'âme de l'art, et l'élément variable comme son corps" ["Consider, if you will, the eternally subsisting part as the soul of art, and the variable one as its body"]. Duality is one of the ideas that Baudelaire never really calls into question, never negates, and the fact that this is so has to do with the very nature of his argument about that duality, namely, that it is irretractable and irredeemable, and that thus any effort at thought or artistic creation necessarily falls back into the multiple no matter how much it may strive for unity. For proof of this, we need not go further than Baudelaire's theory of duality in the very paragraph we have been considering. When he claims that beauty is double evn though the impression it makes is unified, even his own duality is double, since the unity of impression that he describes is necessarily linked to the duality of the beautiful. When its impression is unified, that impression of unity in turn cannot help but be subsumed under the duality of the beautiful, since the beautiful as Baudelaire describes it here is now itself doubled, consisting in the duality of the way it truly is as well as in the impression that it makes. Unless Baudelaire is suggesting that beauty can appear without sensuous presentation, that is, without a perceiver who receives that unified impression, then the duality of beauty is itself doubled when we consider the role of the unity of impression.

To make sense of the Baudelairean logic of duality as it manifests itself in the essay, we need to take a step back from it and examine the philosophy that informs Baudelaire's implied and stated theories of esthetic production as well. For Baudelaire's metaphysics of duality does not merely exist *alongside* the duality of modern beauty but rather as an essential and determining *aspect* of it. But what does this all have to do with "Le peintre de la vie moderne?" To get there, we need to make one more detour, this time to Baudelaire's drafts of prefaces for the 1861 edition of *Les Fleurs du Mal*. The first of these is crucial because it establishes a link between le Bien and le Beau. Baudelaire sounds a familiar note when he attacks the notion of progress in full ironic mode: "Malgré les secours que quelques cuistres célèbres ont apportés à la sottise naturelle de l'homme, je n'aurais jamais cru que notre patrie pût marcher avec une telle vélocité dans la voie du *progrès*" ["Despite the aid that some famous pedants brought to man's natural stupidity, I would never have believed that our country could walk with such speed in the way of *progress*"] (OC1: 131). Rather than aspiring to the eternal changelessness of the divine, humanity is horrified by that vision of changelessness and seeks to overcome it. Baudelaire's first draft preface deals only briefly, but forcefully, with the question of beauty and the good:

> J'avais primitivement l'intention de répondre à de nombreuses critiques et, en même temps d'expliquer quelques questions très simples, totalement obscurcies par la lumière moderne: qu'est-ce que la Poésie? Quel est son but? de la distinction du Bien d'avec le Beau; de la Beauté dans le Mal; que le rythme et la rime répondent dans l'homme aux immortels besoins de monotonie, de symétrie et de surprise. (131)

[I at first had the intention to respond to numerous critiques and, at the same time, to explain some very simple questions, totally obscured by modern light: what is Poetry? What is its goal? The distinction between the Good and the Beautiful, Beauty in Evil, that rhythm and rhyme resonate in man with the immortal needs of monotony, symmetry, and surprise.]

He renounces his plan of developing these explanations, he says, after realizing it would be useless to explain "quoi que ce soit à qui que ce soit" ["anything at all to anyone at all"]. But before abandoning his development, Baudelaire provides a key insight to the relation between his esthetics and his metaphysics here: human beings have eternal need of both monotony and surprise; hence the possibility of rhythm and rhyme both to set up and potentially to violate expectations. In terms of metaphysics, we can see a putting into play of a foundational Baudelairean dualism involving the problem of *Ennui*, a direct correlate with the "monotony" he evokes here in his mention of rhythm and rhyme. We know that *Ennui* is marked from the very outset of *Les Fleurs du Mal* as a monster and that this fall into stasis is sometimes desired by the poet but is more often deplored as the monstrous state that it is. Entanglement within *ennui* gives rise to the desire for action, and often violent action, as a way to shake off the stagnation.

This action can, as we have seen, take the form of satanic revolt, which cancels *ennui* by violent blasphemy or of violence toward another or oneself. Poems that feature such acts of violence respond to the esthetic and metaphysical desire for both monotony and surprise. Such is the case in "Je t'adore à l'égal de la voûte nocturne" ["I Adore You as Much as the Nocturnal Vault ... "] for instance, whose conventions of love lyric are transformed in the last lines of the poem into an attack: "Je m'avance à l'attaque, et je grimpe aux assauts,/Comme après un cadavre un choeur de vermisseaux" ["I advance to attack, and I climb to assault,/Like a swarm of maggots after a cadaver" (87)] (OC1: 27). The tension between monotony and surprise is even more marked in a poem such as "A celle qui est trop gaie" ["To One Who Is Too Gay"] which begins not so much in conventional love lyric as in sheer banality and calculated artlessness: "Ta tête, ton geste, ton air/Sont beaux comme un beau paysage; /Le rire joue en ton visage/Comme un vent frais dans un ciel clair" ["Your head, your bearing, your gestures/Are fair as a fair countryside;/Laughter plays on your face/Like a cool wind in a clear sky" (151)] (OC1: 156), only to end in a far more vividly described violent act than the one in "Je t'adore ... ": This is of course the famous lines:

Ainsi je voudrais, une nuit,
Quand l'heure des voluptés sonne,
Vers les trésors de ta personne,
Comme un lâche, ramper sans bruit.

Pour châtier ta chair joyeuse,
Pour meurtrir ton sein pardonné,
Et faire à ton flanc étonné
Une blessure large et creuse. (OC1: 157)

[Thus I should like, some night,
When the hour for pleasure sounds,
To creep softly, like a coward,
Toward the treasures of your body,

To whip your joyous flesh
And bruise your pardoned breast,
To make in your astonished flank
A wide and gaping wound (153)]

This violent surprise is also the self-inflicted torture of "L'héautontimorouménos," which takes on an important theological resonance when read in the light of the traditional characterization of humanity under the condition of original sin as *incurvatus in se*.

The rupture that produces human duality also renders the poetic act itself violent. Baudelaire says as much in the last sentence of "Le Confiteor de l'artiste" ["The Artist's *Confiteor*"]: "L'étude du beau est une duel où l'artiste crie de frayeur avant d'être vaincu" ["Studying the beautiful is a duel in which the artist shrieks with fright before being defeated" (4)] (OC1: 279). Many other poems also feature a necessary act of violence toward the object of art which the poet represents as necessary in order to create the poem. Such is the case in "Je t'adore à l'égal de la voûte nocturne":

Je t'adore à l'égal de la voûte nocturne,
Ô vase de tristesse, ô grande taciturne,
Et t'aime d'autant plus, belle, que tu me fuis,
Et que tu me parais, ornement de mes nuits,
Plus ironiquement accumuler les lieues
Qui séparent mes bras des immensités bleues.

Je m'avance à l'attaque, et je grimpe aux assauts,
Comme après un cadavre un choeur de vermisseaux,
Et je chéris, ô bête implacable et cruelle!
Jusqu'à cette froideur par où tu m'es plus belle! (OC1: 27)

I adore you as much as the nocturnal vault,
O vase of sadness, most taciturn one,
I love you all the more because you flee from me,
And because you appear, ornament of my nights,
More ironically to multiply the leagues
That separate my arms from the blue infinite.

I advance to attack, and I climb to assault,
Like a swarm of maggots after a cadaver,
And I cherish, implacable and cruel beast,
Even that coldness which makes you more beautiful. (87)

Here the conception of beauty resembles the one in the poem "La beauté," where it is only by a violent act that the poet could hope to break the stoic, silent stance of a beauty that is nearly totally inaccessible to the poet: "Je suis belle, ô mortels! comme un rêve de pierre,/Et mon sein, où chacun s'est meurtri tour à tour,/Est fait pour inspirer au poète un amour/Eternel et muet ainsi que la matière" ["I am fair, O mortals! like a dream carved in stone,/And my breast where each one in turn has bruised himself/Is made to inspire in the poet a love/As eternal and silent as matter" (59)] (OC1: 21). This beauty does not inspire poetic creation but, rather, hinders it by inspiring mute love on the part of the poet, a silence that he would have to break in order to craft a poem which, one supposes, would never be adequate to portray the beauty that he adores in silence unless it were, as in "Je t'adore à l'égal...," to transform the beauty in such a way as to kill it.

We are now in a position to return to "Le Peintre de la vie moderne," since the other section of the essay that takes up the famous definition of art as consisting of the eternal and the transitory also returns, in a brief but evocative and telling phrase, to the kinds of metaphysical and theological questions we have been considering. Section IV contains the most famous iteration of Baudelaire's characterization of the task of the artist, which is to "tirer l'éternel du transitoire" ["draw out the eternal from the transitory"] (OC2: 694). This is in the context of a discussion of whether artists should dress their subjects in ancient costume or the clothing of their own time. Here is how Baudelaire defends the use of contemporary costume: "Cet élément transitoire, fugitif, dont les métamorphoses sont si fréquentes, vous n'avez pas le droit de le mépriser ou de vous en passer. En le supprimant, vous tombez forcément dans le vide d'une beauté abstraite et indéfinissable, comme celle de l'unique femme avant le premier péché" ["This transitory, fugitive element, whose metamorphoses are so frequent, you do not have the right to disdain it or do without it. By suppressing it, you necessarily fall into the void of an abstract and undefinable beauty, such as that of the only woman before the first sin"]. What is this prelapsarian woman doing here? Baudelaire's phrasing is surprising, not least for the incongruous use of the word "tombez" ["fall"] here. In the context of a discussion of the first sin, the reader expects the fall to refer to entry into the condition of original sin. But here, intriguingly, the fall is not into sin but rather a leap back to the condition of innocence. Since it is clear that Baudelaire is arguing *against* the avoidance of the contemporary in art, his comparison suggests that what we might at first glance consider to be ideal beauty—that before the fall—is in fact undesirable for art: "the void of an abstract and undefinable beauty" is to be shunned and hence Baudelaire's appeal to the contemporary embodiment of beauty.

And here we arrive at the theological crux of Baudelaire's argument: if the abstract beauty of the prelapsarian woman is to be avoided at all costs, that means that sin is the very condition of art itself. If beauty were accessible without the embodied form of painting or poetry, there would be no need of art-making at all. It is thus not as a reparatory or compensatory gesture that we make art, nor is it in order to wallow in the perverse pleasures of evil, but rather in order, paradoxically, to avoid falling back into a state of innocence, in which beauty remains a void because it has no form. All art, then, depends on the fall, and on an irredeemable fall at that. Cioran agrees with Baudelaire on this point. He writes in the *Cahiers*:

> L'écrivain c'est le triomphe du vieil homme, des vieilles tares de l'humanité; c'est l'homme *avant* la Rédemption. Pour l'écrivain, le Rédempteur n'est pas venu, effectivement; ou son action rédemptrice n'a pas réussi. L'écrivain se félicite de l'erreur d'Adam, et ne prospère que dans la mesure où chacun de nous la renouvelle et la prend à son compte. C'est l'humanité tarée dans son essence qui constitue la matière de toute *œuvre*. On ne crée qu'à partir de la Chute. (C 580)

> [The writer is the triumph of the old man, of the old stains of humanity; it is man *before* Redemption. For the writer, the Redeemer has not come, actually, or his redemptive action did not succeed. The writer is glad about Adam's error, and only prospers to the extent that each one of us renews it and takes it as his own. It is humanity stained in its essence that constitutes the material of every *work*. One only creates from the basis of the Fall.]

It is by a necessarily violent act, which aligns itself with the transitory, that the artist succeeds or at least attempts to create the artwork, not so much to create beauty itself but rather to give it form, without which it would remain in the void. Hence the second section of "Je t'adore..." with its "Je m'avance à l'attaque" ["I advance to attack"] makes more sense in the broader Baudelairean conception of artistic creation, which the poet describes in "Le soleil" ["The Sun"] as "ma fantasque escrime" ["my fanciful fencing" (281)] (OC1: 83). The word recurs in "Le Peintre de la vie moderne" with reference to Guys:

> Maintenant, à l'heure où les autres dorment, celui-ci est penché sur sa table, dardant sur une feuille de papier le même regard qu'il attachait tout à l'heure sur les choses, s'escrimant avec son crayon, sa plume, son pinceau, faisant jaillir l'eau du verre au plafond, essuyant sa plume sur sa chemise, pressé, violent, actif, comme s'il craignait que les images ne lui échappent, querelleur quoique seul, et se bousculant lui-même. (OC2: 796)

> [Now, at the hour when others are sleeping, this one is bent over his table, shooting at a piece of paper the same glance that he just now was attaching to things, fencing with his pencil, his pen, his brush, making gush forth the water from the glass to the ceiling, wiping his pen on his shirt, hurried, violent, active, as if we were afraid that the images would escape him, quarrelsome even though alone, and jostling himself.]

Art is necessarily violent, whether that violence has an external object, or is turned against the artist himself, or whether it seems to have no object whatsoever, as in the passage I have just quoted, where it is not blood that springs forth but rather an innocent glass of water.

Baudelaire's prose poems are the locus of the most extensive development of the link between ethics and esthetics in light of the asoteriological worldview that he works out in *Les Fleurs du Mal*; significantly, given what we have just seen in terms of the relationship of violence and esthetic creation, several key moments in the prose poems put violence and esthetic creation center stage in a way that simultaneously explores the ethical relation to the other, and in doing so, the relation to self. In that sense, by developing the consequences of the split self that Baudelaire had already identified in *Les Fleurs du Mal*, the prose poems become the site of the ironic ethical encounter as that has been described by Gary Handwerk:

> Irony is a response to and not just an expression of the fragmentation of the human world it accepts as inevitable. Rather than trying to define or fix identity, it opens out into the dialogue, the response where identity can come into being. Irony provokes a movement toward intersubjective coherence by exposing the unacknowledged seams of personal identity. It is a testing for rather than an assumption of shared values, hence it necessarily oscillates back to the here and now, grounding the transcendental moment of doubt in the real encounter. In its fullest operation, irony is the expression of the mind in search of what will suffice. (173)[5]

While the prose poems are often set in the modern city, the problems they pose defy attempts to read the poems reductively as a manifestation of experiences that could only be possible in that urban environment. The generalized nature of the characters and the setting encourage a wider philosophical and esthetic lens, and the poems themselves actively resist attempts to provide a single exhaustive interpretation. One of the most hyperbolically violent and puzzling of these poems is "Assommons les pauvres!" ["Let's Beat up the Poor!"] which provides an intriguing window into the relation of ethics and esthetics in the prose poems. The opening presents the move from abstract concerns to lived experience, with the poet representing himself "confiné dans [sa] chambre" ["shut [...] up in [his] room"] for two weeks, reading books "à la mode dans ce temps-là" ["fashionable at that time" (121)] (OC1: 357). This is not quite a representation of abstract contemplation, for we are given to believe that the works the poet has been reading are those of popular utopian socialists, "tous ces entrepreneurs de Bonheur public" ["all those managers of public happiness"]. But the principle of absorbing an idea until one is drawn to test the idea empirically is consonant with Baudelaire's general interest here in portraying the lived consequences of his asoteriological atheology. The poet claims to have "digested" and "swallowed" the contents of his reading, the effect of which is a state bordering on "le vertige ou la stupidité" ["vertigo or idiocy"]. What emerges from his reading is "le germe obscur d'une idée supérieure à toutes les formules de bonne femme dont j'avais récemment parcouru le dictionnaire. Mais ce n'était que l'idée d'une idée, quelque chose d'inifiniment vague" ["the dim seed of an idea better than all the old wives' formulas I had recently perused in the encyclopedia. But it was only the idea of an idea, something infinitely hazy" (121)] (OC1: 358). It is at this point that the poet takes to the street, inspired by a voice that he hears which, in contrast to Socrates' demon, is "un grand affirmateur, […] un Démon d'action, un Démon de combat" ["A great approver, […] a Demon of action, or Demon of combat" (122)] (358). The status of the poet's idea is never explicitly clarified after this, since the idea is transfigured by, or clarified by, or worked out through, the violence he inflicts on a beggar he encounters. It is the Demon that speaks the maxim that the poet will attempt to demonstrate by action: "Celui-là seul est l'égal d'un autre, qui le prouve, et celui-là seul est digne de la liberté, qui sait la conquérir" ["He alone is equal to another, if he proves it, and he alone is worthy of freedom, if he can conquer it" (122)] (358). While the poet succeeds in convincing the beggar of this definition of liberty and equality and sending him off to beat others as he has been beaten, it is, first of all, never clear that such convincing is equivalent to establishing the truth of the maxim and, second of all, that we are to accept the sincerity of the maxim.

While the poem moves us from books into the street, from contemplation to action, it does not go so far as to allow the reader to decide definitively whether the poem at hand is meant to be taken as a parody or not. The lack of any clearly discernible "message" is not only what makes the poem intriguing; it is also what maintains the duality that sustains any Baudelairean articulation of the self or philosophy of creation.[6] The violence of the creative act is not redeemed by coming to rest in a determinate meaning but is rather left in dynamic suspension: what we have in "Assommons les pauvres" is both a satire of theories of equality *and* the performance of genuine equality. It is not so much a case of undecidability between two (or more) options as it is a simultaneity of contrasting interpretive possibilities, so that the action performed by the poem forces the reader back to the contemplative moment akin to the one from which the poet had emerged at the beginning of the poem. The reader, unlike the poet-character, contemplates unresolvable duality, a condition which, by virtue of Baudelaire's asoteriology, no form of action could cancel or transcend.[7]

The impossibility of redemptive political action implies another important shift that Baudelaire accomplishes in this poem, namely, from the political to the ethical. For while Baudelaire may have lost faith in political transformation in the wake of the events of 1851, the prose poems often put ethical relations, in the broad sense of encounters with and relations to others, center stage, as "Assommons les pauvres" certainly does. That is not to say that there is a discernible "moral" at work in the texts, nor is the ethical merely reducible to compassion for the suffering of others, although that is certainly visible in the texts as well. But the ethical, as opposed to the political, relationship is primary in *Le Spleen de Paris*, for while explicitly political positions appear under the sign of mocking irony, such as in "Le Miroir" ["The Mirror"], where a character invokes the "immortal principles" of 1789 to justify his looking at himself in the mirror (OC1: 344), or indeed in "Assommons les pauvres," where the initial target of satire was Pierre-Joseph Proudhon, as an earlier version of the poem attests, ethical relations are not consistently ironized and in fact often seem to spring from genuine compassion on the part of the poet.[8] By removing the specificity associated with Proudhon's ideas in particular, Baudelaire generalizes the political into the ethical. In so doing, he emphasizes the equality of human beings that is at the base of the implied ethics of the prose poems, an equality established not politically but rather theologically, as a result of Baudelaire's faithful insistence on the primacy of original sin. But we should go further and say that it is not exactly the theological notion of original sin but rather, as I have been arguing, the atheological notion of *irredeemable* original sin that establishes the equality of the ethical relation, since removing the possibility of redemption also removes one more potential source of inequality: if all are equal under original sin, an unequal relation would result from the division of humanity into the saved and the damned. But since no such division is possible in Baudelaire's metaphysics, the possibility of equal ethical relation remains always open. And thus when the poet says to the beggar who has just returned his blows, "Monsieur, *vous êtes mon égal*" ["Sir, *you are my equal*" (123)] (OC1: 359), we cannot read the same kind of irony as we could in "Le Miroir," where the political, as opposed to existential, equality posited by the speaker is clearly the site of irony and ridicule.[9]

The equality posited in "Assommons les pauvres!" may well be a satire of Proudhon, but it is never *only* that; again, the duality inscribed in the interpretation of the poem itself testifies to the duality introduced with original sin *and* points the way toward ethical relation not beyond but *within* that condition, coterminous with the irony. That irony and duality are also what allow equality and violence to coexist and even seem mutually dependent in this poem. And the violence that inaugurates the ethical equality here points to another aspect of Baudelaire's logic of the fall, namely, the impossibility of acting meaningfully upon the equality posited in the poem. As Steve Murphy notes, if the beggar does as the narrator suggests at the end of the poem and gives half his money to those who take his beating and give it back to him, as he had done to the narrator, there will be an ever-diminishing quantity of money shared, since the beggar will be giving half of a half of the original sum, and so on, "whereas the bourgeois will always have, in principle, his half of the purse, an alegebra of disparity where the inequality will be maintained" (Murphy 431). The turn to action where the poem suspends itself would thus perpetuate actual inequality based on the principles of ethical equality, yet another manifestation of the impossibility, in Baudelaire's world, of maintaining a non-dualistic and unironic take on equality. The distance between the theoretical equality effected by unredeemed original sin and the actual political or economic inequality that it produces when put into practice comes to be figured, for those who refuse the coming-to-an-end of the poem and extend its action of the poem beyond the poem's actual stopping point, as another fall into the duality of both affirming and denying the possibility of realized or realizable ethical equality. It is from this, I would argue, that stems what Steve Murphy identifies as the late Baudelaire's mode of thought: "not an affirmative ideology, but an ensemble of convictions of which the most tenacious would be, perhaps, intuitions and inferences of a negative and fatalistic order" (160).

Such fatalism is on view in *Le Spleen de Paris* in poems such as "Chacun sa chimère" ["To Each His Chimera"], whose setting "sous un grand ciel gris, dans une grande plaine poudreuse" ["under a huge gray sky, on a huge dusty plain" (9)] (OC1: 282), removes it from any definable place and time. The characters are no more recognizable historically; they are presented as generalized figures, each of whom is carrying "sur son dos une énorme Chimère" ["an enormous Chimera on his back" (9)] (282). They are traveling, but they know neither why nor where. When the poet inquires where they are headed, one of them responds that "il n'en savait rien, ni lui, ni les autres; mais qu'évidemment ils allaient quelque part, puisqu'ils étaient poussés par un invincible besoin de marcher" ["he knew nothing about it, not he, nor the others; but that obviously they were going somewhere, since they were driven by an irresistible need to walk" (9)] (282). While this setting stands in contrast to poems such as "Assommons les pauvres," clearly set in a contemporary urban street, I would argue that Baudelaire's atemporal and temporally specific poems do not exist in tension but rather in complementarity. Rather than seeing the urban poems of either *Les Fleurs du Mal* or *Le Spleen de Paris* as a descent from, or an alteration of, Baudelaire's more metaphysically inflected poems, the most fruitful readings underscore the continuity between the historically specific and more generalized settings in Baudelaire. The shock of the contemporary urban experience extends from, and is informed by, the same asoteriology that guides all of Baudelaire's work. To be able to see the space of a poem as simultaneously historically grounded and specific *and* metaphysically generalized is part of participating in the kind of double vision that Baudelaire encourages and which is written into the fabric of his ideas of irony and the fall.

The undifferentiated space of "Chacun sa chimère" enacts such a penetration of the metaphysical into the historical. For Jérôme Thélot, the gray and powdery landscape of this poem enacts the "abolition of the separation between sky and earth" (*Violence* 74); the space of the poem is "that of modern democracies," a metaphysical space situated either before or after culture, a time of no time (74). The space is thus historically specific and metaphysically generalized; on this reading, it represents the historical bringing to concreteness of the metaphysical void that Baudelaire has theorized. The relationship between the historical and the metaphysical, far from unilinear or determining in one direction or the other, is dynamic in Baudelaire, with historical reality both providing the conditions of the disclosure of the metaphysical reality and shaping the way it is theorized. Central to all of this, for Baudelaire, is the act of esthetic creation itself. The creation of a poem is a fall from the virtual or possible into the actual, an intervention that is consequence and product of the fall. Thélot reads the poem as the "Chimère des chimères, dernière folie du langage intérieure au langage: violence de la violence" ["Chimera of chimeras, last madness of language, interior to language: violence of violence"] and adds: "the Chimeras of the walkers, their condemnation which is their myth, are known and understood: and pronounced, [...] a coagulation of words, fantasies, prejudices, by which walking becomes wandering, the city becomes a desert, and dialogue becomes silence" (*Violence* 84). In a move similar to the one that the poet makes in "Le Cygne" ["The Swan"], everything becomes allegory, but the poem is not reducible to simple allegorical status. Rather, the creation of the poem participates itself in the kind of falling that it describes.

Baudelaire's poetry is, for Thélot, a self-knowing phenomenon: "Of what is poetry capable? Knowing itself, and by that, stripping us of the fascinations which constitute but also condemn us" (85). Cioran's notion of ludicity and his status as "le détrompé" ["the one without illusions"] are echoed here in these claims about poetry's epistemological function. The knowledge which, as we saw in a comment of Walter Benjamin's that is fully worked out in Baudelaire, is a knowledge of evil alone is inscribed in "Chacun sa chimère" at the end of the poem when the poet moves from merely observing the passing figures to contemplating what he saw: "Et pendant quelques instants je m'obstinai à vouloir comprendre ce mystère; mais bientôt l'irrésistible Indifférence s'abattit sur moi, et j'en fus plus lourdement accablé qu'ils ne l'étaient eux-mêmes par leurs écrasantes Chimères" ["And for a few moments I persistently tried to understand this mystery. But soon insurmountable Apathy swooped down upon me, and I was more heavily oppressed than they were themselves by their overwhelming Chimeras" (10)] (283). The poet represents his thought as a striving, an effort of the will to understand, but he ultimately sinks back into indifference or, we could say, indifferentiation, fading back into the landscape itself and dissolving the distinction between observer and observed that he had maintained while watching the travelers. He becomes, so to speak, a fellow traveler by the end of the poem, becoming one with the others by virtue of the burden he now feels in its full force in his own body after having observed it in others. In doing so, he joins the company of those having the resigned look of those who are "condamnés à espérer toujours" ["condemned to hope forever" (9)] (283). Once again the moment of lucidity on the poet's part cancels, it seems, the condemnation to hope and reveals the unredeemable quality of the condition the poet describes. Hope is traded for lucidity, and the poem ultimately suggests that the lucidity is preferable to the eternally unfulfilled and unfulfillable hope that pushes these travelers on. So while the poet is assimilated to the travelers by the crushing weight of the burden he carries, he is at the same time differentiated by the difference in kind of the burden. "Chacun sa chimère" performs this simultaneous identity and distance from others on the part of the poet, in the context of the poem itself, emerging from nothingness and returning there by the resistance to closure that is a hallmark of the endings of Baudelaire's poems in both verse and prose.

The inertia and inaction of the end of "Chacun sa chimère" stand in tension with poems that involve a sudden and irrational burst of action, such as "Assommons les pauvres" and another of the most famous of the prose poems, "Le Mauvais vitrier" ["The Bad Glazier"]. The first half of the poem features the poet speaking as a sort of moralist, presenting generalized observations and enumerating several examples of the phenomenon of "des natures purement contemplatives et tout à fait impropres à l'action" ["characters, purely contemplative and completely unsuited for action" (13)] (OC1: 285) who sometimes are given to uncharacteristic and violent bursts of action. In the second half of the poem, the poet indicates that he himself is among this group and narrates an anecdote about his having invited a glazier to climb the many flights to his apartment, only to chase him away for not having any colored panes of glass to sell in the impoverished neighborhood where he was hawking his wares. The action culminates in the narrator throwing a flower pot on the glazier's head, causing him to fall back and break his merchandise while the narrator continues to cry out "la vie en beau!" ["Make life beautiful!" (15)] (287). The enigmatic anecdote is rich terrain for interpretation, with its staging of relationships involving commercial culture, economic disparity, and the role of art, with passing references to competing hermeneutic claims of medicine and religion as well, in the narrator's affirmation that the inspiration toward action that he is describing is "hystérique selon les médecins, satanique selon ceux qui pensent un peu mieux que les médecins" ["hysterical according to physicians, satanic according to those who think a little more lucidly than physicians" (14)] (286). The tale seems allegorical, but one is not certain of what exactly, and it can certainly be read as parody of "La chanson du vitrier" ["The Song of the Glazier"] by Arsène Houssaye, but any attempt to pin the text definitively to one particular interpretation is bound to leave the whole incompletely accounted for.

Critical commentary on this poem tends to focus more on its second half, that is, on the action more than on the abstract reflection of the first half. After enumerating several examples of those contemplative natures that sometimes explode into action, in a key transitional paragraph, the poet poses an epistemological question about his last example, which is an enthusiastic embrace, by a usually shy man, of an old man in public: "Pourquoi? Parce que … parce que cette physionomie lui était irrésisitiblement sympathique? Peut-être; mais il est plus légitime de supposer que lui-même il ne sait pas pourquoi" ["Why? Because … because he found his expression irresistibly likeable? Perhaps; but it is more legitimate to assume that he himself does not know why" (14)] (286). Unknowing is thus at the heart of the poem; whether the poet is discussing others' motivations or his own, belief in a hypothesis is as far as he can go in terms of an explanatory account of behavior. In the final short paragraph before the anecdote in the second half begins, the poet indicates that he himself has been drawn to the sudden crises of action "qui nous autorisent à croire que des Démons malicieux se glissent en nous et nous font accomplir, à notre insu, leurs plus absurdes volontés" ["which justify our belief that some malicious Demons slip into us and, without us knowing it, make us carry out their most absurd wishes" (14)] (286). Once again, Baudelaire refuses to accord credibility to a scientific hypothesis of hysteria and prefers an explanation that, this time, floats somewhere between the theological and the philosophical, the "malicious Demons" evoking either Christian devil-like creatures or figures such as Descartes' hypothetical "evil genius" dedicated to deceiving Descartes about everything he knows to be true or, as Steve Murphy suggests, "the word can have the etymological meaning of 'protective genie'" as it does in "Assommons les pauvres!" (Murphy 364). The tale that the poet then recounts seems to pick up where "Chacun sa chimère" left off, in the state of indolence: "Un matin je m'étais levé maussade, triste, fatigué d'oisiveté, et poussé, me semble-t-il, à faire quelque chose de grand" ["One morning I had awakened sullen, sad, and worn out with idleness, and I felt impelled to do something great"(14)] (286). As we saw in *Les Fleurs du Mal*, the temptation to action as a corrective to the kind of *ennui* evoked here will ultimately prove futile, since no action can bring about the desired effect of the cancelation of existence. Like the poet asking the avalanche to carry him away, the poet of "Le mauvais vitrier" wishes to transcend inertia and pass into action, a wish that he already reveals to be detrimental to him by his own comment on his first action: "et j'ouvris la fenêtre, hélas!" ["and I opened the window, alas!" (14)] (286). This poem never returns to the contemplative state that is the normal mode of being for this poet, but if we were to project the action beyond the end of the poem, the poet would be likely to return to the state of contemplation and inaction that he claims is proper to his nature.

We also must return, invariably, to the unknown, the "he does not know why" that is at the heart of this poem. The action narrated in the second half does not so much replace the contemplation that precedes it so much as it provides a variation that is in continuity with that contemplation; the doing and the inability to provide a definitive interpretation of the action go hand in hand here. What the poem does open up, though, is the ethical relation to the other. When the poet opens the window, he transgresses the boundary that kept the contemplative self isolated from the street, thus imposing the question of the relation to the others with whom he shares the literal space of the city and the metaphorical space of reflection. Will the other person he encounters turn out to be interchangeable with the self, as the victim of the violence in "L'héautontimorouménos" had been? While the action represented in the poem tends to confirm the hypothesis that we explored earlier of contemplation as always necessarily linked to evil, as contemplation *of* evil, it frustrates any further attempt to make clear sense of the precise relation of action to contemplation or of the poet to the other. The poem does posit such a relation, however, even if, in its complexity, it is not reducible to intellectual understanding. The action of the poem, in contrast to that of "Assommons les pauvres!," is not the testing of a hypothesis, a descent into the street to determine whether reality corresponds to theories about it. Thus, any question about the motivation of the poet or the outcome of the poem sends us back to the center, to the "he does not know why" that unites poet, victim, and reader here via that very incomprehensibility.

Even the most basic questions about the poem turn out to be unanswerable once the reader begins to inquire about them. The speaking subject, for instance, is usually taken to be a poet; such a reading chimes with that character's insistence on beauty, an esthetic concern that seems to trump all others for him. Jérôme Thélot has proposed, however, that it is not the narrator but the glazier who is the figure of the poet here. He outlines a complex process of substitution initiated by the moment of reflection immediately following the narrator's invitation to the glazier to come up ("Cependant je réfléchissais" ["Meanwhile I was thinking" (14)] [286]):

> [*Reflect*—reflect in a mirror, represent the reflexive consciousness. Baudelaire doubles himself in writing, dreamer and glazier, […] executioner and victim, to reflect and reveal the sacrificial structure of consciousness, the genesis of the self by the expulsion of the Other, who is the brother. The glazier attains the

consciousness of the dreamer by the cry separating him from the crowd and by the ascension leading him to the chamber of art. But crying out and raising himself, he *is* the dreamer, who cries and consecrates himself to art. Such that in this cry and this elevation—or this violence and this forgetting, […]—it is self-consciousness that the glazier, the dreamer, attains. Reflexivity, self-consciousness, derives from sacrifice and from the misunderstanding of the double, which are a sacrifice and misunderstanding of self. Identification of self with self operates by doubling, and consciousness is dreamy, discriminating. *To operate*—to cut and make a work, slice and write—, is to be. (*Violence* 105–6)

On this reading, the narrator plays the role not of the poet but of the public, seeking a simple transformation of "ugly" reality into a more appealing vision via art. One would be right to be skeptical about such a view lining up with Baudelaire's esthetics, which challenge all conventional and popular notions of beauty. The violence that Baudelaire seeks to enact is not on those who do not provide rosy optimism but rather on those who seek that as the principal source of value in art.

At any rate, Thélot's argument is more complicated than that, suggesting as it does that the poem breaks down the division between narrator and glazier, not in order to evoke a solipsistic world where everything is a product of the narrator's own consciousness but rather to use Baudelaire's notion of ironically divided subjectivity in order to imagine a new relationship to the other that both allows the narrator to identify with the glazier and also to call for his sacrifice, an act of necessary violence that becomes also a violence inflicted on the self. We have, then, an ethics of equality that can invoke identity only because I am other to myself just as I am identified with another:

In the second moment of the Baudelairean relation to the first person one happens upon, the other is lost: he becomes the Other, the tyranny of the human face […]. Hatred substitutes for the presence of one's fellow the threat of an enemy, and obfuscating the gaze that it distorts into a vision […] it dreams up a rival in place of the neighbor. Moment of violence. This glazier is my obstacle. Art, tyrannical religion of the poet, imposes that the other be misunderstood in his proper being. It fears above all this passage in front of the staircase of its temple, of this simply simple passerby. "When Vengeance beats its infernal reminder,/ And of our faculties makes itself the captain"—according to "Reversibility"—, hatred, dream and art associate together in the same discriminating *operation*: they erase the trace of charity, transfigure the brother and forbid speech. (104–5)

"Le mauvais vitrier" thus complicates the esthetico-ethical relation that we saw operating in "Je t'adore à l'égal …," where esthetic creation demands the destruction of the subject in order to effect the esthetic transformation. In "Le mauvais vitrier," the esthetic act also creates the ethical relation that establishes both distance and proximity between the self and the other, a kind of substitutability that allows for an ethical relation that does not preclude violence toward the self, but at the same time it allows the recognition of equality in the other, a collapsing of the space between self and other that is enacted in poem by the transfer of the flower pot from the narrator's hands to the glazier's head.

The violence of the falling flower pot and the shattered glass cannot said to be redemptive here; it does not *create* the ethical relation so much as enact or *reveal* it. At the same time, though, the violence in the poem cannot be called senseless either: the narrator's own motivations are clear (his frustration with the lack of colored panes), and within the logic of the creation of the poem there is also a motivation, namely, the necessarily violent act that brings the poem into being, the violent rupture in the ordinary that makes the story worth recounting and the poem worth discussing. Still, though, the sense that would be conferred on the act if it were in fact redemptive is not in operation here, and, given the importance of the ethical relation that is established in this poem, one cannot simply identify a merely esthetic impetus to the violence. In that sense, this poem stands in contrast to other, earlier, Baudelaire poems that seem to privilege art for art's sake, the notion that, as Baudelaire himself puts it, poetry "n'a pas la Vérité pour objet, elle n'a qu'Elle-même" ["does not have Truth for its object, it has only Itself"] (OC2: 333). The action in "Le mauvais vitrier" stands in contrast to those poems that feature eternal waiting, such as "Le goût du néant" ["The Taste for Nothingness"] or "Le mauvais moine" ["The Bad Monk"]:

> —Mon âme est un tombeau que, mauvais cénobite,
> Depuis l'éternité je parcours et j'habite;
> Rien n'embellit les murs de ce cloître odieux.
>
> Ô moine fainéant! quand saurai-je donc faire
> Du spectacle vivant de ma triste misère
> Le travail de mes mains et l'amour de mes yeux? (OC1: 16)
>
> [—My soul is a tomb where, bad cenobite,
> I wander and dwell eternally;
> Nothing adorns the walls of that loathsome cloister.
>
> O lazy monk! When shall I learn to make
> Of the living spectacle of my bleak misery
> The labor of my hands and the love of my eyes? (39)]

Bertrand Marchal sees in Baudelaire's art-for-art's-sake stance a source of both sin and redemption: a sin of pride as a kind of idolatry and a kind of "rédemption par soi et pour soi" ["redemption by and for oneself"]: "The bad monk is still a monk, not only by his solitude—this time an essential solitude—, but also because art, which has no other primary material than the 'sad material' of the poet, assumes, in its way, a redemptive function" (139). There is a tension here between the infinite waiting implied by the question posed at the end of the poem and the fact that what we are reading is, of course, a finished poem; that tension tends to implicate the poetic subject further in the ironically doubled subjectivity at play in "Le mauvais vitrier." That ironic subjectivity calls into question the extent to which we can affirm a sense of esthetic redemption, à la Nietzsche, in Baudelaire. "Le mauvais vitrier," I would argue, calls into question the possibility of such an estheticist stance by affirming that it is not possible to engage in esthetic creation without creating an ethical relation to an other and that this relation automatically removes us from the realm of the purely esthetic, thus canceling the redemptive value of it, or at least moving it into the realm of the temporary and the inconclusive.

We can recall here Cioran's notion of the temporary salvation to be found in poetry: "Exercice ou revélation, qu'importe. Nous lui demandons, nous autres, qu'elle nous délivre de l'oppression, des affres du discours. Si elle y réussit, elle fait *pour un instant*, notre salut" ["Exercise or revelation, what does it matter? We ask of it, we others, that it deliver us from oppression, from the torments of discourse. If it succeeds, it makes, *for an instant*, our salvation"] (Pl 400–1). And in fact that temporary release, along with the nonchalance of the "what does it matter," finds direct resonance in the final sentence of "Le mauvais vitrier," which returns to the theological register: "Mais qu'importe l'éternité de la damnation à qui a trouvé dans une seconde l'infini de la jouissance?" ["But what does an eternity of damnation matter to someone who has experienced for one second the infinity of delight?" (15)] (OC1: 287) Like so many of the Baudelaire poems we have examined, this one too eschews definitive conclusion, sending the reader back to the center of the poem and its affirmation of unknowing: "Why […] he does not know why." It is hard to see the poem as redemptive, given the eternal lapse back into the contemplation that was broken only momentarily by the burst of action that establishes the ethical relation without thereby seeing any redemptive value in it; rather, the ethical relation is produced by the impossibility of redemptive violence, which would end the ethical relation by destroying the other as victim. The temptation to act functions here like the temptation to conclude: neither one can effect permanent change, and neither one can bring redemption. And with such an ambiguous conclusion, the reader too is brought into ethical relation with the poet and forced to recognize that a definitive conclusion would also be the death of the work of art, which would exist as stale artefact if ever removed from the dynamic interpretive relation between poet and reader, yet another manifestation of the way the ethical and esthetic relations are inextricably intertwined for Baudelaire.

What emerges as a key feature of the ethical relation as it is posited in the prose poems is that it is a form of solidarity without communication. As Jean-Luc Steinmetz indicates:

Le Spleen de Paris no longer carries any of the sentimental and idealist illusions that *Les Fleurs du Mal* contained. But the very movement that draws us to the other is just as strong there […]. Without placing the mark of original sin in the foreground (which he affirms in his journals), Baudelaire is persuaded of the non-communication between men. Besides, he does not at all wish to enter the crushing era of equality, since he insists above all on preserving his identity, his uniqueness. [...] The book occupies a border zone, where philosophers, doctors, and moralists can be evoked. For the new poetry understands itself to be situated at this intersection of the mind, heart, and body, in this drama of the incarnation, which no doubt forbids that the other be more than a rival. (155)

One could multiply examples of figures evoked as deserving pity in the prose poems, but moments of communication are rare, and what Steve Murphy, referring to "Les Yeux des pauvres" ["The Eyes of the Poor"] has labeled a "manque de communication d'âmes" ["lack of communication of souls"] (269) dominates intersubjective relationships throughout the poems, for reasons we have been exploring. If the other presents him or herself as a rival, as Steinmetz claims, this is in part due to the violent nature of the doubled subjective relationship to oneself as well in Baudelaire, and it does not cancel the possibility of ethical relation, although it does seriously compromise, as I have argued, a political relation. The ethical relationship that is mediated by the theological allows for a relation to the other that is based on little to no contact with that other, an abstracted relation that remains valid even though the actual moments of encounter represented in the prose poems are almost always marked by the impossibility of contact, gross misunderstandings, or violence. In "Le mauvais vitrier," even the violence is effected without contact between the characters, with the flower pot bridging the considerable spatial gap that separates them at the end of the poem. The flower pot thus brings together and separates the characters; its fall, with all of the remnants of the theological that that notion might contain here, both establishes and destroys the distance between the characters, and that simultaneous distance and proximity is emblematic of the ethical relationship as it is established in the prose poems generally.

Even the intersubjective relationships that are not marked by violence also feature the simultaneous distance and proximity that has emerged in all the poems we have been considering. Such is the case in "Mademoiselle Bistouri" ["Miss Scalpel"], where the title character's presumed insanity provides a barrier toward the kind of real solidarity that might have been provoked by the narrator's sympathy for her. The narrator's evening encounter is disconcerting on account both of the woman's delusions (she is sure the narrator is a doctor) and of her sexual interest in doctors and their bloody operating clothes. There is a sort of *dialogue de sourds* as the narrator at first attempts to correct the woman's mistaken impression that he is a doctor, and then asks questions, as an analyst might, about why she has the impressions that she has and for how long she has had a fetish for surgeons. The whole exchange is presented rather matter-of-factly, with just this comment from the narrator at the end of the dialogue: "Quelles bizarreries ne trouve-t-on pas dans une grande ville, quand on sait se promener et regarder? La ville fourmille de monstres innocents" ["What weirdness you find in big cities, when you know how to walk about and look! Life swarms with innocent monsters" (118)] (OC1: 355). The poem is unusual in that the narrator plays the role of the rationalist seeking to understand or perhaps to diagnose Mademoiselle Bistouri (Murphy 548–9), as opposed to other poems, such as "L'Etranger" ["The Stranger"], where the first-person speaker is, rather, himself the aberrant case subject to questioning, or "Le mauvais vitrier," in which, as we just saw, the narrator derides attempts at scientific or medical explanation and suggests that traditional notions of the demonic would be more apt in terms of accounting for aberrant cases. But he ultimately renounces the possibility of accounting for Mademoiselle Bistouri in these terms, and ends the poem idiosyncratically with a prayer to a God "qui avez peut-être mis dans mon esprit le goût de l'horreur pour convertir mon coeur, comme la guérison au bout d'une lame" ["who have perhaps placed a taste for horror in my mind in order to convert my heart, like a cure at knife point" (118)] (OC1: 356), asking him to have pity on the insane and asking whether they can truly be monsters in the eyes of the Creator "qui sait pourquoi ils existent, comment ils *se sont faits* et comment ils auraient pu *ne pas se faire*" ["who knows why they exist, how they *were made* and how they might have been able *not to be made*" (118)] (OC1: 356). The tone becomes increasingly tentative as the poem reaches its conclusion, with the strong affirmation of conversion at knife point governed by a "peut-être" ["maybe"] that has the potential to cancel the entire affirmation, and the totally open possibility that the insane could in fact, by God's inscrutable ways, be monsters, despite God's merciful nature. As J.A. Hiddleston remarks: "the prayer which seems to plead in favor of innocent monsters is as much a challenge to the existence of divine providence and order, as an indication of submission and belief in their reality; it borders on the blasphemous, and […] points not to providence but to a moral anarchy at the heart of the universe" (61). There is simultaneous distance and proximity between Mademoiselle Bistouri and the narrator, who is strangely drawn to her at the same time as he perceives her on the other side of the sanity divide. We have, yet again, a solidarity that stems from distance, and from a shared sense of the unredeemable fall that is no doubt at the root of the tentative nature of the prayer and its inability to assert God's mercy with full confidence. What, then, is the status of the "cure at knife point," a powerful and yet, as presented, entirely metaphorical conversion?

For Edward Kaplan, "Mademoiselle Bistouri" is a crucial moment in what he reads as a progression toward the ethical as the prose poems progress from the beginning to the end of the collection. For him, the poem "most sharply juxtaposes the esthetic and the ethical—and that which transcends them while including both, the religious" (135), and he argues that the conversion evoked by Baudelaire in the prayer is indeed to be understood in a fairly strong religious sense: "Her madness serves no apparent goal, whereas the narrator suggests that his 'taste for horror' should 'convert his heart, like a cure at knifepoint.' He in fact succeeds" (145). Jérôme Thélot reads the scene differently, in the context of the poet's appropriation of Pascal's writings on the "operation" of conversion:

Miss Scalpel *could* operate the conversion of the poet with her weakness, which draws to her his strength, and which already makes the poem *turn* into a final prayer. Baudelaire works with Pascal's lexicon but he displaces the base: conversion is not, for him, an effect of grace, it does not have its origin in God, it does not come from the *strong* transcendence that Augustinian theology aims at under the name of God, since it is an effect of the "horror" suffered by the sick and the poor in spirit: it has its origins not in God but in the other, and it comes from a *weak* transcendence, if this word can still designate the mysterious relation between a worried poet and his former accomplice who is sick from now on. (*L'Immémorial* 26–7)

We could say that, for Thélot, the transcendence that operates here is *so* weak as to dissolve entirely, that what used to be labeled the effect of a divinity is figured here as an entirely human relation. While Baudelaire preserves the shell of theological discourse by putting the talk of "conversion" in the form of a prayer, the ethical relation to the other has bypassed the divine here, an effect which is, I would argue, the final consequence of the refusal of redemption. The cry to God for pity is unaccompanied by any reassurance that it will be heard and answered, and the appeal to God seems to come more from one of "ceux qui sont condamnés à espérer toujours," as the poet puts it in "Chacun sa chimère" (OC1: 283). If the poet's heart is converted in "Mademoiselle Bistouri," it is not to faith and certainly not to the hope of redemption, but rather to a kind of ethical relation that draws the poet and Mademoiselle Bistouri together by the same gesture that also maintains them in an uncancelable distance from one another. This is the ironic duality of the conversion-within-the-fall, a conversion which is itself double because it exists as an effect of empathy without permitting any closer ethical relation, and also because the conversion as Baudelaire describes it here may not even *be* a conversion, since the qualifying "maybe" cancels any strength we might want to attribute to the claim about an actual conversion of any sort here. This ethical relationship between the two individuals in the poem can be generalized to the level of the community, where the conditions for a sense of connection between subjects are both established and prevented by the solidarity that, under the sign of irony, both unites and divides communities just as it divides the individual subjectivity from itself. The ethical relationship is thus generalized to include even the subject's own relation to itself.

Admittedly, this leads us to a potentially unsatisfying answer about the nature of the ethical relation in Baudelaire, in that the relation is left open, under the sign of the conditional mood and the eternal qualifying "maybe," but to go beyond this risks failing to do justice to the openness of Baudelaire's own texts, which both call for and resist attempts at closure in terms of meaning. To raise the question of the possibility of ethical "progression" throughout the collection of prose poems is to cede to the desire to conclude, a teleological orientation which, as I have argued throughout this study, is common to both philosophy and poetry. The fact that in individual poems as well as across the scope of both *Les Fleurs du Mal* and *Le Spleen de Paris* (both on their own terms and in relation to each other) the sense of a conclusion is weakened by the poetry's tendency to circle back on itself, suggests the extent to which Baudelaire refuses the linear, teleological orientation that comes with a philosophical and esthetic model based on the logic of redemption. Reading the prose poems draws us, as readers, into the circular structure of the frustrated desire to conclude, since the reader plays an essential role in the process of deriving meaning from the prose poems. In that sense,

Baudelaire renews the relationship between himself and the "hypocrite lecteur, –mon semblable, –mon frère" ["hypocritish reader, –my fellow, –my brother" (5)] (OC1: 6), and once again, as it had been in *Les Fleurs du Mal*, this relationship is at once an esthetic and ethical one whereby the poet posits both proximity to and distance from the reader in the same way as the narrator of so many of the prose poems is both near to and separated from the other subjects he encounters. As Steve Murphy notes, the dominant esthetics and ethics of the prose poems consists in "never handing over to the reader a simple value judgment as an author-authority, but allowing him a more active role in the reception of the text" (635). The reader is called upon not to complete the work by arriving at a definitive interpretation but rather by residing in the doubleness and uncertainty of the poems themselves, inhabiting the space of unredeemed irony that both allows the esthetic act and reinforces the ethical bond between poet and reader, which becomes emblematic of the solidarity of non-redemption among all human subjects generally, enacted in relationship with one's own doubled self and with those one encounters on the page or on the streets in a community without communication.

Esthetic creation thus enacts, even (and especially) through the violence it inflicts on the objects from which the creation stems, an esthetic and ethical relationship that extends the realm of the possible, as Paul Audi has noted:

> Créer ne veut pas dire produire un objet, un objet doté d'une matière et d'une forme [...]; créer veut dire conférer, par cette production même, une nouvelle puissance à l'esprit, une puissance capable, par l'instauration du sens que la création effectue, d'ouvrir le champ des possibles à une extension nouvelle. (335–6)

> [Creating does not mean producing an object, an object provided with a matter and a form, [...]; creating means conferring, by this very production, a new power to the mind, a power capable, by the instauration of meaning that creation effects, of opening the field of possibilities to a new extension.]

But, as we have seen Audi himself note, creation does not limit itself to the possible, since to do so would be to restrict phenomena to the realm of the virtual as opposed to the actual, a realm Audi has metaphorically labeled "paradise" and from which one must fall in order to enact creation. The work of art that also effects an ethical relation to self and others, as well as between the author and reader, inaugurates solidarity without ever closing off the ethical relation by making it changeless. Such changelessness is the mark of the virtual, and thus to establish a relationship at all is to acknowledge the need to remain within the actual, the unredeemed and unredeemable situation that generates relationship in the first place.

As in *Les Fleurs du Mal*, then, there is in *Le Spleen de Paris* a resistance to conclusion and a frustration of attempts to approach the work systematically or linearly. Such are, as I hope to have demonstrated, key effects of the attempt to think and write beyond redemption. As this verse and prose poetry yield a rich set of conceptual questions, bringing the poetry closer to theoretical writing in some senses, so too recent theoretical writing has veered from systematic approaches toward the fragmentary, the tentative, and the suggestive. I turn now, to conclude, to Jean-Luc Nancy and Giorgio Agamben's attempts to think within (a)theological structures but beyond the notion of redemption. In this, their work is in continuity with Baudelaire's own "writing beyond salvation." Nancy's recent writings on Christianity and its "autodeconstruction" can provide insight into the way theological discourse functions in Baudelaire, whereas our excursions into Baudelaire's poetry can shed light on Nancy's ideas of the way Christian discourse is not simply surpassed or superceded, but rather moves beyond itself while retaining something of the force of the theological. As Aukje van Rooden explains, in a description that resonates strongly with what we have demonstrated in Baudelaire regarding the interplay between the (a)theological and the ethical, for Nancy "the notion of *poiesis*" provides a "view not only of creation but also of community, of our being together in the world," which Nancy "tries to understand as an act, a *praxis*, rather than as a fulfilled work or a closed figure" (van Rooden 185–8). One of the ideas that Nancy borrows from the traditional Christian register in order to show how it empties itself of its own "religious" content is that of adoration, a concept that guides the second volume of his analysis of the "deconstruction of Christianity." The definitions that Nancy offers of adoration are multifaceted; they open onto questions as a poem might, rather than closing off the field of definition the way a systematic philosophy might seek to do. Nancy returns to these sorts of characterizations of adoration several times in his book, altering the focus, and thus our conception of adoration, a bit each time. That multifaceted nature of his definitions is also a feature of adoration itself:

> Adoration signals a relationship to a presence that it would be out of the question to bring "here," that must be known and affirmed as essentially "elsewhere," with the effect of opening the "here." It is therefore not a presence in the accepted sense of the word. It is not the presence of anything in particular, but that of the opening, the dehiscence, the breach, or the breaking out of the "here" itself. (*Adoration* 9)

Here we see Nancy's struggle with articulating a new meaning for familiar terms such as "presence" that would both surpass and retain the theological force of the concept. In language that leans heavily on a philosophy (or theology) of negation, Nancy establishes presence as a kind of pure presence that would be the presence of nothing, that becomes opening itself. Further in the text, Nancy affirms that "'adoration' simply means: attention to the movement of sense, to the possibility of an address that would be utterly new, neither philosophical nor religious, neither practical nor political nor loving—but attentive" (20). Nancy's suggestion of pure openness echoes the pure virtuality that for Paul Audi is the paradise from which we must fall in order to have an actuality at all, a fall epitomized for Audi by esthetic creation. And so Baudelaire's poem on the theme of adoration ("Je t'adore à l'égal … "), which actualizes the fall from adoration into creation and its concomitant destruction, can be read as an interhistorical reply to Nancy.

Nancy argues in *Adoration* in favor of maintaining the open by resisting attempts to fill the empty space left by Christianity upon its departure:

Materialisms, positivisms, scientisms, irrationalisms, fascisms or collectivisms, utilitarianisms, individualisms, historicisms, legalisms, and even democratisms, without mentioning all the relativisms, skepticisms, logicisms—all duly atheist— will have been attempts, more or less pitiful or frightening, to occupy this place, with greater or lesser dissimulation of the effort to do so, for one had, after all, become somewhat aware that this was not what needed to be done.

Such is still, and on a renewed basis, our responsibility: to keep the place empty, or better still, perhaps, to ensure that there shall be no more place for an instance or for a question of a "reason given" ["raison rendue"], of foundation, origin, and end. (33)

Nancy's procession of –isms recalls Cioran's condemnation of successive attempts to effect progress in humanity whether from scientific developments or political movements, as well as Baudelaire's critique of progress. It resonates, too, with Agamben's conception of "the open":

It is not easy to think this figure—whether new or very ancient—of that life that shines in the "saved night" of nature's (and, in particular, human nature's), eternal, unsavable survival after it has definitively bid farewell to the logos and to its own history. It is no longer human, because it has perfectly forgotten every rational element, every project for mastering its animal life; but if animality had been defined precisely by its poverty in world and by its obscure expectation of a revelation and a salvation, then this life cannot be called animal either. It surely "does not see the open," in the sense that it does not appropriate it as an instrument of mastery and knowledge; but neither does it remain simply closed in its own captivation. (*Open* 90–1).

Commenting on this passage, Colby Dickson reminds us that Agamben "aims to restore humanity to its intended present moment, not one in which the human subject, as the centerpiece of Western, rational thought, would reign over all of creation, but rather, a present wherein the human animal might reappear in its originary environment" (*Agamben* 119). The present moment, or moment of presence, seems fated to move, in Nancy and Agamben alike, into a future or past, whether it be the originary status evoked here by Dickson or the seemingly always deferred future moment when Nancy's empty place would truly be empty. The conceptual restlessness that is revealed here suggests the trace, or more than a trace, of soteriological thinking whereby a kind of redemption is imagined, even if it impossible to achieve, or an impossibly innocent origin is conceived, but in a way that is recognized to be non-human in that such an originary state does not and cannot correspond to humanity as it is defined in actual lived post-lapsarian existence. Boyan Manchev has argued that Nancy is "explicitly opposed" to messianic rhetoric:

despite the fact that the project of deconstucting Christianity comprises many categories that imply a messianic horizon (the event to come or the empty signal announcing it), Nancy is explicitly opposed to messianic rhetoric. Thus, in the opening to *Concealed Thinking*, he writes: "For my part, I remain reticent about the vocabulary of the messianic" (*La pensée dérobée* 14n1). Indeed Nancy presents himself as one of the major critics of messianic logic and therefore of negative ontologies. (Manchev 265)

Being reticent about the messianic is not, of course, the same as successfully eliminating it from one's thought, which is a move that many contemporary thinkers find as desirable as it is difficult to accomplish. While Manchev is right that Nancy's negative ontology "does not end in an absolute event" (264), it nevertheless bears the mark of a look forward to redemption of the eternally open, or of the community that would be accomplished by *poiesis*, a transposition of esthetic salvation to a newly invented, and perhaps purely conceptual, political one.

The Agamben of *The Open* is in fact more willing than Nancy to retain a notion of redemption, since he contrasts the savable and the unsavable in terms of the question of relation to knowledge: "To articulate a zone of nonknowledge—or better, of a-knowledge—means [...] not simply to let something be, but to leave something outside of being, to render it unsavable" (*Open* 91). Agamben implies here that to be is to be savable, precisely the contrary of the relationship to knowledge that the other thinkers we have examined establish between redemption and knowledge. For these others, the realm of knowledge, not nonknowledge, is the one which renders the existent being unsavable, and it is this condition of irredeemability that these writers have sought to come to terms with. Agamben's notion of redemption is unrelated to a divinity, but it is no less real and operative in his thought, and especially his political thought. He defines redemption in *The Coming Community* as "the irreparable loss of the lost, the definitive profanity of the profane" (*Coming* 102). Colby Dickinson underscores that this conception of redemption requires not that we act in order to effectuate our redemption but rather that we refrain from acting:

> What it singularly requires is that we stop creating the representations of ourselves and our bodies that continue to plague us and to weight us down as so much unnecessary baggage. We are thereby called instead to let things appear as they already are, in "whatever" form they present themselves. This is to invoke a state that, in effect, removes salvation—as traditionally characterized—from us entirely. There is nothing to be saved, then, because we have regressed "beyond" salvation—we have been profaned. "We can have hope only in what is without remedy. [...] (The innermost character of salvation is that we are saved only at the point when we no longer want to be. At this point, there is salvation—but not for us.)" (*Coming* 102). (*Agamben* 139)

The notion of salvation existing, but not for us, resonates with Agamben's notion, explored in chapter one, of a "pure" salvation that would be salvation without an object, a variation on asoteriological thinking that both retains and cancels the notion of salvation, which by traditional definition must have an object of the action.

There is thus no true attempt to move beyond the logic of redemption in Agamben, but rather an explicit effort to redefine the concept in a way that steers clear both of a theistic account and of secular political moves toward an ideal. Agamben's quasi-messianic vision cannot but stand opposed to Nancy's attempt to keep open the space cleared by Christianity's auto-deconstruction. Any future-oriented thinking, such as Agamben's notion of the "coming community" implies, cannot help pulling back toward a teleological orientation, even if one maintains that the "coming" of that community is infinitely deferred. As Baudelaire and Cioran have helped us to see, a thorough embedding in the present is the proper temporal orientation of asoteriology. In that sense, Nancy's approach gets us closer to a move beyond the logic of redemption. In one of his more lyrical characterizations of adoration, he claims it is

> nothing other [...] than the movement of singing that comes to the throat and the lips for no reason, from nowhere [...]. The murmur and stammering of a celebration and an invocation, of an exclamation that comes from before language and outlasts it. A salutation without salvation, which salutes existence, a stranger to the opposition between the saved and the lost, the blessed and the damned" (*Adoration* 64)

Nancy's play on the French word *salut*, which means both salutation and salvation, accomplishes a crucial shift in thinking about redemption, and a more promising way of moving beyond the logic of redemption by redefining it as an acknowledgement of the other in a present moment, an acknowledgement that carries no trace of traditional theological redemption beyond the linguistic correspondence between the two terms in French. By refusing to populate the space of the open with positive political content, Nancy in effect shifts the terrain from the political to the ethical at the same time as he moves from the sacred to the immanent: "In this new world, where the relations of men among themselves radically take over from the common or collective relation to divine powers, relation itself somehow comes to occupy the place of the sacred" (*Adoration* 50). Another of Nancy's definitions of adoration also underscores the importance of non-transcendent relation:

> Adoration: the movement and the joy of recognizing ourselves as existents in the world. Not that this existence is not tough, thankless, shot through with grief. Yet this grief is not the price we pay in order to reach another world. It redeems nothing, but at least we can, insofar as we do not give up on living, salute and name some beings from time to time. To adore passes through naming, saluting the unnameable that the name hides within it and that is nothing other than the fortuitousness of the world. (62)

Christina Smerick describes Nancy's approach to redemption in terms that directly echo Agamben's: "the kind of salvation indicated by Nancy, and maintained in the face of criticism from Derrida and others, is a salvation that saves nothing, except that it saves us from believing in other worlds, worlds we fantasize about escaping to if we could just believe correctly. […] We need to be saved from belief, particularly belief in salvation" (Smerick 36). Yet the direct echo of Agamben's notion of "saving nothing" fails to do justice to the real distance that Nancy takes from messianic thinking, which neither Agamben nor Benjamin before him manages to effect.[10] It moves Nancy closer to the asoteriological thinking of Cioran and Baudelaire, as evidenced by Smerick's contention that, for Nancy, "we need to be saved from […] belief in salvation," which echoes Cioran's assertion in *De l'inconvénient d'être né*, which I cited in chapter four: "La certitude qu'il n'y a pas de salut est une forme de salut, elle est même *le* salut. À partir de là on peut aussi bien organiser sa propre vie que construire une philosophie de l'histoire. L'insoluble comme solution, comme seule issue … " ["The certainty that there is no salvation is a form of salvation, it is even salvation itself. From there one can organize one's own life as well as construct a philosophy of history. The insoluble as solution, as the only way out … "] (Pl 886). This return to the terrain mapped out by Cioran reminds us of the difficulty of overcoming the logic of redemption, as opposed to merely recharacterizing our definition of it. By identifying this point of commonality between Cioran's thought and Nancy's, we remain within the paradoxical situation outlined by Cioran's writings on redemption, and already present in the passage just quoted: the liberation from redemption, characterized as itself a kind of redemption, merely redefines the terms despite the author's desire to move beyond the category entirely.

When Nancy makes the move, quoted above, to defining adoration as "the movement […] of recognizing ourselves as existents" in a world "shot through with grief" that "redeems nothing," he joins Baudelaire in articulating what a life lived in full recognition of the impossibility of redemption would look like. When Nancy shifts the terrain from saving to naming, he does so in a way prefigured by Baudelaire in poems such as "Hymne":

À la très chère, à la très belle
Qui remplit mon coeur de clarté,
À l'ange, À l'idole immortelle,
Salut en l'immortalité !

Elle se répand dans ma vie
Comme un air imprégné de sel,
Et dans mon âme inassouvie
Verse le goût de l'éternel.

Sachet toujours frais qui parfume
L'atmosphère d'un cher réduit,
Encensoir oublié qui fume
En secret à travers la nuit,

Comment, amour incorruptible,
T'exprimer avec vérité ?

Grain de musc qui gis, invisible,
Au fond de mon éternité!

À la très bonne, à la très belle
Qui fait ma joie et ma santé,
À l'ange, à l'idole immortelle,
Salut en l'immortalité! (OC1: 162)

[To the dearest, fairest woman
Who sets my heart ablaze with light,
To the angel, the immortal idol,
Greetings in immortality!

She permeates my life
Like air impregnated with salt
And into my unsated soul
Pours the taste for the eternal.

Sachet, ever fresh, that perfumes
The atmosphere of a dear nook,
Forgotten censer smoldering
Secretly through the night,

Everlasting love, how can I
Describe you truthfully?
Grain of musk that lies unseen
In the depths of my eternity!

To the dearest, fairest woman
Who is my health and my delight
To the angel, the immortal idol,
Greetings in immortality! (471)]

Read in conjunction with the passage from Nancy, this poem seems almost an illustration of it: Baudelairean adoration passes through naming while remaining unable actually to name, thus "saluting the unnameable that the name hides within it." The woman is never quite equivalent to the terms used to describe her, which pass from the plausible "idole" through the comparative "comme un air" through the metaphorical "sachet" and "grain de musc." The woman is reduced to an odor, a weightless sensual property which is noticed and then passes away, leaving the "goût de l'éternel" to remain unfulfilled in this poem that never actually enacts any kind of transcendence and whose "salut" can be read simultaneously as à greeting and a bidding farewell.

The lack of contact in the poem preserves the woman, since the adoration featured in "Hymne" is markedly different from the one in "Je t'adore à l'égal..." precisely because in the latter poem, contact is established, a contact whose violent encounter destroys the life of the woman in order to produce "cette froideur par où tu m'es plus belle!" ["that coldness which makes you more beautiful"] (OC1: 27). These two prototypical encounters in *Les Fleurs du Mal* become transformed in *Le Spleen de Paris* to a different kind of ethical relation midway between the adoration-without-contact of "Hymne" and the intimate contact that destroys the object in "Je t'adore à l'égal ... ," a relation marked by what Steinmetz described as "non-communication between men" (Steinmetz 155). This relation permits encounter without sacrifice of its object, a new model based even more solidly in a notion of original sin that prevents, on account of the solidarity that could only be broken by a logic of redemption that divides the saved from the damned, a unilateral destruction of an object.[11]

In Nancy's move to an ethics of relation, he renders his philosophy in some sense consonant with pessimism as it has been characterized by Joshua Foa Dienstag, for whom pessimism is

> what used to be called an "ethic" and what today might be called a "technique of the self" or a "form of life." More modestly, pessimism is a philosophical sensibility from which political practices can be derived. It is a proposed stance from which to grapple with a world that we now recognize as disordered and disenchanted. It includes judgments about history and the possible course of our civilization, but it is not really a detailed set of predictions about future politics or economics. [...] Pessimism's goal is [...] to edify us about our condition and to fortify us for the life that lies ahead. (Dienstag xi)

Pessimism thus carves a space for ethical relation by identifying common ground for humanity in its boundedness to time. Here, Baudelaire's notion of original sin joins Cioran's reflections on the "fall into time" and Nancy's philosophy of recognition of existence in an unredeemable world. This interhistorical reading, which links Nancy's most recent writings to Baudelaire's, emphasizes the importance of the relation to the other that emerges, not despite, but rather on account of, the refusal of redemption and the need to draw all of the attendant consequences. It is a relation that Jacques Derrida also aligns with Jean-Luc Nancy at the very end of his book on him:

> And let it be—blessed, like a benediction still unthinkable, an exasperated benediction, a benediction *accorded* to his "exasperated consent" and in accordance with it, a benediction without any hope of salvation, an ex-hoped-for [exespéré] *salve*, an incalculable, unpresentable salutation in advance renouncing Salvation (as should any salute worthy of the name).
>
> Just *salut*, greeting without salvation; just a *salut* on the way. [Un salut sans salvation, un salut juste à venir] (*Touching* 310)

In Derrida's closing remark, we see all the ambiguity of the notion of salvation and, especially, the difficulty of doing away with it. For what is the status of the "ex-" in the "exespéré?" The hope is clearly not simply relegated to the past, since it is also "à venir," an expression that brings back nearly the full force of the messianic, which is precisely the category one would try to surpass when reorienting *salut* as greeting rather than salvation. The very nature of the French language makes it impossible, for any philosopher deeply attuned to language, to separate salvation and greeting in the word *salut* (and adoration as well, as in the ceremony known as *le salut du saint sacrement*). To arrive at "just *salut*," it would need to always be "on the way," eternally deferred, and thus awaited, which is the etymological root of *espérer*, which returns us to the domain of hope that Derrida and Nancy had, presumably, attempted to move beyond, an attempt which is, I would claim, ultimately a failed one. Baudelaire comes closer, in his encounter without communion, in his complicity that is not *even* a greeting, to reorienting a conception of human encounter away from redemption, showing along the way how such a distancing also facilitates the esthetic *and* ethical relation while rejecting, it is true, any notion of community, whether actual or, like Nancy's and Agamben's, always "to come."

Notes

Introduction

1   For more on the history of the term *incurvatus in se* in the context of a contemporary theological account of sin, see Jenson.

2   See, for instance, "Elévation" (OC1: 10).

3   I borrow the term "interhistorical" from Hilary Thompson. See "Time and Its Countermeasures" 98.

4   "De Maistre et Edgar Poe m'ont appris à raisonner" (OC1: 669).

Chapter 1

1   Compagnon's own list of characteristics of the antimoderns does include those categories however: "counter-revolution, anti-Enlightenment, pessimism, original sin, the sublime, vituperation" (18). Strictly speaking, then, Baudelaire might not fulfill Compagnon's criteria, and Compagnon's study includes chapters on nineteenth-century figures such as Chateaubriand, de Maistre, and Renan but not on Baudelaire. Still, as I will argue, it is the originality of Baudelaire's *kind* of antimodernity, as opposed to that of these other figures, that he occupies such a crucial position in the modern/antimodern plane.

2   See Pichois' note in Baudelaire OC2: 707, n.2.

3   For example: "Histoire de ma traduction d'*Edgar Poe*. Histoire des *Fleurs du mal*, humiliation par le malentendu, et mon procès" ["Story of my translation of *Edgar Poe*. Story of the *Fleurs du mal*, humiliation by misunderstanding, and my trial"] (OC2: 685).

4   See Jacques Derrida's remarks on aphorism: "Un aphorisme authentique ne doit jamais renvoyer à un autre. […] Mais qu'on le veuille ou non, qu'on le voie ou non, des aphorismes s'enchaînent ici, *comme* aphorismes, et en nombre, numérotés. Leur série se plie à un ordre *irréversible*. […] Lecteur, visiteur, au travail!" ["An authentic aphorism must never refer to another. […] But whether we want it or not, whether we see it or not, aphorisms link up here, *as* aphorisms, and in number, numbered. Their series folds to an *irreversible* order. […] Reader, visitor, to work!"] (*Psyché* 513).

5   Sylvain David recognizes a similar pattern in Emil Cioran, who defines the absolute via reference to Baudelaire's "L'héautontimorouménos": "Beyond doubt remains a will, if not a need, to believe. […] If one cannot hope to reassume one day an innocent and original faith in the universe, the possibility remains of flight forward […]. Besides, this exercise of dangerous intellect seems to correspond to certain esthetic practices of modernity […]: 'I am the wound and the knife,' there is our absolute, our infinity" (David 104).

6 Critchley situates Freud within a line of "post-Christian" attempts to think through original sin. A more complex case is that of Heidegger: "Heidegger's ideas of thrownness, facticity, and falling were explicitly elaborated in connection with Luther's conception of original sin and the anthropology of the primal Christianity in Paul. It is a phenomengically refined conception of original sin that allows Heidegger to explain the endless human propensity towards evasion and flight from taking responsibility for oneself. Although such a responsibility can be momentarily achieved in authentic resoluteness, it can never arrest the slide back into inauthenticity. The concept of original sin is still very much with us" (Critchley 109).

7 For John Gray a notable shift from pessimism to an unlikely optimism has been the mark of contemporary neo-conservativism, in sharp contrast to thinkers such as de Maistre: "Neo-conservatives have been distinguished by their belligerent optimism, which links them with a powerful utopian current in Enlightenment thinking and with the Christian fundamentalist faith that evil can be defeated" (*Black* 33). Likewise, Gray dismisses descriptions of George W. Bush's politics as Manichean: "The followers of Mani were subtle thinkers who accepted that evil could never be eliminated. Talk of ending evil is no more Manichean than it is Augustinian. It is an expression of Christian postmillennialism, which harks back to the belief of the first Christians that the blemishes of human life can be wiped away in a benign catastrophe" (34).

8 Cf. Agamben's comments in *The Signature of All Things* about creation and redemption not being "separate but rather [they] persist in a single place, where the work of salvation acts as a kind of a priori that is immanent in the work of creation and makes it possible" (108).

9 Françoise Meltzer has offered a critique of de Man's position, arguing that "the present for Baudelaire acts as a place from which to see the past on the one hand and the future on the other—not as interdependent but as endlessly, irrevocably noncontiguous. […] [T]he moment in Baudelaire is the position from which the past and the future irrevocably reassert themselves […]; the present is the place that allows for this realization; and that place is the lived moment" (Meltzer 214).

10 Tomoko Masuzawa provides a Benjaminian reading of this poem and concludes that "the singular achievement of Baudelaire, as Benjamin seems to assess it, lies in the particular form in which these two orders of time [*Erlebnis* and *Erfahrung*] are finally collapsed—not mediated, not chosen between" (529).

11 This self-tormented consciousness has much in common with the Augustinian notion of sin as man's condition of being *incurvatus in se*. See Jenson for an analysis of the legacy of this idea in Christian theology.

12 See also "Le Squelette laboureur" ["Skeleton with a Spade"] and its skepticism about *néant* and repose after death: "Voulez-vous […]/Montrer que dans la fosse même/Le sommeil promis n'est pas sûr; // Qu'envers nous le Néant est traître;/Que tout, même la Mort, nous ment,/Et que sempiternellement/Hélas! il nous faudra peut-être // Dans quelque pays inconnu/Ecorcher la terre revêche/Et pousser une lourde bêche/Sous notre pied sanglant et nu?" [Do you wish […]/To show that even in the grave/None is sure of the promised sleep; // That Annihilation betrays us;/That all, even Death, lies to us,/And that forever and ever,/Alas! we shall be forced perhaps // In some unknown country/To scrape the hard and stony ground/And to push a heavy spade in/With our bare and bleeding feet? (315)] (OC1: 94).

13 Debarati Sanyal argues that in this poem, as in Baudelaire's poetry generally, "irony [...] is continually reframed in a context disclosing the underlying violence of acts of knowing the self and the other," a move that gives rise to irony as "counterviolence" to the traumatic shock of the modern (36).

14 On this paratext, reprinted in OC1: 1075–6, see William Olmstead, who argues that the note allows us to "gain a privileged view of how Baudelaire restaged earlier poetry to suit his changed religious and political views," allowing him to "dramatiz[e] evil at once sympathetically and judgmentally" (Olmstead 109).

15 See OC1: 1078.

16 I analyze this poem in more detail in Chapter 3.

17 Here my interpretation differs from that of Claude Pichois, for whom Peter's denial is an act not of cowardice but of vengeance, since Pichois associates the remorse in the poem with Christ's supposed regret at having duped mankind. Peter thus becomes, according to Pichois, "a man whose eyes were opened" (OC1: 1078). My interpretation turns on questions of knowledge or consciousness as well, but of a very different subject, namely, the inability of Jesus or anyone to cancel inaction by carrying out revolt to the bitter end.

18 As Jonathan Culler has noted, the devil plays an ambiguous role throughout Baudelaire's collection: "What happens in the opening poem [...] happens in the collection as a whole: the poems with an important framing function claim that the Devil is ubiquitous, but subsequent poems do not tell us whether the scenes or movements they narrate are examples of the Devil's work" (Culler 92).

Chapter 2

1 Steiner 156. My comments on Benjamin's intended structure for the Baudelaire book draw on Steiner's descriptions.

2 See also Jacobs' exploration of the persistence of redemption in Benjamin's later work as well: "In Benjamin's work from beginning to end, ironically, this complicity and interchangeability of a banal concept of redemption with that of the Fall is at play. This is what takes place in 'Towards the Image of Proust,' for example, where Benjamin's reader might be lured into finding either a nostalgia for a lost past (in a temporality of fall) or a celebration of its recuperation as redemption. What takes place instead is the production of the dialectical image" (Jacobs 112).

3 On the question of fashion in the *Arcades Project*, see Richard Wolin, whose remarks indicate that Benjamin ultimately situates fashion as a manifestation of the always-the-same, rather than a potentially redemptive break from sameness: "Benjamin's object was to demonstrate the manner in which the always-the-same of prehistory manifests itself in the modern, insofar as the modern manifests itself as the always-the-same. The purpose of this intention was not to attempt to discover rudiments of archaic life in the modern per se, but rather to unmask the idea of the modern itself—i.e., the idea of an endless stream of consumer goods or 'fashion'—as that of eternal recurrence or the always-the-same" (Wolin 129).

4 Pop-Curseu identifies diverging engagement with Nietzsche on the part of Benjamin and Fondane as well, but goes on to note Benjamin's comment in *Central Park* 20 ("The heroic in Baudelaire is always the sublime form under which the demonic

manifests itself, and spleen manifests its vile and barbarous form") as one that "Fondane himself could have written" in his book on Baudelaire (Pop-Curseu 151).

5 Olivier Salazar-Ferrer rightly questions, however, the potential blindness of Fondane's position when it comes to the political stakes of a philosophy of antirational action: "His plea for a return to myth and an affective participation in the real, his critique of the idea of culture and his attack on the rationalism inherited from the Enlightenment place him in a delicate situation in the ideological landscape of the 1930s," when Fascism was attracted to these ideas (*Fondane* 167).

6 Ramona Fotiade identifies the roots of this view in the writings of Lev Chestov who "argues that knowledge, as opposed to life, brought about a need for certainty […]. More accurately, knowledge introduced a rational dimension into language (and implicitly into experience), which underpins any theory of meaning, as ideal meaning or meaning-in-itself, constituted independently of the variable conditions of experience and of the thinking subject's existence" (Fotiade 54).

7 For analysis of Fondane's views of the fall in comparison with those of André Breton's, and in light of the critique of surrealism that Fondane advances, see Fotiade 23–5.

8 "And if [Baudelaire] deserved his life? If, contrary to commonplaces, men only ever had the life they deserved?" (Sartre 18).

9 Fondane's epigraph reads "L'ivresse de l'art est plus propre que toute autre, à jeter un voile sur les terreurs du gouffre" (BEG 11). The exact quotation from Baudelaire is "L'ivresse de l'Art est plus apte que toute autre à voiler les terreurs du gouffre" (OC1: 321).

10 Divorcing God from reason leaves Fondane with a conception of an irrational, tyrannical God that chimes with some of Baudelaire's references to a divinity who takes pleasure in human suffering. As Olivier Salazar-Ferrer summarizes in his analysis of Fondane: "Arbitrary and incomprehensible, beyond good and evil, it is a terrible God who can only be approached through trial. He is the God of Job and of the sacrifice of Isaac by Abraham or the one of the scandalous Christ chasing the merchants from the temple and who dies abandoned on the cross. […] All social religion with its dogmas, prohibitions, rituals, and forms of collective life will be foreign to him" (*Fondane* 132).

11 Ramona Fotiade summarizes the relationship between the fall, knowledge, and freedom as both Chestov and Fondane theorize it: "Death is inscribed in the Knowledge of Good and Evil and initiates a drive for knowledge that remains at all times opposed to the principle of Life. […] In contrast to the philosophy of the finitude of being, which places man under the imperative of the Law and defines his existence in relation to death, Chetsov and Fondane advance the project of a philosophy of Life, which is also a philosophy of unlimited freedom" (Fotiade 203–4).

12 On this passage in Baudelaire and its sources in Augustine and Pascal, see Starobinski "Notes" 148–54. Starobinski affirms that "far from being a delusional plan of Baudelaire's, the 'fine conspiracy' would be the scenario of one of his nightmares" (153) and that we need to read "belle" ironically here, as Baudelaire uses it thus in many other instances in his journals.

13 For another characterization of the *gouffre* in Fondane, see Salazar-Ferrer: "Resulting from the melting of the rational foundation of the whole of our certitudes, the *gouffre* designates the sudden consciousness of the illusion of the whole of our rational and idealist convictions. It appears in particular when the values of the good, the

true and the beautiful melt away, and with them, the comfort of Stoic, Christian, or nineteenth-century progressive moralities. This melting happens for Fondane under the power of traumatic events that do not integrate in logics of consolation or justification" (*Fondane* 207–8).

Chapter 3

1   For a more detailed analysis of this idea, see Clemens 50–1.
2   Colby Dickson notes that according to Agamben, poetry "becomes an atheological enterprise because it must reinvent the way in which theology has been understood from its inception as an attempt to speak the truth of language's origin, a truth which [...] language itself cannot state" ("Poetic" 211).
3   Aggeler's translation does not reproduce the alteration in punctuation.
4   For more details, see OC1: 931–2.
5   For a fuller reading of this poem, see my "Baudelaire with Badiou."
6   I analyze the way the "nous/vous" opposition functions here in more detail in "Résonance, accord, voyage."
7   Jean Starobinski links "L'héautontimorouménos" to "L'irrémédiable" by way of the kind of self-reflexive consciousness that prevents both consciousness and poetry from coming to an end. About the latter poem, Starobinski writes: "'Consciousness of Evil' is the result of all allegorical images that prefigure it. And at the same time it sends us back to what was the first word of the poem: 'An Idea,' as if a circle was beginning again, and if the irremediable aspect of melancholy destined the fall repeat itself indefinitely" (*La mélancolie* 45).

Chapter 4

1   See also Weller's analysis of this passage (155).
2   Peter Sloterdijk provides an amusing but apt characterization of Cioran's compositional process: "He produces books by compiling the text provided by his inner employees. They present their material in irregular sessions—aphorisms from the blasphemy department, observations from the misanthropy studio, gibes from the disillusionment section, proclamations from the press office of the circus of the lonely, theses from the agency for swinging on the edge, and poisons from the editorial office for the despisal of contemporary literature. Formulating the thought of suicide is the only job that remains in the chief editor's hands; this involves the practice on which all further sequences of repetition depend" (80).
3   Aurélien Demers summarizes Cioran's view as follows: "Nothing and no one can save us because we are necessarily alone, and God can only be a monstrous nothingness or a monster of annihilation [...]. Far from being a solution, salvation, just like God, transfigures itself—or defigures itself—in its opposite" (Demers 154).
4   Cf. Simona Modreanu's remark that for Cioran, "the religious cannot be a question of content but only of intensity" (*Cioran* 34). In a letter, Cioran calls prayer "a temptation and an impossibility, an unrealizable necessity" (Cioran and Guerne 59).

5 Cioran makes a similar comment in an interview: "Ce sont les deux Français auxquels je pense le plus. J'ai cessé de les lire il y a très longtemps, mais je pense plus que de raison à Baudelaire, et à Pascal. Tout le temps, je me réfère à eux, je me sens une sorte d'affinité souterraine avec eux" ["Those are the two Frenchmen of whom I think the most often. I stopped reading them a very long time ago, but I think more than is reasonable about Baudelaire and Pascal. All the time, I refer to them, I feel a sort of underground affinity with them"] (*E* 40).

6 "A negative heroism, though, in that the hero of a universal of the fall or decomposition does not have to fight against an exterior peril but, on the contrary, enters into conflict with his own interiority. Already Walter Benjamin, inspired by Baudelaire, considered that modernity had produced its own exemplary or heroic figures with the lesbian, the prostitute, the Apache, or the suicide since, rather than use up their strength to fight in the name of a cause or an ideal, these deviant types represented in his eyes the quintessence of inversion and self-destruction. [...] Cioran takes up in his own way this idea of personal sacrifice, of a vain exploit, but at a strictly individual level: contrary to the models [...] retained by [Benjamin], he aspires less to destroy himself physically than to demolish systematically in himself the least idea, image, or illusion that he could have in common with his contemporaries. From his point of view, the only heroic gesture still possible to modern man is that exemplary one of 'thinking against oneself' (*TE* 821)" (David 15).

7 See "A une heure du matin" ["At One O'Clock in the Morning" (16–17)] (OC1: 288).

8 While Cioran often identifies salvation as the most problematic doctrine of Christianity, he also implicates another foundational notion, incarnation, which he sees as yielding an unjustified hubris that aligns itself to Western notions of progress in the modern period: "L'Incarnation est la flatterie la plus dangereuse dont nous ayons été l'objet. Elle nous aura dispensé un statut démesuré, hors de proportion avec ce que nous sommes. En haussant l'anecdote humaine à la dignité de drame cosmique, le christianisme nous a trompés sur notre insignifiance, il nous a précipités dans l'illusion, dans cet optimisme morbide qui, au mépris de l'évidence, confond cheminement et apothéose. Plus réfléchie, l'Antiquité païenne, mettait l'homme à sa place" ["The Incarnation is the most dangerous flattery of which we have been the object. It will have given us an immoderate status, out of proportion with what we are. By raising the human anecdote to the dignity of cosmic drama, Christianity has fooled us about our insignificance, it had led us into illusion, into that morbid optimism which, against the evidence, confuses progression with apotheosis" (Pl 641–2).

9 As Modreanu writes: "Being unable to adhere to a spontaneous 'yes' or a tortured 'no,' Cioran first adopts a logic, then a sort of metaphysics of the excluded middle [...] founded on the 'voluptuousness of the contradiction' and a certain nobility of lamentation that dilutes its tears in the subtleties of paradox" (*Cioran* 122).

10 Such a view of messianism as an informing structural principle allows us to go beyond moments when messianism is a thematic concern of Cioran's which he associates with less complex concepts such as his critique of progress: "Le Messie à venir, le vrai, on comprend qu'il tarde à se manifester. La tâche qui l'attend n'est pas aisée: comment s'y prendrait-il pour délivrer l'humanité de la *manie du mieux*?" ["The Messiah to come, the true one, we understand that he is late showing himself. The task awaiting him is not easy: how would he go about delivering humanity from the *mania of the best*?"] (Pl 881).

Chapter 5

1   As Aurélien Demers has noted, Cioran proposes three potential ways to escape from
    the consequences of the fall, those of the child, the primitive person, and the insane.
    All of these states are states of unconsciousness, though; so as long as a human subject
    is fully conscious, the effects of the fall remain operative. See Demers 167.

2   Simona Modreanu is right to advocate a balanced approach to Cioran's problematic
    political engagement in his early years: "First, these facts are undeniable and
    hagiographical attempts at obscuring these realities of Cioran's past by certain critics,
    especially Romanian ones, are at least as harmful as the relentlessness deploted by
    certain others, especially French ones, to place him among the accused of history"
    (*Cioran* 18).

3   If Cioran refuses the idea of progress, he also rejects the idea that the modern period
    has seen an escalation of catastrophe. He writes in a letter in 1969: "What I noticed
    is that people may understand the horror of the modern world but not the horror
    of the world itself, which is at the Heart of my fears and which, even though I am an
    unbeliever, makes me hold monasticism in such esteem" (Cioran and Guerne 151).

4   In an analysis that echoes Audi's discussion of potentiality and creation, William
    Watkin points out that according to Agamben, one common feature of both literature
    and philosophy is that "both seem to founder on an aporia between potentiality and
    actuality." See his analysis of the "productive negation" at stake in both poetry and
    philosophy in Watkin 44.

5   See François Raffoul's commentary on this passage as it relates to larger questions of
    Nancy's philosophy of world and the deconstruction of Christianity (Raffoul 24).

6   One remarkable effect of this always already occurring fall is, however, an ability
    to read and understand Cioran's aphorisms, which depend on irony. According to
    Simona Modreanu: "To understand a Cioran text, […] one has to have already
    understood it! The je-ne-sais-quoi of irony answers a kind of precomprehension
    always already present in the receiver" (*Dieu* 59).

7   For analyses of Cioran's relationship to gnosticism, see Modreanu *Dieu* 147–200 and
    Jérôme Laurent 264–9.

8   Michel Jarrety identifies Cioran's "passion of undeliverance" and its concomitant
    suffering as a "sensation of being and a sign of election" (Jarrety 120), a sign of the
    speaking subject's quasi-Romantic tragic superiority.

9   Cf a similar passage where Cioran invokes his simultaneous lucidity and delusion:
    "Un enfant, des enfants tous, incapables de voir ce que vous seul avez vu, vous, le
    plus détrompé des mortels, sans aucune illusion sur autrui et sur soi. Mais vous en
    garderez une malgré tout: celle tenace, indéracinable, de croire ne point en posséder"
    ["A child, all of them children, unable to see what only you have seen, you the most
    illusion-free of mortals, without any illusion about others and yourself. But you will
    keep one even so: the tenacious, unuprootable illusion of not having any"] (Pl 567)

10 Patrice Bollon underscores the permanent coexistence of lucidity and delusion in
    Cioran, "the demand for the most illuminating lucidity *and* the need for the most
    obscurantist illusion, the search for wisdom *and* acquiescence to the most vile
    drives, a mystical movement toward holiness *and* attachment to the most atheistic
    materialism […]! As if the affirmer and negator coexisted in him permanently and
    about all things" (Bollon 150).

11 For an insightful reading of the way Cioran cultivates rather than refuses paradox, see David 85–106.

12 One should perhaps add that the impermanence of salvation is also related to the impermanence of ideas in Cioran's writing, which Edward Said identifies as a source of suffering: "What makes him suffer particularly, he thinks, is his incapacity to 'happen.' Like Rameau's Nephew he sees the world, and his writing thus expresses a series of positions taken, but only provisionally. […] Ineluctably the difficulties he encounters make him return to a consciousness of the impasse of writing itself" (Said 174).

13 Sylvie Jaudeau calls this the lucidity of the "last man" in Cioran: "In a magesterial inversion, fallen man can pride himself on the incomparable privilege of living in full consciousness of his mortal destiny. […] Characterized by lucidity, [his consciousness] forgets the illusions immanent in time and reconsiders history while depriving it of its aura. It envisages it from the perspective of the 'last man,' that new species which has ceased to confuse becoming and absolute and to make historical time sacred as the ancients did by rendering it complicit with the atemporal or with a transcendent absolute that they placed in paradise, the end of time, or other utopias" (Jaudeau 40–1).

14 For a discussion of pessimism and disappointment in Cioran, see Acquisto, "Epistèmologic."

15 "Je disais l'autre jour à un ami que, tout en ne croyant plus à l'écriture, je ne voudrais pas y renoncer, que travailler était une illusion défendable et qu'après avoir gribouillé une page ou seulement une phrase, j'avais toujours envie de siffler" ["I was saying the other day to a friend that, even while no longer believing in writing, I did not want to renounce it, that working was a defensible illusion and that after having scribbled a page or only a sentence, I always had a desire to whistle" (*O* 1651).

Chapter 6

1 Bersani offers a critique of Walter Benjamin on precisely the grounds that, even in his weak version of messianism, "art itself gets reduced to a kind of superior patching function" (1). See also Kathleen Kerr-Koch's discussion of "aspects of Benjamin's work that leave the readers apprehensive, in particular in the way that he appropriates material from strong and systematic but politically dangerous thinkers and uses them for his own purposes. The question as to what extent Benjamin's work becomes complicit with the atrocities of the time, however, is certainly a real one" (78–9).

2 Audi also evokes Benjamin Fondane's book on Baudelaire which "can be—not to say *should* be—considered as one of the most important contributions to esth/ethic theory that we have ever received from the past" (245).

3 On deconstruction as "textual messianism," see Reynolds.

4 See 1 Corinthians 7:29-32. Simon Critchley also appropriates the notion of the "as not" for an atheistic faith. See *Faith* 177–83.

5 For an insightful reading that identifies political potential in the violence and ethical irony of the prose poems, see Sanyal 53–94.

6 As Richard Burton notes, "The very fact that ["Assommons les pauvres!"] can be plausibly interpreted either as an incitement to revolutionary violence (in a left-wing, proto-Marxist sense) or as a nihilistic *reductio ad absurdum* of all forms of leftism

already locates it at or close to the point […] where the opposition between left and right ceases to be operable" (363).

7   Françoise Meltzer comments: "In 'Assommons', we are witness to a theological and political strabismus as if the poet were remembering Proudhon's social theories with one eye and reading Maistre on original sin with the other. Such recording is not an attempt to write modernity; it is rather a reeling, a pitching" (17).

8   On Proudhon and "Assommons les pauvres," see Murphy 404–12.

9   See, though, Hiddleston's reading of "Le miroir" which sees evidence of the poet's emphasis on original sin at work in this poem as well: "he has a right to regard his ugliness by whatever standard that moral ugliness itself may desire, and not in the light of the truly immortal principle of original sin which defines man's places both in time and society. There can be no point in such a self-examination since it will lead to no change in the individual: it is as if the Devil had turned into Narcissus in a world where mirrors do not have the kindness to shatter" (80–1).

10 Smerick recognizes this refusal of salvational logic earlier in her essay: "Nancy does not suggest 'salvation'—or certainly not the sort of salvation the Western mentality has come to expect (no spit-curled Superman will fly in from another world, no spirit penetrates flesh in order to redeem it for eternity). In fact, those sorts of rescue fantasies may be what destroy us, for they suggest a power play by some Other who will save us all, and thus they collapse again into dominance and unity" (31).

11 There are resonances here with Georges Bataille's analysis of the way the definitive end of divine immanence brings about a state in which destruction in the "here-below" is always creative. As a consequence of that end of immanence, "production alone is accessible and worthy of interest here-below; the principle of nonproductive destruction is given only in the beyond, and it cannot have any value for the here-below" (*Theory* 89–90).

Works Cited

Acquisto, Joseph. "Baudelaire with Badiou: Event and Subjectivity in 'L'Héautontimorouménos.'" In *Thinking Poetry: Philosophical Approaches to Nineteenth-Century French Poetry*, edited by Joseph Acquisto. New York: Palgrave Macmillan, 2013, 185–201.

———. "Épistémologie et esthétique de la déception chez Proust et Cioran." *Revue Romane* 45:1 (2010), 117–30.

———. "Résonance, Accord, Voyage: La politique du poétique chez Baudelaire et Rancière." *Revue des Sciences Humaines* 314 (Avril–Juin 2014), 73–86.

Adorno, Theodor W. *Minima Moralia*. trans. E.F.N. Jephcott. London: Verso, 2005.

Agamben, Giorgio. *The Coming Community*. trans. Michael Hardt. Minneapolis: University of Minnesota Press, 1993.

———. *The End of the Poem*. trans. Daniel Heller-Roazen. Stanford: Stanford University Press, 1999.

———. *The Man without Content*. trans. Georgia Albert. Stanford: Stanford University Press, 1999.

———. *The Open*. Stanford: Stanford University Press, 2004.

———. *The Time that Remains*. trans. Patricia Dailey. Stanford: Stanford University Press, 2005.

———. *The Signature of All Things*. trans. Luca d'Isanto with Kevin Attell. New York: Zone Books, 2009.

———. *The Kingdom and the Glory*. trans. Lorenzo Chiesa. Stanford: Stanford University Press, 2011.

———. *Nudities*. trans. David Kishik and Stefan Pedatella. Stanford: Stanford University Press, 2011.

Alexander, Ian. "The Consciousness of Time in Baudelaire." In *Studies in Modern French Literature*, edited by L.J. Austin, Garent Rees and Eugène Vinaver, 1–17. Manchester: Macnhester University Press, 1962.

Audi, Paul. *Créer*. Lagrasse: Verdier, 2010.

Baer, Ulrich. *Remnants of Song: Trauma and the Experience of Modernity in Charles Baudelaire and Paul Celan*. Stanford: Stanford University Press, 2000.

Bataille, Georges. *Inner Experience*. trans. Leslie Anne Boldt. Albany: State University of New York Press, 1988.

———. *Theory of Religion*. trans. Robert Hurley. New York: Zone Books, 1989.

Baudelaire, Charles. *Correspondance*, edited by Claude Pichois. Paris: Gallimard, 1973.

———. *The Flowers of Evil*. trans.William Aggeler. Fresno: Academy Library Guild, 1954.

———. *Œuvres complètes*, edited by Claude Pichois. Paris: Gallimard: 1975–6.

———. *The Parisian Prowler*. trans. Edward K. Kaplan. Athens: University of Georgia Press, 1997.

Bénichou, Paul. "Le Satan de Baudelaire." In *Les Fleurs du Mal*, edited by André Guyaux and Bertrand Marchal. Paris: Presses Universitaires de la Sorbonne, 2003, 9–23.

Benjamin, Walter. *Illuminations*. trans. Harry Zohn. New York: Schocken Books, 1968.

———. *The Origin of German Tragic Drama*. trans. John Osborne. London: Verso, 1998.

———. *Arcades Project*. trans. Howard Eiland and Kevin McLaughlin. Cambridge: Belknap Press, 1999.

———. *The Writer of Modern Life*, edited by Michael W. Jennings. Cambridge: Belknap Press, 2006.

Bersani, Leo. *The Culture of Redemption*. Cambridge: Harvard University Press, 1990.

Bollon, Patrice. *Cioran l'hérétique*. Paris: Gallimard, 1997.

Burton, Richard. *Baudelaire and the Second Republic*. Oxford: Clarendon Press, 1991.

Calinescu, Matei. *Five Faces of Modernity*. Durham: Duke University Press, 1987.

Cavaillès, Nicolas. *Cioran malgré lui—Ecrire à l'encontre de soi*. Paris: CNRS Editions, 2011.

Cioran, Emil. *Entretiens*. Paris: Gallimard, 1995.

———. *Cahiers*. Paris: Gallimard, 1997.

———. *Œuvres*. Paris: Gallimard, 2011.

Cioran, Emil and Armel Guerne. *Lettres 1961–1978*, edited by Vincent Piednoir. Paris: L'Herne, 2011.

Clemens, Justin. "The Role of the Shifter and the Problem of Reference in Giorgio Agamben." In *The Work of Giorgio Agamben: Law, Literature, Life*, edited by Justin Clemens, Nicholas Heron and Alex Murray, 43–65. Edinburgh: Edinburgh University Press, 2008.

Compagnon, Antoine. *Les Antimodernes*. Paris: Gallimard, 2005.

Critchley, Simon. *Very Little … Almost Nothing*. London: Routledge, 2004.

———. *The Faith of the Faithless*. London: Verso, 2012.

Culler, Jonathan. "Baudelaire's Satanic Verses." *Diacritics* 28:3 (Fall 1998), 86–100.

David, Sylvain. *Cioran: Un héroïsme à rebours*. Montreal: Presses Universitaires de Montréal, 2006.

De Lussy, Eric. "Réception de *Baudelaire et l'expérience du gouffre*." *Cahiers Benjamin Fondane* 15 (2012), 36–58.

Demers, Aurélien. *Le pessimisme jubilatoire d'Emil Cioran*. Doctoral Thesis. Université Jean Moulin Lyon 3, 2007.

De Man, Paul. *Blindness and Insight*. Minneapolis: University of Minnesota Press, 1983.

Derrida, Jacques. *Psyché: Inventions de l'autre*. Paris: Galilée, 1987.

———. *Acts of Literature*. New York: Routledge, 1992.

———. *On Touching—Jean-Luc Nancy*. trans. Christine Irizarry. Stanford: Stanford University Press, 2005.

Dickinson, Colby. *Agamben and Theology*. London: T&T Clark, 2011.

———. "The Poetic Atheology of Giorgio Agamben: Defining the Scission between Poetry and Philosophy." *Mosaic* 45:1 (March 2012): 203–17.

Dienstag, Joshua Foa. *Pessimism: Philosophy, Ethic, Spirit*. Princeton: Princeton University Press, 2006.

Fondane, Benjamin. *La conscience malheureuse*. Paris: Denoël et Steele, 1936.

———. *Baudelaire et l'expérience du gouffre*. Paris: Seghers, 1972.

———. *Le Lundi existentiel et le dimanche de l'histoire*. Paris: Editions du Rocher, 1990.

———. *Faux traité d'esthétique*. Paris: Méditérrannée, 1998.

———. *Le mal des fantômes*. Paris: Verdier, 2006.

Fotiade, Ramona. *Conceptions of the Absurd*. Oxford: Legenda, 2001.

Froidevaux, Gérald. *Baudelaire: Représentation et modernité*. Paris: J. Corti, 1989.

Goodstein, Elizabeth. *Experience without Qualities: Boredom and Modernity*. Stanford: Stanford University Press, 2005.

Gray, John. *Heresies*. London: Granta, 2004.

———. *Black Mass*. New York: Farrar, Straus and Giroux, 2007.

Guedj, Dominique. "Visages du malheur dans la pensée de Fondane et « importance » du *Baudelaire*." In *Une poétique du gouffre: Sur Baudelaire et l'experience du gouffre de Benjamin Fondane*, edited by Monique Jutrin and Gisèle Vanhese, 109–27. Soveria Mannelli: Rubbetino, 2003.

Habermas, Jürgen. "Walter Benjamin: Consciousness-Raising or Rescuing Critique." In *On Walter Benjamin*, edited by Gary Smith, 90–128. Cambridge: The MIT Press, 1988.

Handwerk, Gary. *Irony and Ethics in Narrative: From Schlegel to Lacan*. New Haven: Yale University Press, 1985.

Hannoosh, Michele. *Baudelaire and Caricature: From the Comic to an Art of Modernity*. University Park: The Pennsylvania State University Press, 1992.

Heidegger, Martin. "What Is Metaphysics?" In *Basic Writings*, edited by David Farrell Krell, 91–112. New York: Harper and Row, 1977.

Hiddleston, J. A. *Baudelaire and* Le Spleen de Paris. Oxford: Clarendon, 1987.

Jackson, John E. *La Mort Baudelaire*. Neuchâtel: A la Baconnière, 1982.

Jacobs, Carol. *In the Language of Walter Benjamin*. Baltimore: The Johns Hopkins University Press, 1999.

Jameson, Fredric. *The Modernist Papers*. London: Verso, 2007.

Jarrety, Michel. *La morale dans l'écriture: Camus, Char, Cioran*. Paris: Presses Universitaires de France, 1999.

Jaudeau, Sylvie. *Cioran ou le dernier homme*. Paris: José Corti, 1990.

Jauss, Hans Robert. *Towards an Aesthetic of Reception*. trans. Timothy Bahti. Minneapolis: University of Minnesota Press, 1982.

Jennings, Michael. *Dialectical Images: Walter Benjamin's Theory of Literary Criticism*. Ithaca: Cornell University Press, 1987.

Jenson, Matt. *The Gravity of Sin*. London: T&T Clark, 2006.

Jutrin, Monique. "Relecture de *Baudelaire ou l'expérience du gouffre*: Vers une lecture de participation." In *Une poétique du gouffre: Sur Baudelaire et l'experience du gouffre de Benjamin Fondane*, edited by Monique Jutrin and Gisèle Vanhese, 13–21. Soveria Mannelli: Rubbetino, 2003.

———. *Avec Benjamin Fondane au-delà de l'histoire*. Paris: Parole et Silence, 2011.

———. "Fondane aux prises avec Baudelaire." *Cahiers Benjamin Fondane* [online].

Kerr-Koch, Kathleen. *Romancing Fascism: Modernity and Allegory in Benjamin, Shelley, de Man*. New York: Bloomsbury, 2013.

Laurent, Jérôme. "Plotin et la gnose." In *Cioran*, edited by Laurence Tacou, 264–9. Paris: L'Herne, 2009.

Liiceanu, Gabriel. *Itinéraires d'une vie: EM Cioran*. Paris: Editions Michalon, 1995.

Manchev, Boyan. "Ontology of Creation." In *Re-treating Religion: Deconstructing Christianity with Jean-Luc Nancy*, edited by Alena Alexandrova and Ignaas Devisch et al., 261–74. New York: Fordham University Press, 2012.

Marcel, Gabriel. "Un allié à contre-courant." In *Cioran*, edited by Laurence Tacou, 222–3. Paris: L'Herne, 2009.

Marchal, Bertrand. "Baudelaire, Barbier Gautier et le mauvais moine." *L'Année Baudelaire* 6 (2002), 127–41.

Marder, Elissa. *Dead Time: Temporal Disorders in the Wake of Modernity*. Stanford: Stanford University Press, 2001.

Martin, Mircea. "Le *Baudelaire* de Fondane ou comment un poète refuse l'approche esthétique de la poésie." In *Une poétique du gouffre: Sur Baudelaire et l'experience du gouffre de Benjamin Fondane*, edited by Monique Jutrin and Gisèle Vanhese, 231–46. Soveria Mannelli: Rubbetino, 2003.

Masuzawa, Tomoko. "Tracing the Figure of Redemption: Walter Benjamin's Physiognomy of Modernity." *MLN* 100: 3 (1985), 514–36.

Mauriac, Claude. "L'un des meilleurs écrivains français" In *Cioran*, edited by Laurence, Tacou, 215–18. Paris: Editions de L'Herne, 2009

Meltzer, Françoise. *Seeing Double: Baudelaire's Modernity*. Chicago: The University of Chicago Press, 2001.

Modreanu, Simona. *Cioran*. Paris: Oxus, 2003.

———. *Le Dieu paradoxal de Cioran*. Paris: Editions du Rocher, 2003.

Murphy, Steve. *Logiques du dernier Baudelaire*. Paris: Champion Classiques, 2007.

Mutin, Rachel, "Philosophie du néant et métaphysique du fragment" In *Cioran*, edited by Laurence, Tacou, 238–49. Paris: Editions de L'Herne, 2009.

Nadeau, Maurice. "Un penseur crépusculaire." In *Cioran*, edited by Laurence Tacou, 211–12. Paris: L'Herne, 2009.

Nancy, Jean-Luc. *Adoration*. trans. John McKeane. New York: Fordham University Press, 2013.

———. *The Creation of the World or Globalization*. trans. François Raffoul and David Pettigrew. Albany: State University of New York Press, 2007.

———. *Dis-enclosure: The Deconstruction of Christianity*. trans. Bettina Bergo et al. New York: Fordham University Press, 2008.

Nietzsche, Friedrich. *The Birth of Tragedy*. trans. Shaun Whiteside. New York: Penguin, 1993.

———. *The Gay Science*, edited by Walter Kauffman. New York: Vintage, 1974.

Olmstead, William. "Apostasy Apostasized: The Effects of Censorship and Self-Censorship on Baudelaire's 'Le Reniement de Saint Pierre.'" *Nineteenth-Century French Studies* 36:1–2 (Fall–Winter 2007–8), 109–21.

Parfait, Nicole. *Cioran ou le défi de l'être*. Paris: Editions Desjonquères, 2001.

Pop-Curseu, Ioan. "'Jouer la comédie à soi-même et auix autres': La théatralité de Baudelaire selon Fondane et Benjamin." *Cahiers Benjamin Fondane* 15 (2012), 149–63.

Raffoul, François. "The Creation of the World." In *Jean-Luc Nancy and Plural Thinking: Expositions of World, Ontology, Politics, and Sense*, edited by Peter Gratton and Marie-Eve Morin, 13–26. Albany: State University of New York Press, 2012.

Reynolds, Anthony. "The Linguistic Return: Deconstruction as Textual Messianism." *SubStance* 43:1 (2014), 152–65.

Rimbaud, Arthur. *Complete Works, Selected Letters: A Bilingual Edition*. Chicago: University of Chicago Press, 2005.

Said, Edward. "Amateur d'insoluble." In *Cioran*, edited by Laurence, Tacou, 173–6. Paris: Editions de L'Herne, 2009

Salazar-Ferrer, Olivier. "L'ambivalence du gouffre." In *Une poétique du gouffre: Sur Baudelaire et l'experience du gouffre de Benjamin Fondane*, edited by Monique Jutrin and Gisèle Vanhese, 49–62. Soveria Mannelli: Rubbetino, 2003.

———. *Benjamin Fondane*. Paris: Oxus, 2004.

Sanyal, Debarati. *The Violence of Modernity: Baudelaire, Irony, and the Politics of Form*. Baltimore: The Johns Hopkins University Press, 2006.

Sartre, Jean-Paul. *Baudelaire*. Paris: Gallimard, 1947.

Sloterdijk, Peter. *You Must Change Your Life*. trans. Wieland Hoban. Cambridge: Polity, 2013.

Smerick, Christina. "No Other Place to Be: Globzalization, Monotheism, and *Salut* in Nancy." In *Jean-Luc Nancy and Plural Thinking: Expositions of World, Ontology, Politics, and Sense*, edited by Peter Gratton and Marie-Eve Morin, 27–41. Albany: State University of New York Press, 2012.

Sora, Mariana. "Diogène sous les toits de Paris." In *Cioran*, edited by Laurence Tacou, 224–31. Paris: L'Herne, 2009.

Starobinski, Jean. *La mélancolie au miroir*. Paris: Julliard, 1989.

———. "Notes de lecture." *L'Année Baudelaire* 6 (2002), 143–54.

Steiner, Uwe. *Walter Benjamin: An Introduction to His Work and Thought*. trans. Michael Winkler. Chicago: The University of Chicago Press, 2010.

Steinmetz, Jean-Luc. *Reconnaissance: Nerval, Baudelaire, Lautreamont, Rimbaud, Mallarmé*. Nantes: Cécile Defaut, 2008.

Taylor, Charles. *A Secular Age*. Cambridge: Belknap Press, 2007.

Teboul, Margaret. "Walter Benjamin et Benajmin Fondane devant l'Histoire et le temps." *Cahiers Benjamin Fondane* 14 (2011), 85–114.

Thélot, Jérôme. *Baudelaire: Violence et poésie*. Paris: Gallimard, 1993.

———. *L'immémorial. Etudes sur la poésie moderne*. Paris: Editions Les Belles Lettres, 2011.

Thompson, Hilary. "Time and Its Countermeasures." In *Modernism and Theory: A Critical Debate*, edited by Stephen Ross, 86–98. London: Routledge, 2009.

van Rooden, Aukje. "Intermezzo." In *Re-treating Religion: Deconstructing Christianity with Jean-Luc Nancy*, edited by Alena Alexandrova and Ignaas Devisch et al., 185–8. New York: Fordham University Press, 2012.

Watkin, William. *The Literary Agamben*. London: Continuum, 2010.

Watkin, Christopher. *Difficult Atheism*. Edinburgh: Edinburgh University Press, 2011.

Weber, Max. "Science as Vocation." *Daedalus* 87:1 (Winter 1958), 111–34.

Weller, Shane. *Literature, Philosophy, Nihilism*. New York: Palgrave Macmillan, 2008.

Wolin, Richard. *Walter Benjamin: An Aesthetic of Redemption*. New York: Columbia University Press, 1982.

Zartalouids, Thanos. "Soulblind, or On Profanation." In *The Work of Giorgio Agamben: Law, Literature, Life*, edited by Justin Clemens, Nicholas Heron and Alex Murray, 132–48. Edinburgh: Edinburgh University Press, 2008.

Žižek, Slavoj. *The Puppet and the Dwarf*. Cambridge: The MIT Press, 2003.

Žižek, Slavoj and John Milbank. *The Monstrosity of Christ: Paradox or Dialectic?*, edited by Creston Davis. Cambridge: MIT Press, 2009.

Index